G.I.JOE

OPERATION HISS

G.I. JOE
OPERATION HISS

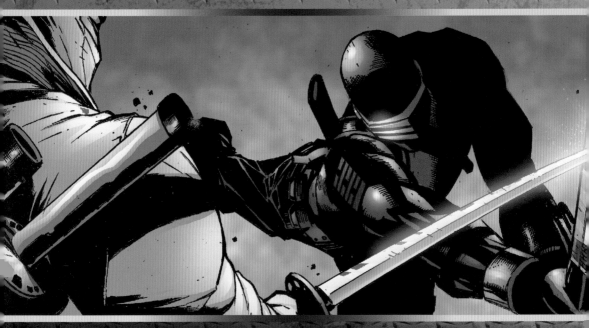

WRITTEN BY: **BRIAN REED**

ART BY: **ALEX CAL, AGUSTIN PADILLA** (ISSUES 1-4),
AND **GIANLUCA GUGLIOTTA** (ISSUE 5)

COLORS BY: **J. BROWN** • LETTERS BY: **CHRIS MOWRY** AND **ROBBIE ROBBINS**

ASSISTANT EDITOR: **CARLOS GUZMAN** • EDITOR: **ANDY SCHMIDT**

COLLECTION EDITS BY: **JUSTIN EISINGER** • COLLECTION DESIGN BY: **SHAWN LEE**

Licensed By:

Special thanks to Hasbro's Aaron Archer, Michael Kelly, Amie Lozanski, Ed Lane, Joe Furfaro, Jos Huxley, Samantha Lomow, and Michael Verrecchia for their invaluable assistance.

www.IDWPUBLISHING.com   ISBN: 978-1-60010-742-9   13 12 11 10   1 2 3 4

IDW ™   Operations: Ted Adams, Chief Executive Officer • Greg Goldstein, Chief Operating Officer • Matthew Ruzicka, CPA, Chief Financial Officer • Alan Payne, VP of Sales • Lorelei Bunjes, Dir. of Digital Services • AnnaMaria White, Marketing & PR Manager • Marci Hubbard, Executive Assistant • Alonzo Simon, Shipping Manager • Angela Loggins, Staff Accountant • Cherrie Go, Assistant Web Designer • Editorial: Chris Ryall, Publisher/Editor-in-Chief • Scott Dunbier, Editor, Special Projects • Andy Schmidt, Senior Editor • Bob Schreck, Senior Editor • Justin Eisinger, Editor • Kris Oprisko, Editor/Foreign Lic. • Denton J. Tipton, Editor • Tom Waltz, Editor • Mariah Huehner, Associate Editor • Carlos Guzman, Editorial Assistant • Design: Robbie Robbins, EVP/Sr. Graphic Artist • Neil Uyetake, Art Director • Chris Mowry, Graphic Artist • Amauri Osorio, Graphic Artist • Gilberto Lazcano, Production Assistant • Shawn Lee, Production Assistant

HAWK ONLINE. JOES REPORT IN.

02/04/0198004-FB

CHINA

2344
6471
47-
J878
7104

G.I. JOE COMM SOFTWARE v3.4
SATELLITE UPLINK ENGAGED
OPERATIVE TRACKING INITIALIZING...

SNAKE EYES AND I ARE IN POSITION, GENERAL.

SCARLETT

DATAFRAME, GIVE ME A VISUAL ON THEIR LOCATION.

CHINA

02/04/0198004-FB

44561
HSH4H
GSFHG
5655S
6HSA8
8R2F-
FHHLA
GN774
4154/
//GLK
NBVFO
AVNNK
LZU45

TRACKING OPERATIVES...
CHINA...
GUANGDONG PROVINCE...

I'M BRINGING THE INFORMATION UP ON YOUR SCREEN NOW, SIR.

DATAFRAME

HERE'S WHERE WE STAND, JOES. AFTER THE EVENTS AT THE POLAR ICE CAP, G.I. JOE HAS BEEN ASKED TO INVESTIGATE THE M.A.R.S. OPERATIONS.

02/04/0198004-FB

GUANGZHOU

44561
HSH4H
GSFHG
5655S
6HSA8
8R2F-
FHHLA
GN774
4154/
//GLK
NBVFO
AVNNK
LZU45

TRACKING OPERATIVES...
CHINA...
GUANGDONG PROVINCE...

THE M.A.R.S. CHINA FACILITY WENT DARK YESTERDAY AFTERNOON. ALL TELECOMMUNICATIONS, ALL COMPUTER NETWORK TRAFFIC—EVERYTHING JUST WENT AWAY.

HAWK

EYES ON THE GROUND REPORT THE FACTORY GATES ARE SEALED UP TIGHT, BUT THAT WORK CONTINUES INSIDE.

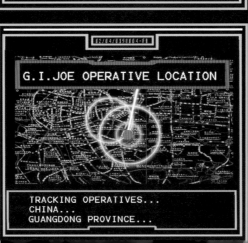

02/04/0198004-FB

G.I.JOE OPERATIVE LOCATION

TRACKING OPERATIVES...
CHINA...
GUANGDONG PROVINCE...

THE CHINESE GOVERNMENT HAS AGREED TO A JOE GROUND OPERATION TO INFILTRATE THE M.A.R.S. FACILITY...

HAWK

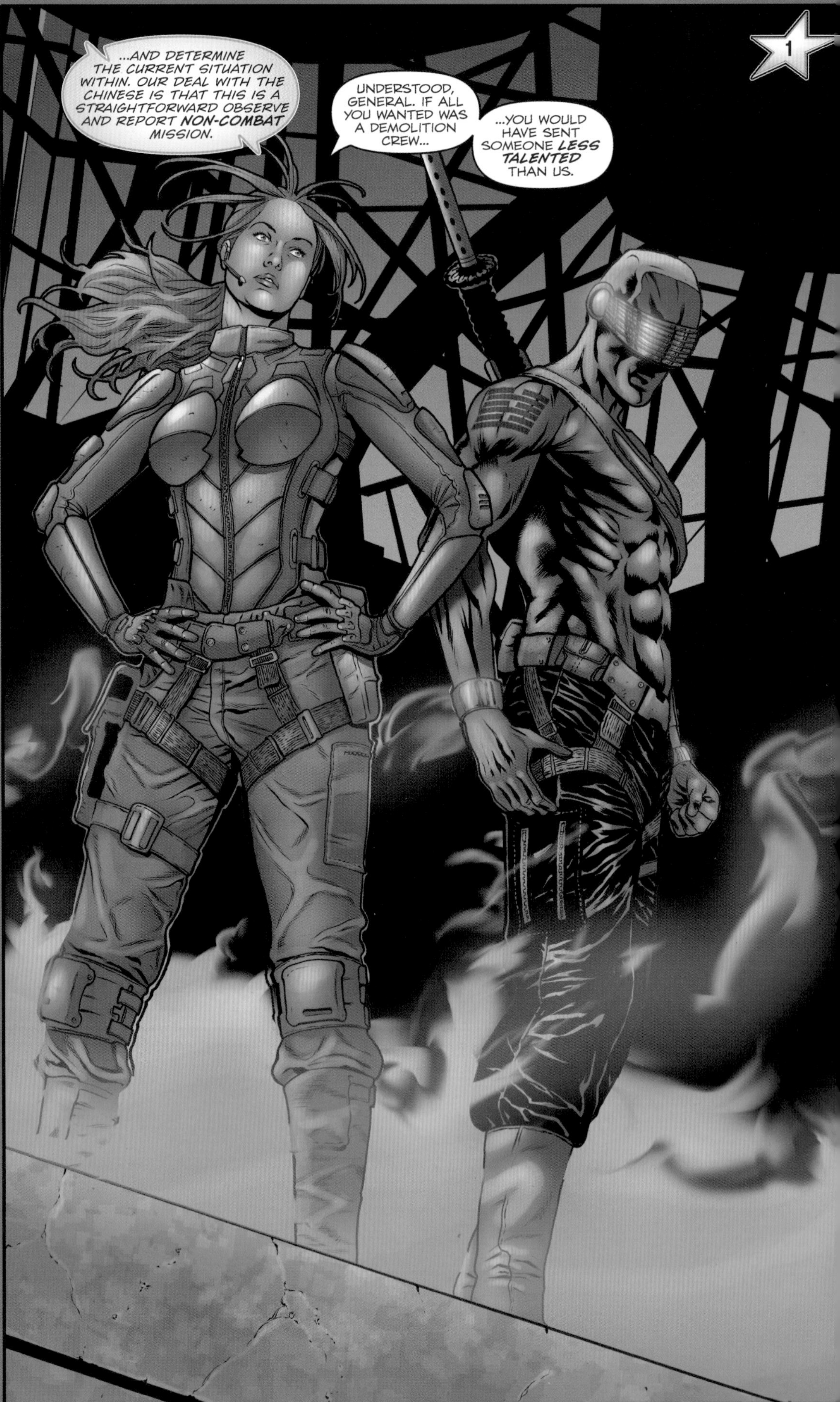
1
...AND DETERMINE THE CURRENT SITUATION WITHIN. OUR DEAL WITH THE CHINESE IS THAT THIS IS A STRAIGHTFORWARD OBSERVE AND REPORT **NON-COMBAT** MISSION.
UNDERSTOOD, GENERAL. IF ALL YOU WANTED WAS A DEMOLITION CREW...
...YOU WOULD HAVE SENT SOMEONE ***LESS TALENTED*** THAN US.

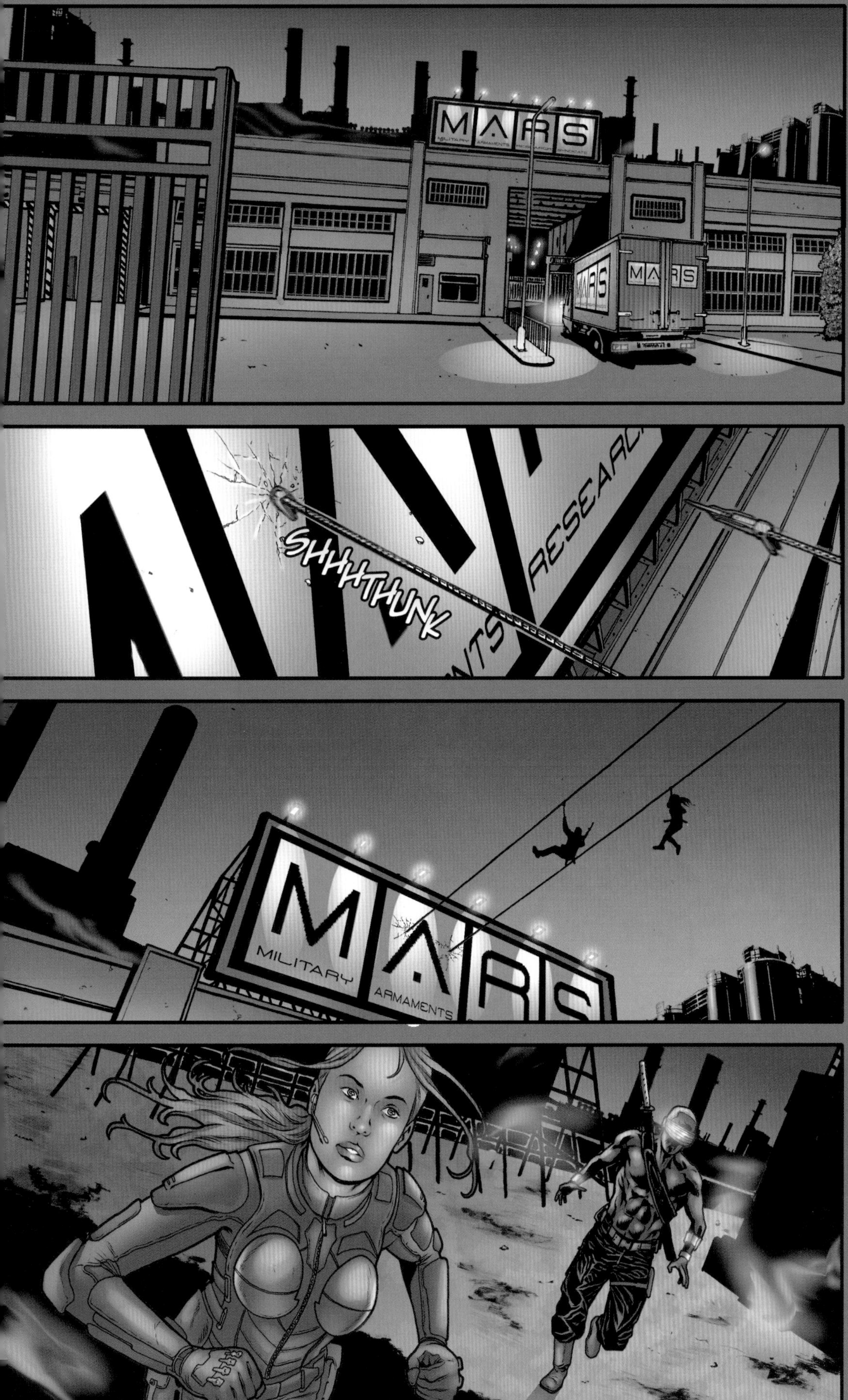
M.A.R.S
SHHHTHUNK
MILITARY
ARMAMENTS

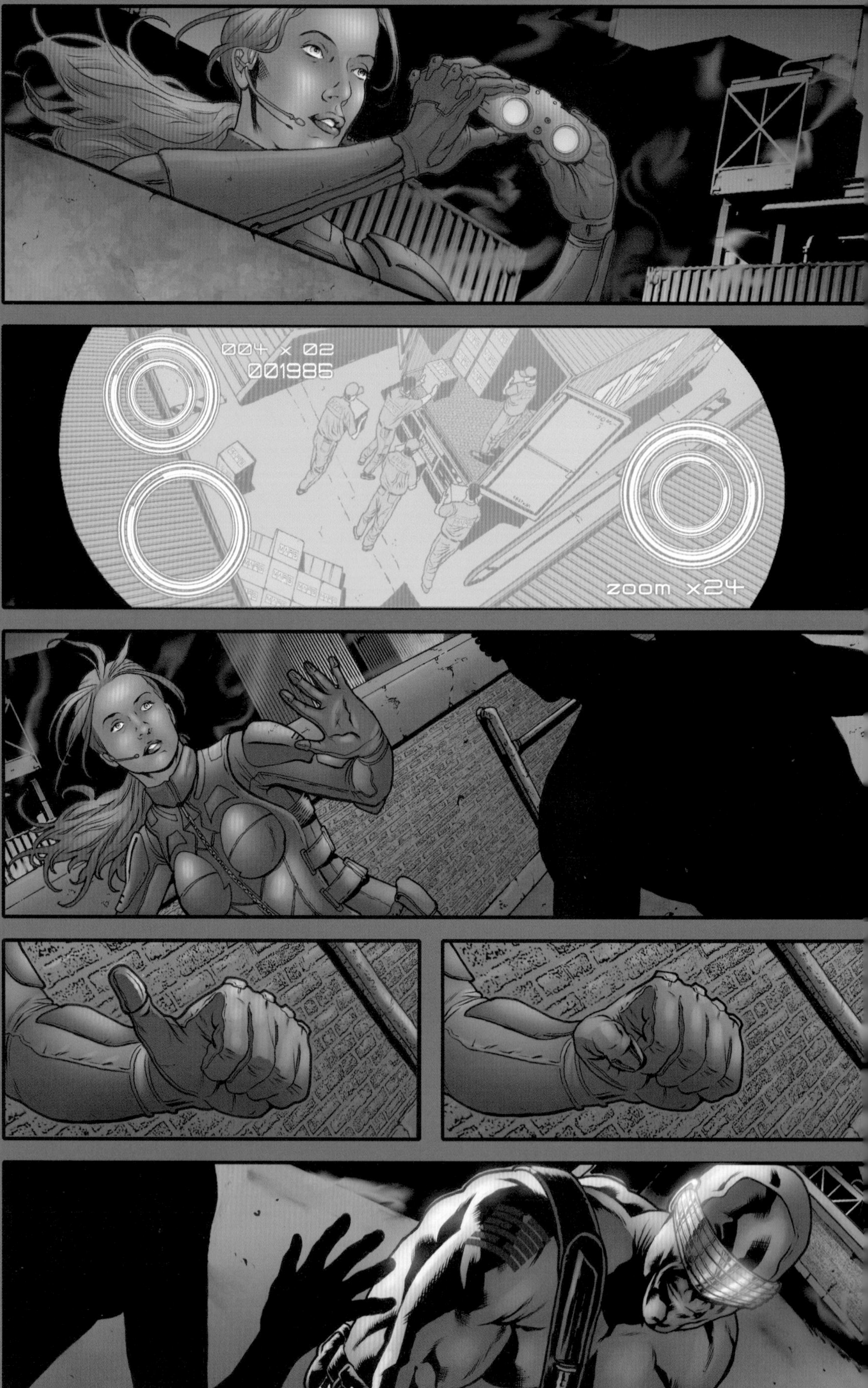
004 x 02
001985
zoom x24

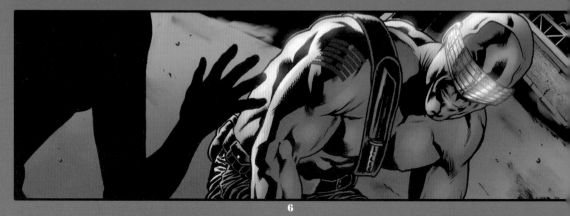

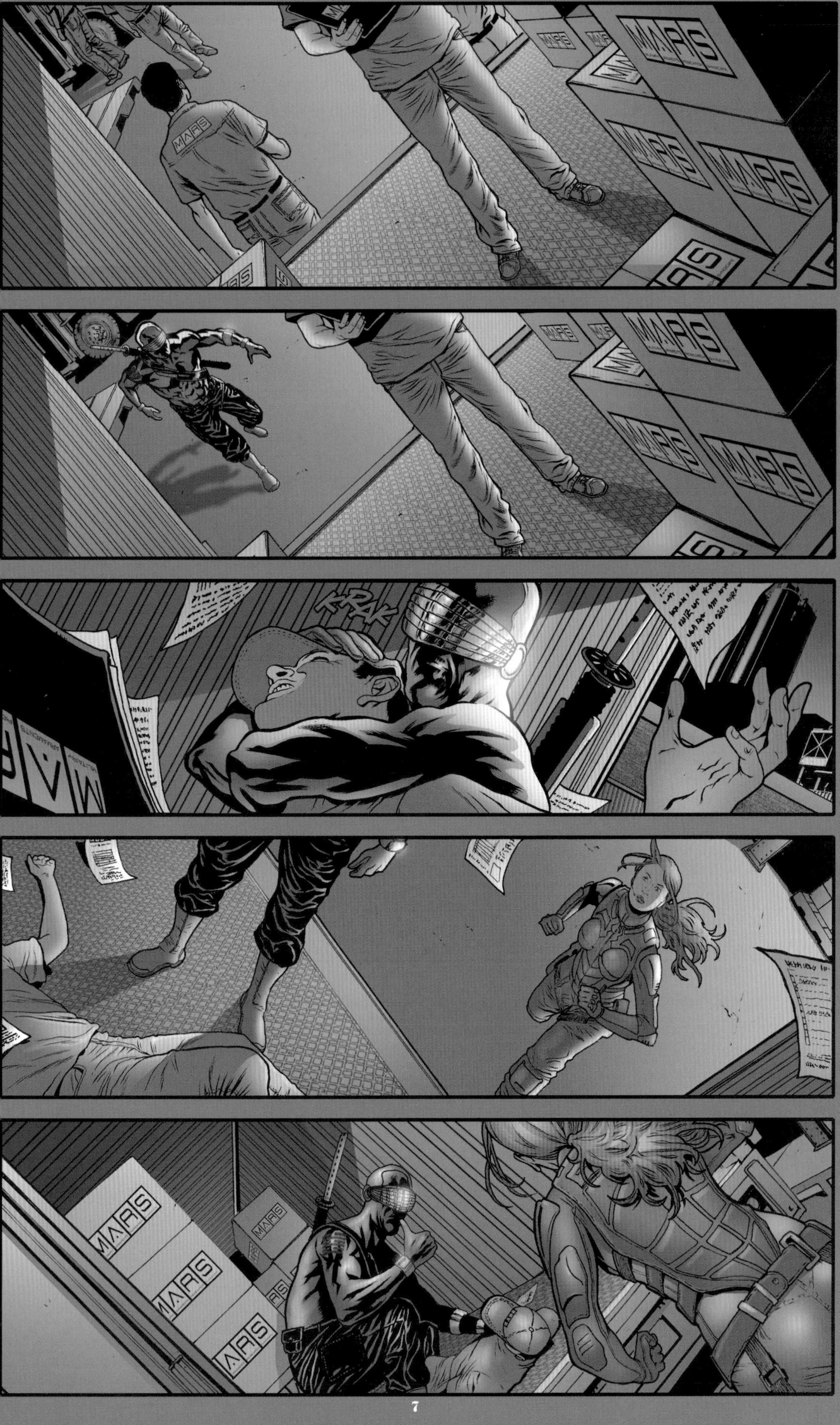
MARS
KRAK

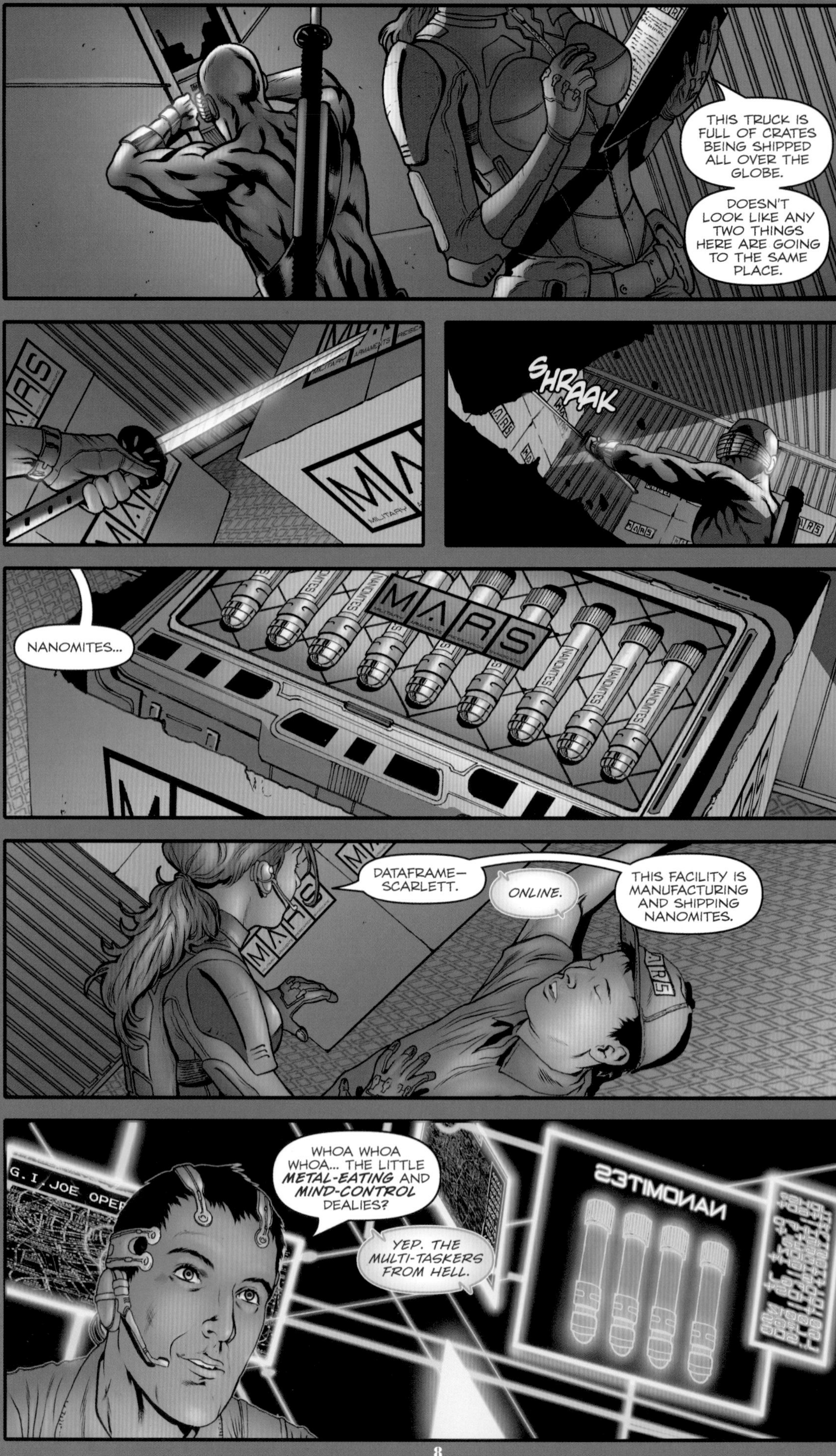
THIS TRUCK IS FULL OF CRATES BEING SHIPPED ALL OVER THE GLOBE.
DOESN'T LOOK LIKE ANY TWO THINGS HERE ARE GOING TO THE SAME PLACE.
SHRAAK
NANOMITES...
DATAFRAME— SCARLETT.
ONLINE.
THIS FACILITY IS MANUFACTURING AND SHIPPING NANOMITES.
WHOA WHOA WHOA... THE LITTLE METAL-EATING AND MIND-CONTROL DEALIES?
YEP. THE MULTI-TASKERS FROM HELL.

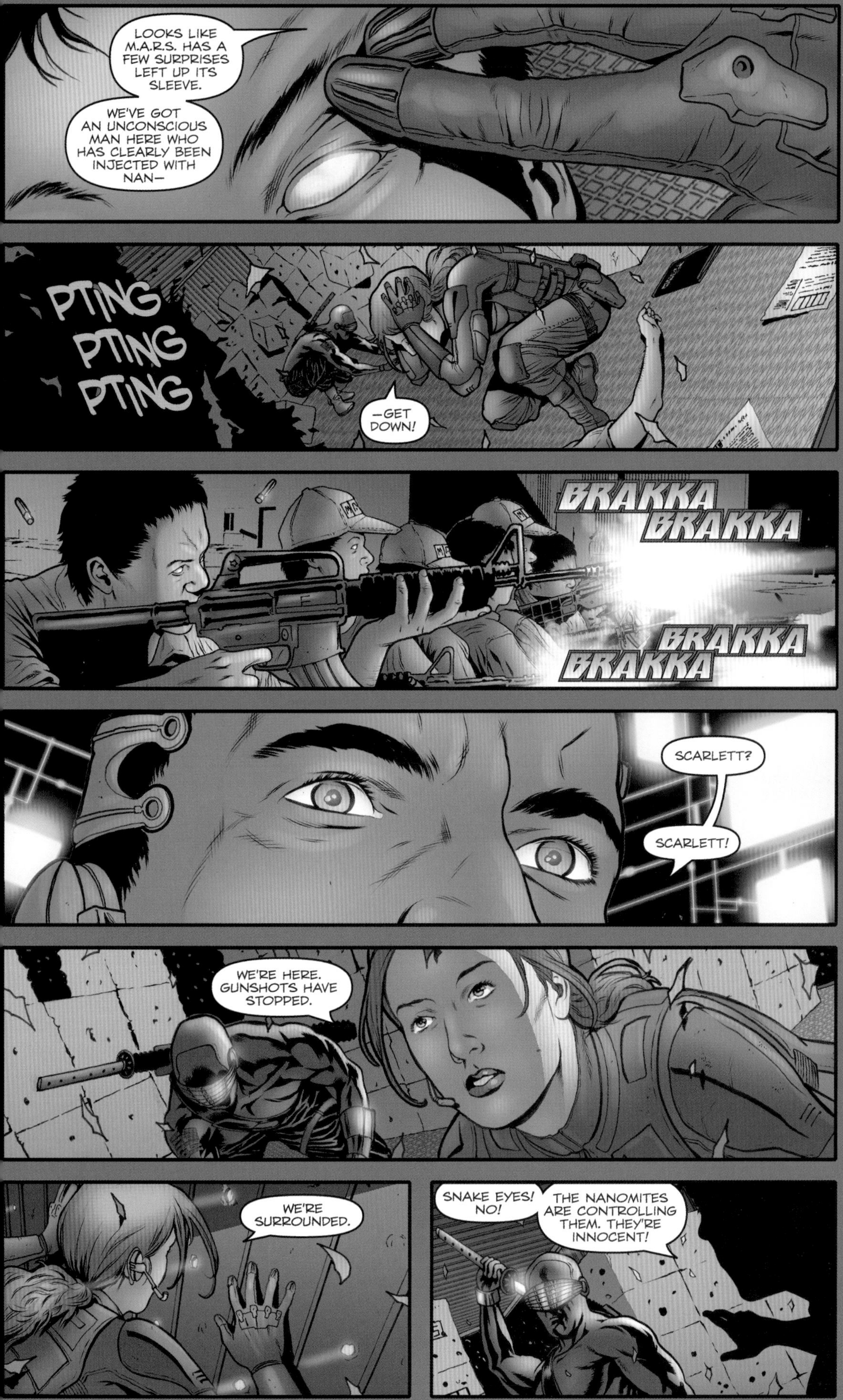
LOOKS LIKE M.A.R.S. HAS A FEW SURPRISES LEFT UP ITS SLEEVE.
WE'VE GOT AN UNCONSCIOUS MAN HERE WHO HAS CLEARLY BEEN INJECTED WITH NAN—
PTING PTING PTING
—GET DOWN!
BRAKKA BRAKKA
BRAKKA BRAKKA
SCARLETT?
SCARLETT!
WE'RE HERE. GUNSHOTS HAVE STOPPED.
WE'RE SURROUNDED.
SNAKE EYES! NO!
THE NANOMITES ARE CONTROLLING THEM. THEY'RE INNOCENT!

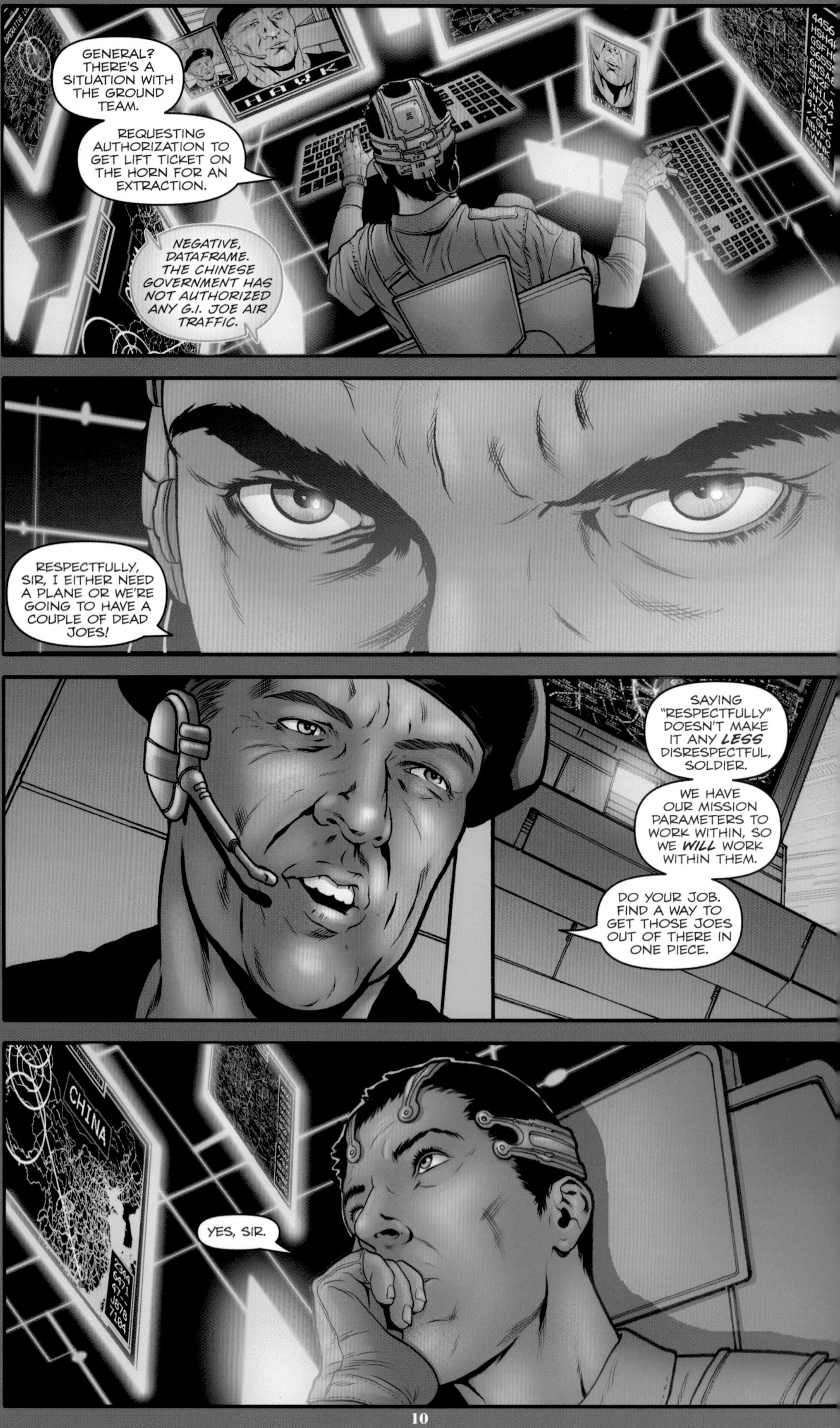
GENERAL? THERE'S A SITUATION WITH THE GROUND TEAM.
REQUESTING AUTHORIZATION TO GET LIFT TICKET ON THE HORN FOR AN EXTRACTION.
NEGATIVE, DATAFRAME. THE CHINESE GOVERNMENT HAS NOT AUTHORIZED ANY G.I. JOE AIR TRAFFIC.
HAWK
RESPECTFULLY, SIR, I EITHER NEED A PLANE OR WE'RE GOING TO HAVE A COUPLE OF DEAD JOES!
SAYING "RESPECTFULLY" DOESN'T MAKE IT ANY LESS DISRESPECTFUL, SOLDIER.
WE HAVE OUR MISSION PARAMETERS TO WORK WITHIN, SO WE WILL WORK WITHIN THEM.
DO YOUR JOB. FIND A WAY TO GET THOSE JOES OUT OF THERE IN ONE PIECE.
CHINA
YES, SIR.

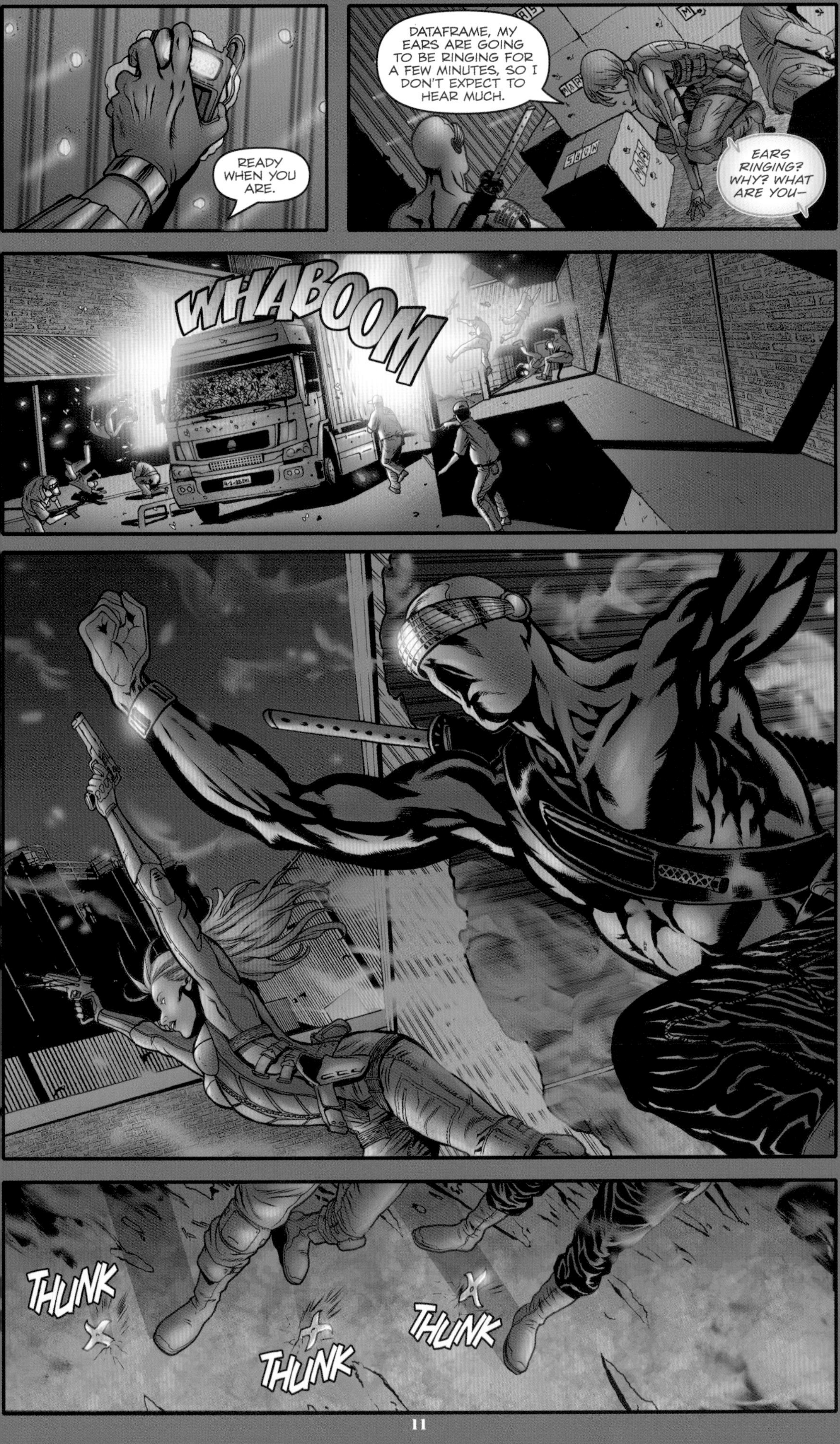
READY WHEN YOU ARE.
DATAFRAME, MY EARS ARE GOING TO BE RINGING FOR A FEW MINUTES, SO I DON'T EXPECT TO HEAR MUCH.
EARS RINGING? WHY? WHAT ARE YOU—
WHABOOM
THUNK
THUNK
THUNK

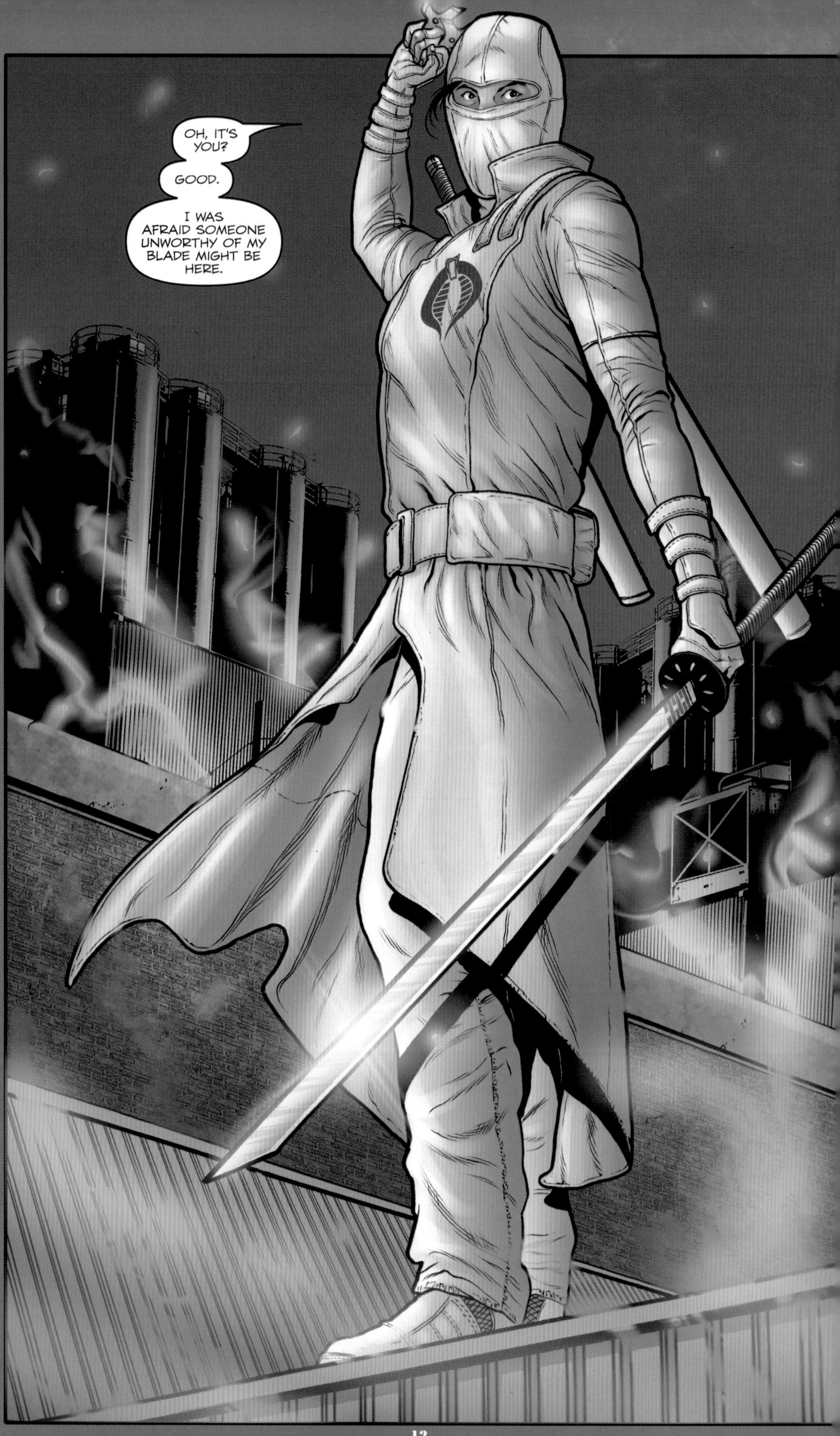
OH, IT'S YOU?
GOOD.
I WAS AFRAID SOMEONE UNWORTHY OF MY BLADE MIGHT BE HERE.

ALL RIGHT, ALL RIGHT...

I'LL GET GOING.

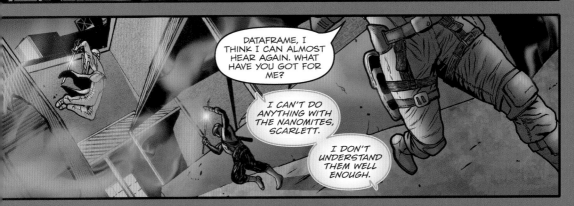

DATAFRAME, I THINK I CAN ALMOST HEAR AGAIN. WHAT HAVE YOU GOT FOR ME?

I CAN'T DO ANYTHING WITH THE NANOMITES, SCARLETT.

I DON'T UNDERSTAND THEM WELL ENOUGH.

WHAT DO YOU HAVE FOR BUILDING SCHEMATICS?

WE HAVE ACCESS TO ALL OF THE M.A.R.S. FILES BEFORE THE FACTORY WENT OFFLINE.

TELL ME WHERE THE COMPUTERS ARE THAT CONTROL THE ASSEMBLY LINES.

AND TELL ME QUICK—

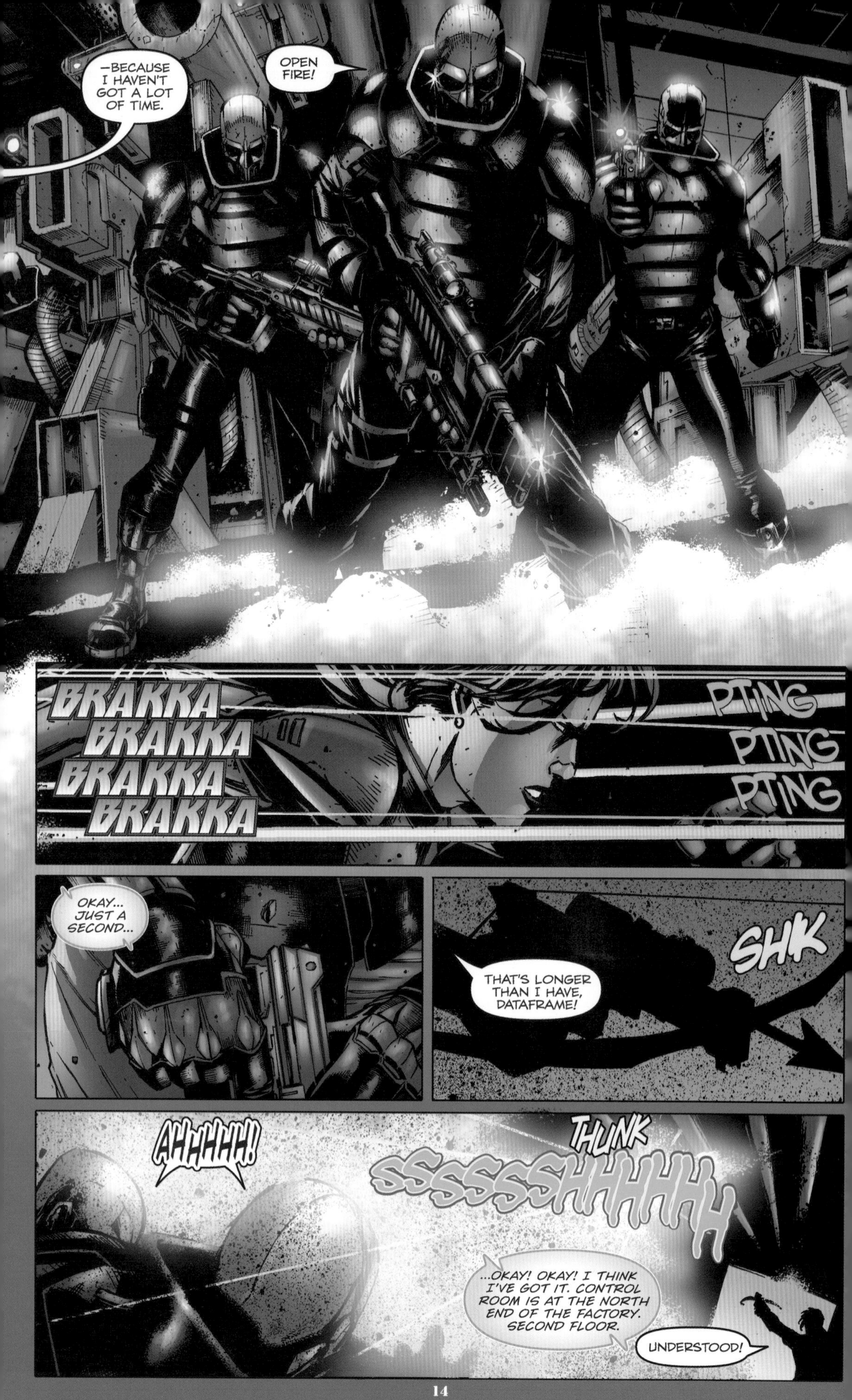
—BECAUSE I HAVEN'T GOT A LOT OF TIME.
OPEN FIRE!
BRAKKA BRAKKA BRAKKA BRAKKA
PTING PTING PTING
OKAY... JUST A SECOND...
THAT'S LONGER THAN I HAVE, DATAFRAME!
SHK
AHHHHH!
THUNK
SSSSSSHHHHHH
...OKAY! OKAY! I THINK I'VE GOT IT. CONTROL ROOM IS AT THE NORTH END OF THE FACTORY. SECOND FLOOR.
UNDERSTOOD!

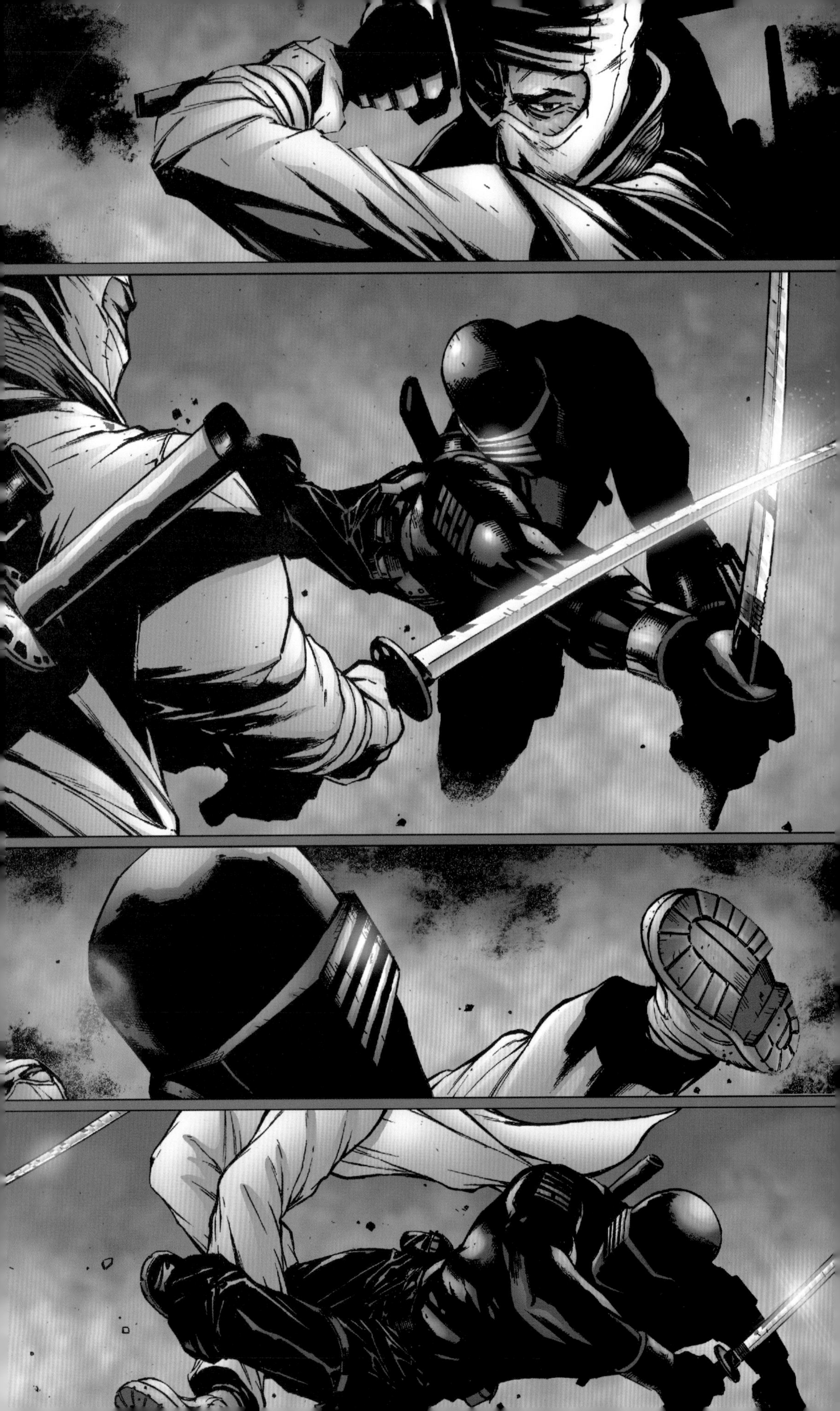

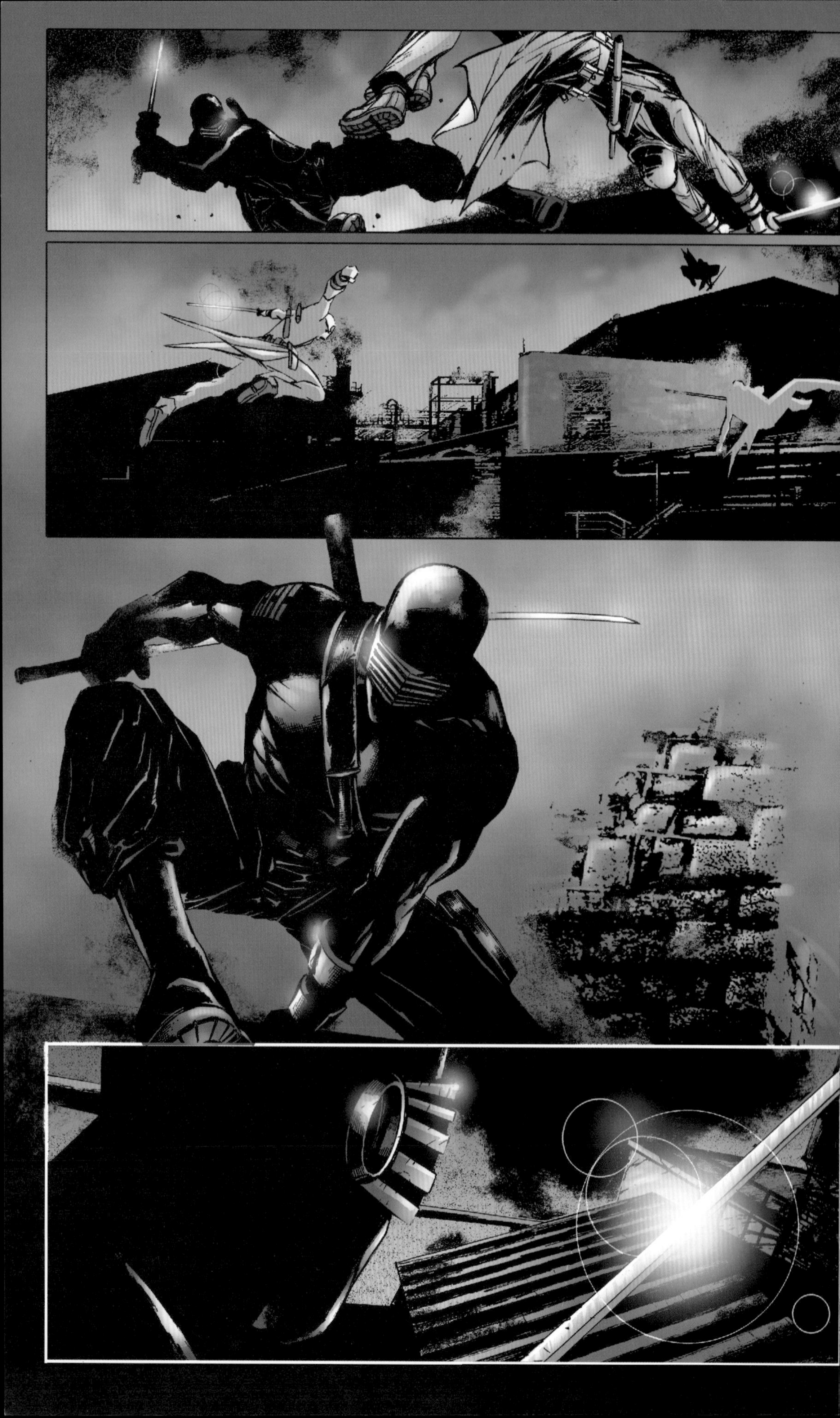

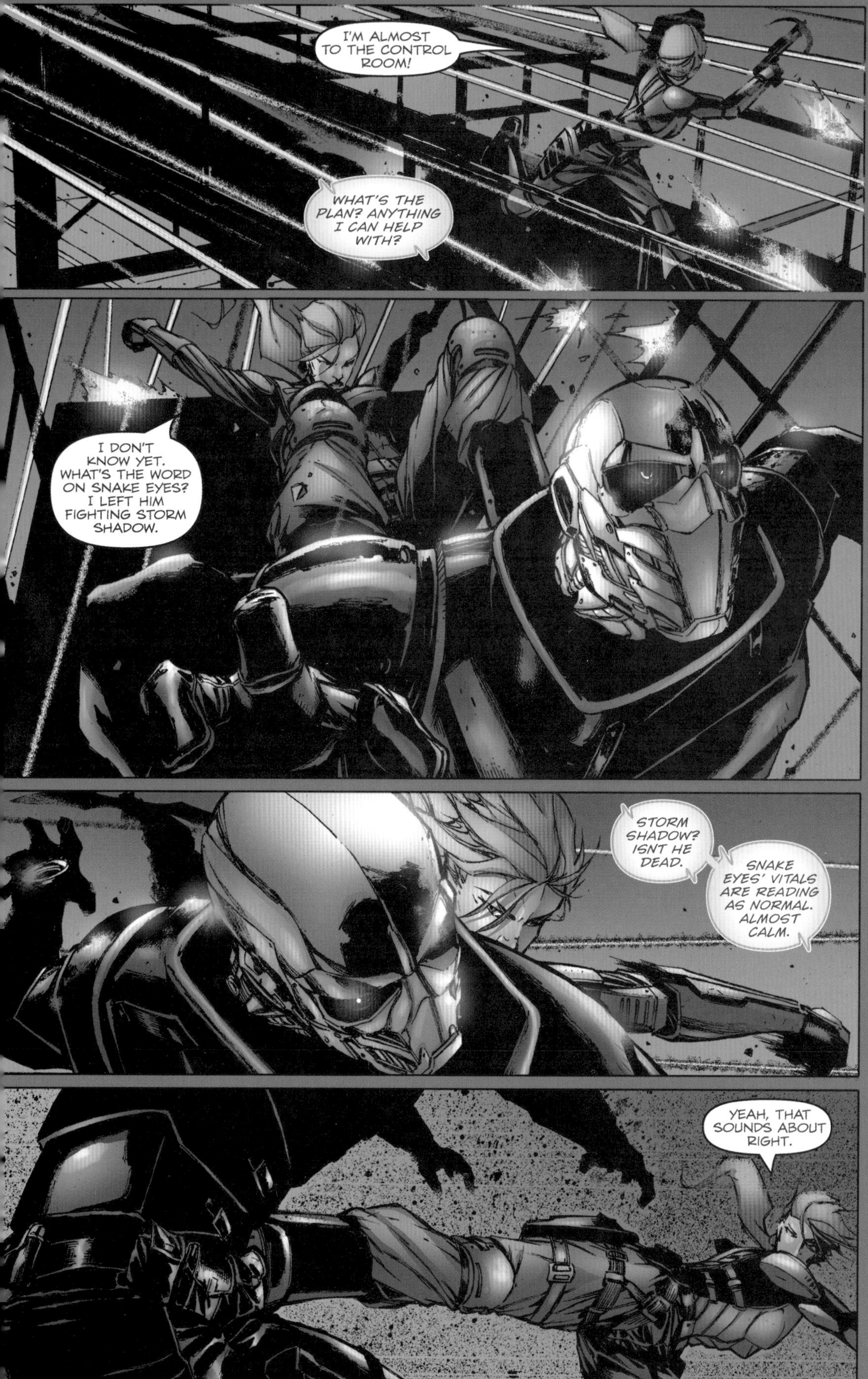
I'M ALMOST TO THE CONTROL ROOM!
WHAT'S THE PLAN? ANYTHING I CAN HELP WITH?
I DON'T KNOW YET. WHAT'S THE WORD ON SNAKE EYES? I LEFT HIM FIGHTING STORM SHADOW.
STORM SHADOW? ISNT HE DEAD.
SNAKE EYES' VITALS ARE READING AS NORMAL. ALMOST CALM.
YEAH, THAT SOUNDS ABOUT RIGHT.

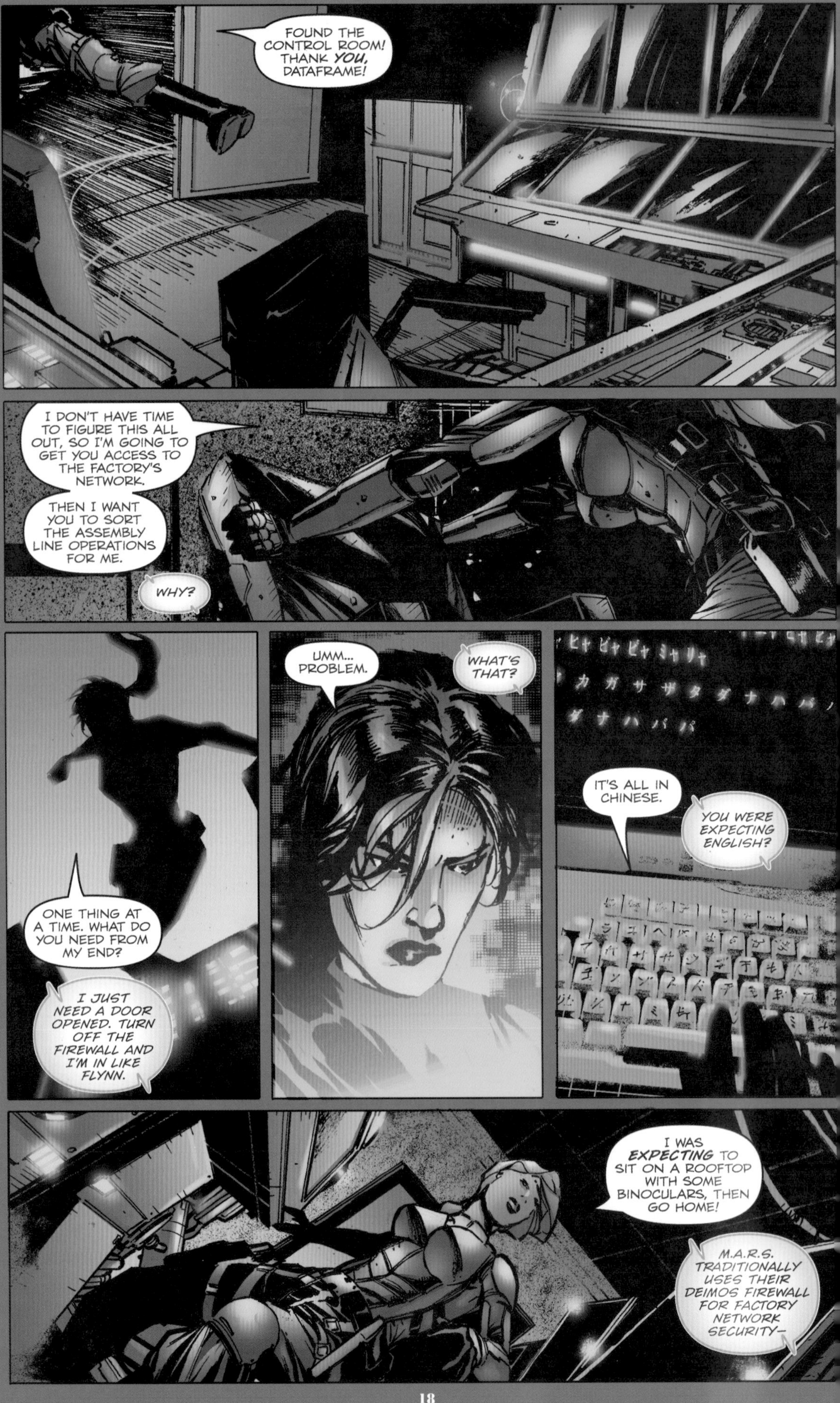
FOUND THE CONTROL ROOM! THANK *YOU,* DATAFRAME!
I DON'T HAVE TIME TO FIGURE THIS ALL OUT, SO I'M GOING TO GET YOU ACCESS TO THE FACTORY'S NETWORK.
THEN I WANT YOU TO SORT THE ASSEMBLY LINE OPERATIONS FOR ME.
WHY?
ONE THING AT A TIME. WHAT DO YOU NEED FROM MY END?
I JUST NEED A DOOR OPENED. TURN OFF THE FIREWALL AND I'M IN LIKE FLYNN.
UMM... PROBLEM.
WHAT'S THAT?
IT'S ALL IN CHINESE.
YOU WERE EXPECTING ENGLISH?
I WAS *EXPECTING* TO SIT ON A ROOFTOP WITH SOME BINOCULARS, THEN GO HOME!
M.A.R.S. TRADITIONALLY USES THEIR DEIMOS FIREWALL FOR FACTORY NETWORK SECURITY—

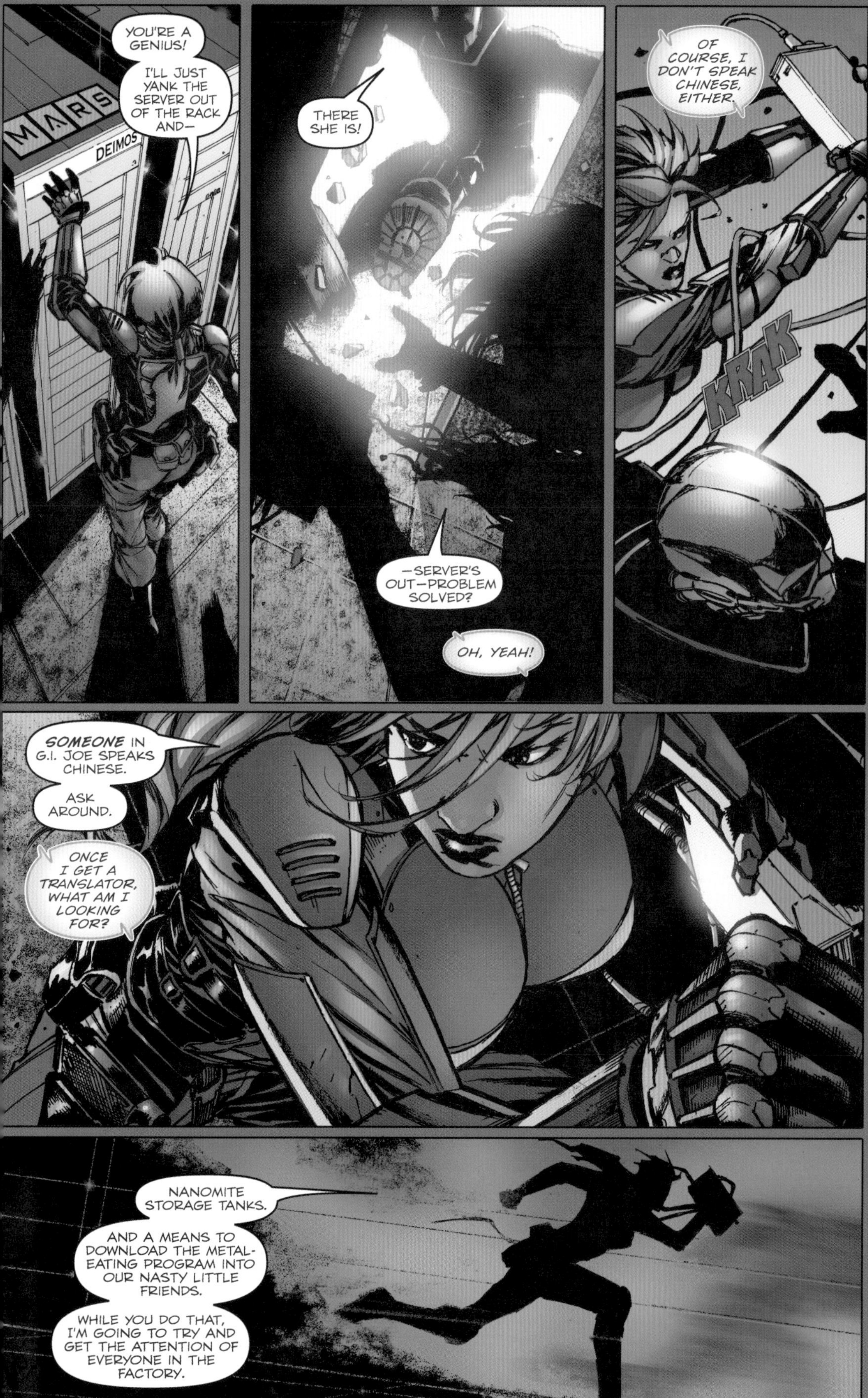
YOU'RE A GENIUS!
I'LL JUST YANK THE SERVER OUT OF THE RACK AND—
MARS
DEIMOS
THERE SHE IS!
—SERVER'S OUT—PROBLEM SOLVED?
OH, YEAH!
OF COURSE, I DON'T SPEAK CHINESE, EITHER.
KRAK
SOMEONE IN G.I. JOE SPEAKS CHINESE.
ASK AROUND.
ONCE I GET A TRANSLATOR, WHAT AM I LOOKING FOR?
NANOMITE STORAGE TANKS.
AND A MEANS TO DOWNLOAD THE METAL-EATING PROGRAM INTO OUR NASTY LITTLE FRIENDS.
WHILE YOU DO THAT, I'M GOING TO TRY AND GET THE ATTENTION OF EVERYONE IN THE FACTORY.

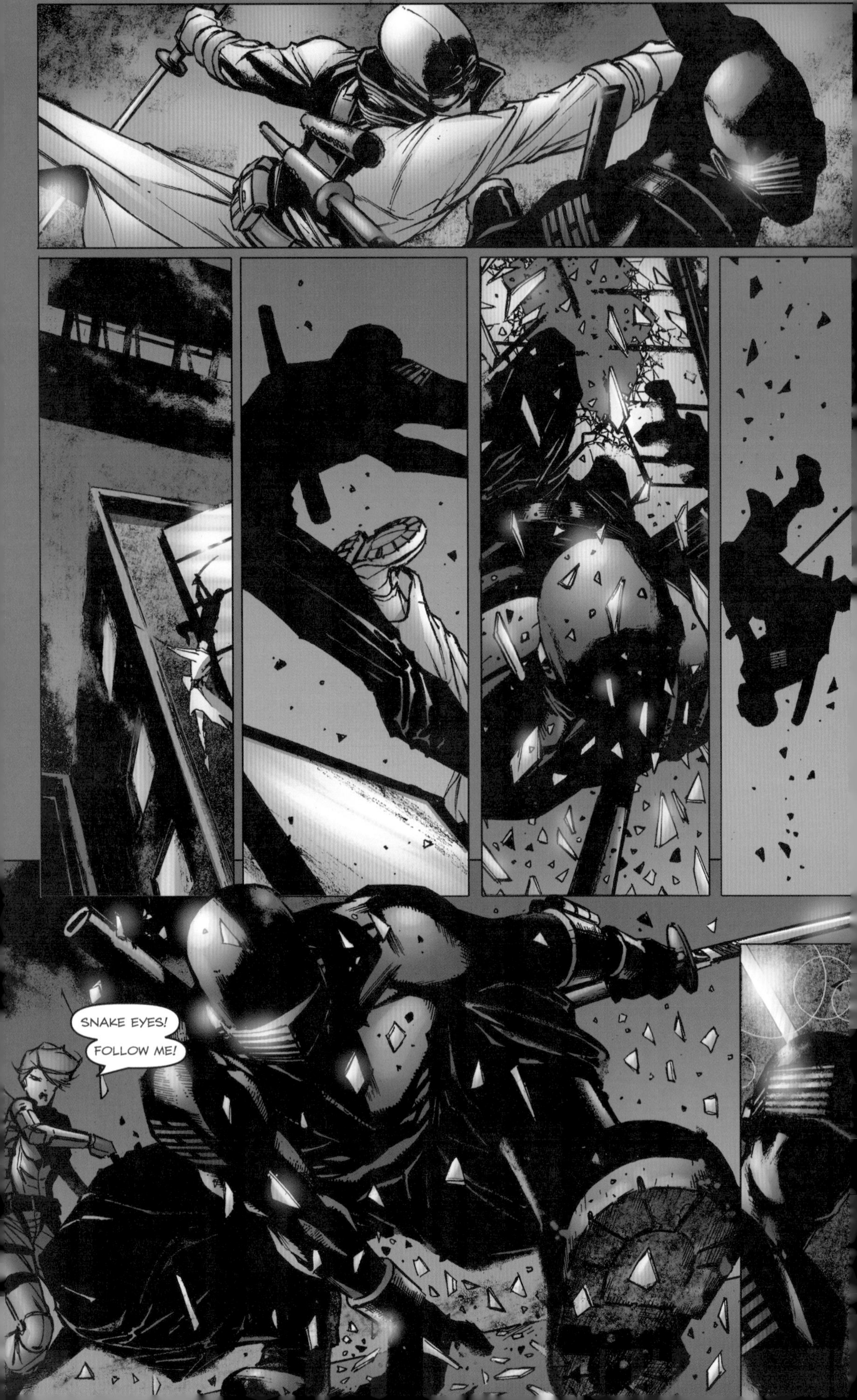
SNAKE EYES!
FOLLOW ME!

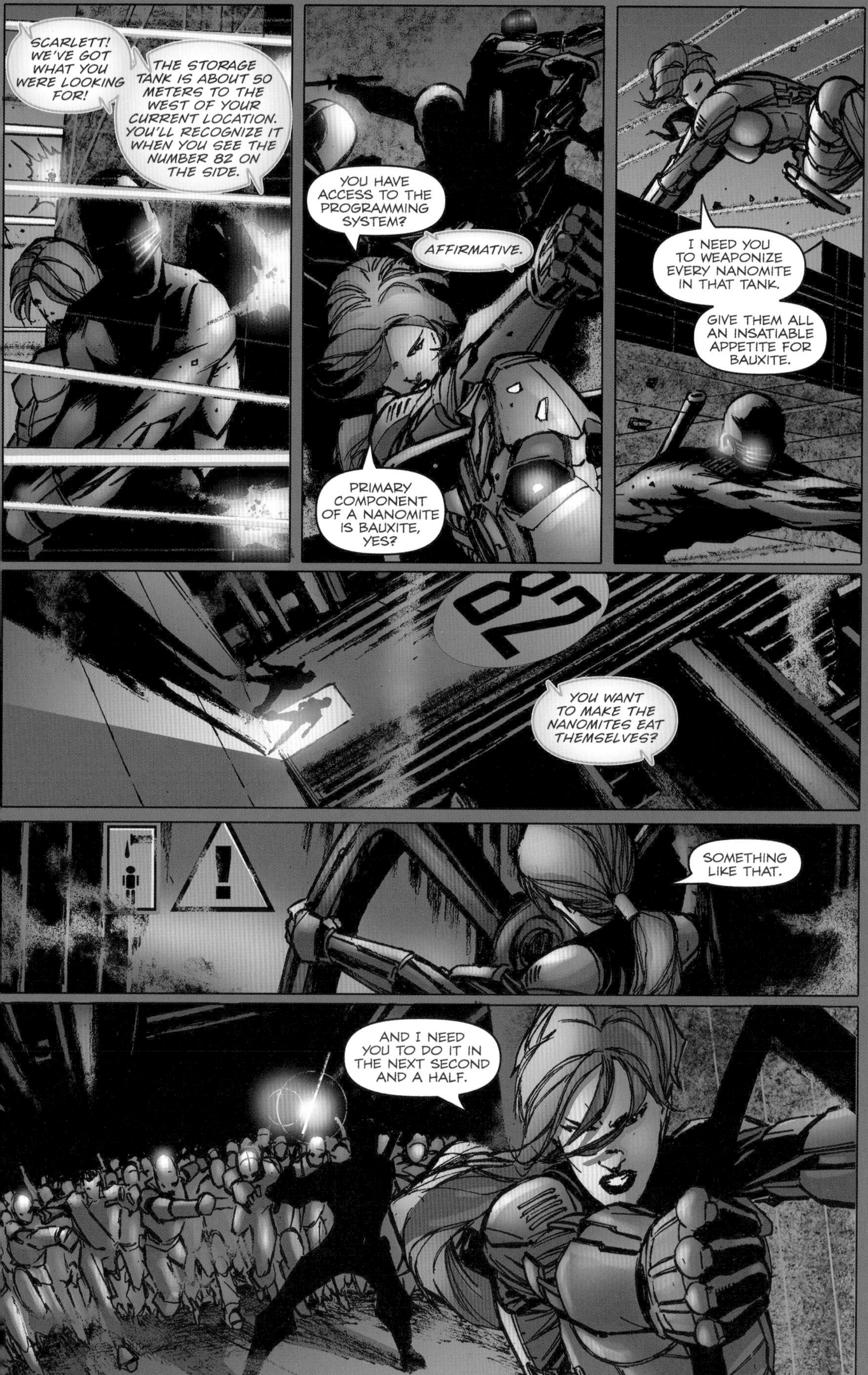

SCARLETT! WE'VE GOT WHAT YOU WERE LOOKING FOR!
THE STORAGE TANK IS ABOUT 50 METERS TO THE WEST OF YOUR CURRENT LOCATION. YOU'LL RECOGNIZE IT WHEN YOU SEE THE NUMBER 82 ON THE SIDE.
YOU HAVE ACCESS TO THE PROGRAMMING SYSTEM?
AFFIRMATIVE.
PRIMARY COMPONENT OF A NANOMITE IS BAUXITE, YES?
I NEED YOU TO WEAPONIZE EVERY NANOMITE IN THAT TANK.
GIVE THEM ALL AN INSATIABLE APPETITE FOR BAUXITE.
82
YOU WANT TO MAKE THE NANOMITES EAT THEMSELVES?
SOMETHING LIKE THAT.
AND I NEED YOU TO DO IT IN THE NEXT SECOND AND A HALF.

UPLOADING NOW!

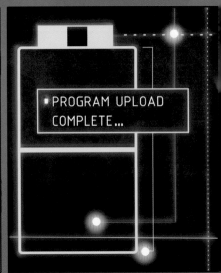

PROGRAM UPLOAD COMPLETE...

FWO OOSH

‹WHAT HAPPENED? WHERE AM I?›

SO, TO RECAP...

...YOU WALKED ONTO THE M.A.R.S. PROPERTY, AND EVERYTHING INSTANTLY WENT TO HELL.

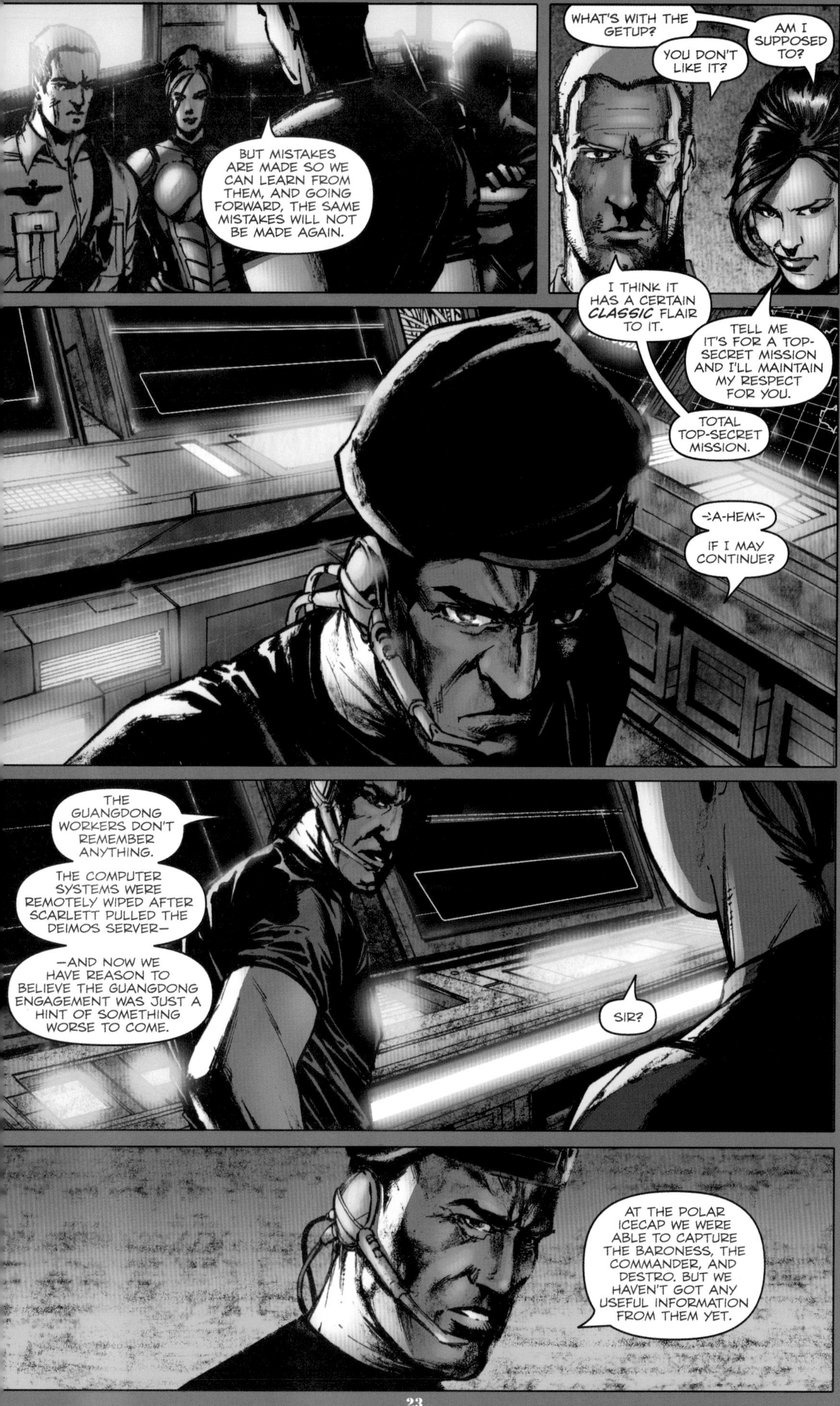
BUT MISTAKES ARE MADE SO WE CAN LEARN FROM THEM, AND GOING FORWARD, THE SAME MISTAKES WILL NOT BE MADE AGAIN.
WHAT'S WITH THE GETUP?
YOU DON'T LIKE IT?
AM I SUPPOSED TO?
I THINK IT HAS A CERTAIN CLASSIC FLAIR TO IT.
TELL ME IT'S FOR A TOP-SECRET MISSION AND I'LL MAINTAIN MY RESPECT FOR YOU.
TOTAL TOP-SECRET MISSION.
-A-HEM-
IF I MAY CONTINUE?
THE GUANGDONG WORKERS DON'T REMEMBER ANYTHING.
THE COMPUTER SYSTEMS WERE REMOTELY WIPED AFTER SCARLETT PULLED THE DEIMOS SERVER—
—AND NOW WE HAVE REASON TO BELIEVE THE GUANGDONG ENGAGEMENT WAS JUST A HINT OF SOMETHING WORSE TO COME.
SIR?
AT THE POLAR ICECAP WE WERE ABLE TO CAPTURE THE BARONESS, THE COMMANDER, AND DESTRO. BUT WE HAVEN'T GOT ANY USEFUL INFORMATION FROM THEM YET.

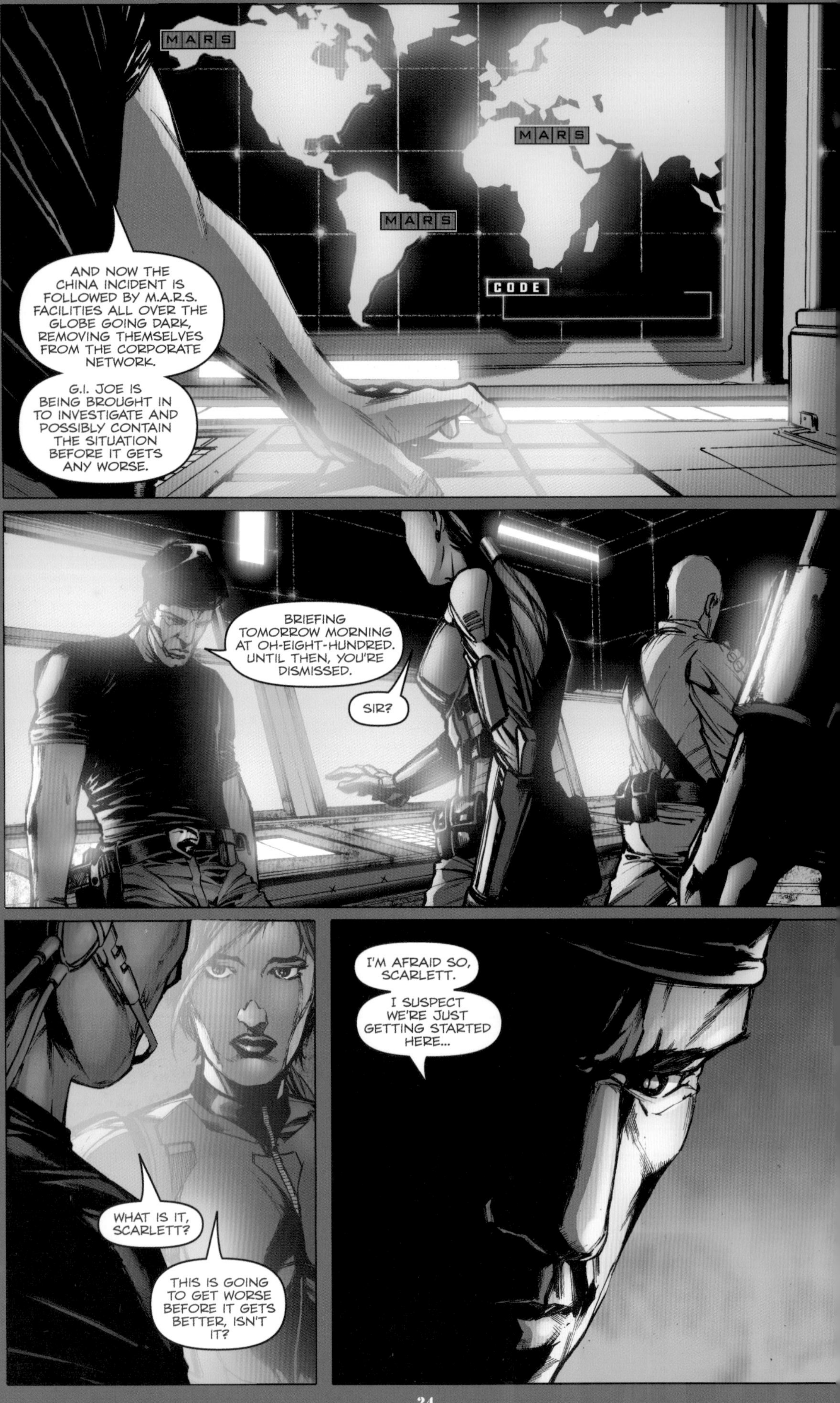
MARS
MARS
MARS
CODE
AND NOW THE CHINA INCIDENT IS FOLLOWED BY M.A.R.S. FACILITIES ALL OVER THE GLOBE GOING DARK, REMOVING THEMSELVES FROM THE CORPORATE NETWORK.
G.I. JOE IS BEING BROUGHT IN TO INVESTIGATE AND POSSIBLY CONTAIN THE SITUATION BEFORE IT GETS ANY WORSE.
BRIEFING TOMORROW MORNING AT OH-EIGHT-HUNDRED. UNTIL THEN, YOU'RE DISMISSED.
SIR?
WHAT IS IT, SCARLETT?
THIS IS GOING TO GET WORSE BEFORE IT GETS BETTER, ISN'T IT?
I'M AFRAID SO, SCARLETT.
I SUSPECT WE'RE JUST GETTING STARTED HERE...

WESTON, ARIZONA

2

STAN'S PLACE

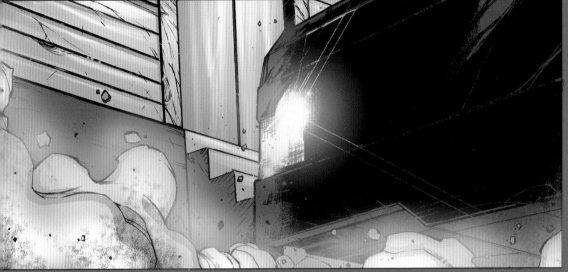

CONRAD "DUKE" HAUSER—STATUS:
INITIATING UNDERCOVER OPERATION

DAVID IRVINE?

YES?

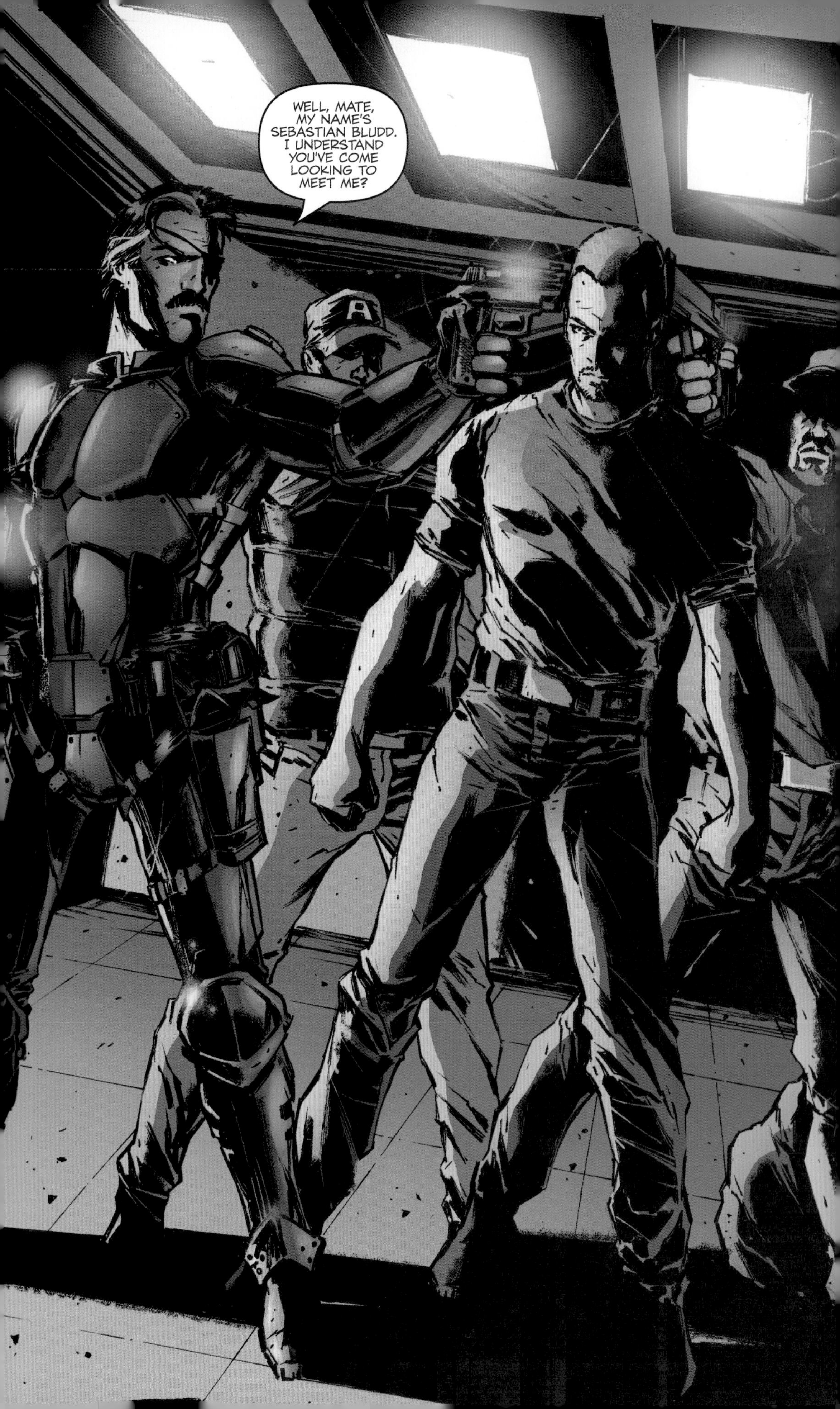
WELL, MATE, MY NAME'S SEBASTIAN BLUDD. I UNDERSTAND YOU'VE COME LOOKING TO MEET ME?

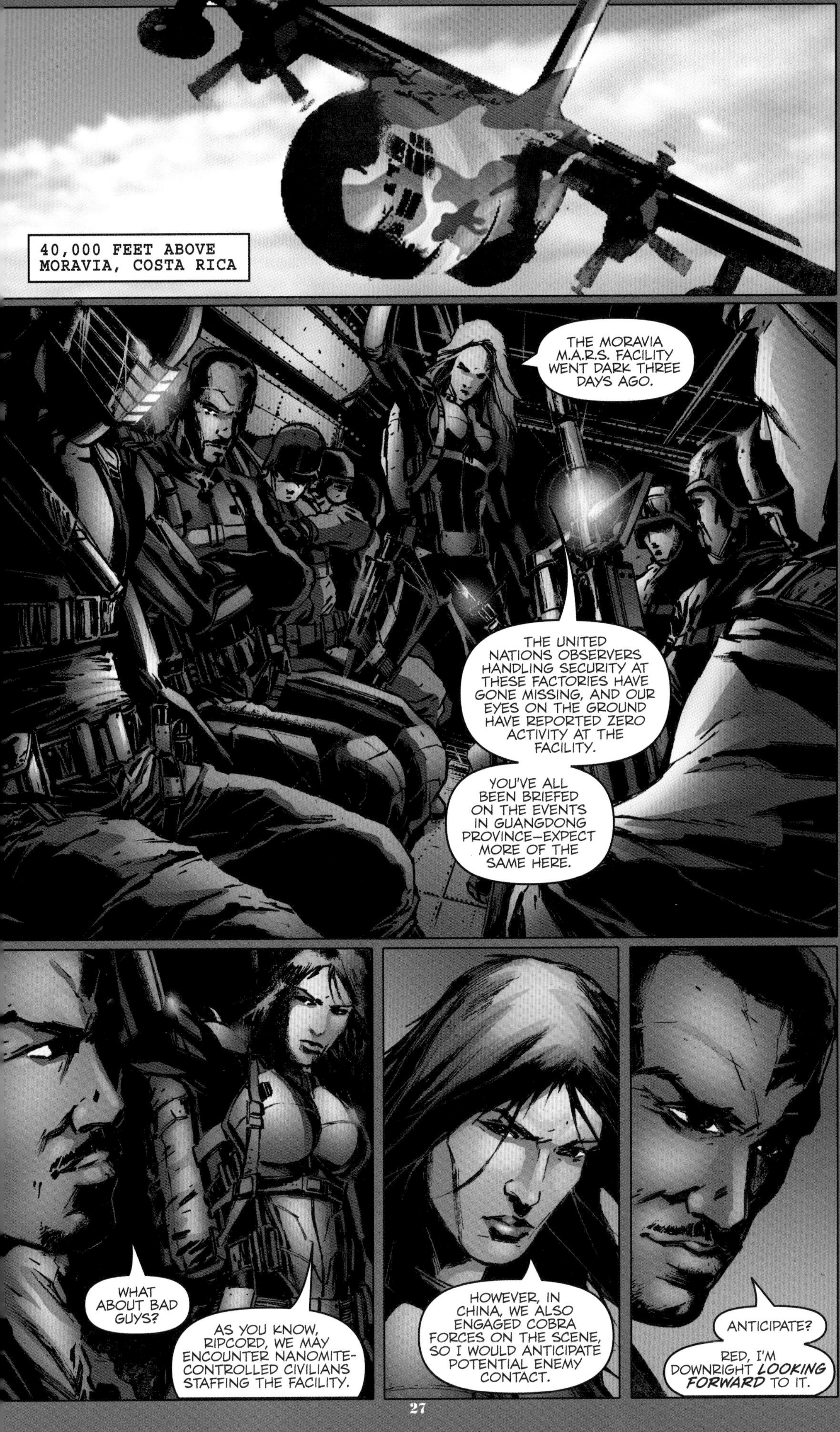
40,000 FEET ABOVE MORAVIA, COSTA RICA
THE MORAVIA M.A.R.S. FACILITY WENT DARK THREE DAYS AGO.
THE UNITED NATIONS OBSERVERS HANDLING SECURITY AT THESE FACTORIES HAVE GONE MISSING, AND OUR EYES ON THE GROUND HAVE REPORTED ZERO ACTIVITY AT THE FACILITY.
YOU'VE ALL BEEN BRIEFED ON THE EVENTS IN GUANGDONG PROVINCE—EXPECT MORE OF THE SAME HERE.
WHAT ABOUT BAD GUYS?
AS YOU KNOW, RIPCORD, WE MAY ENCOUNTER NANOMITE-CONTROLLED CIVILIANS STAFFING THE FACILITY.
HOWEVER, IN CHINA, WE ALSO ENGAGED COBRA FORCES ON THE SCENE, SO I WOULD ANTICIPATE POTENTIAL ENEMY CONTACT.
ANTICIPATE?
RED, I'M DOWNRIGHT ***LOOKING FORWARD*** TO IT.

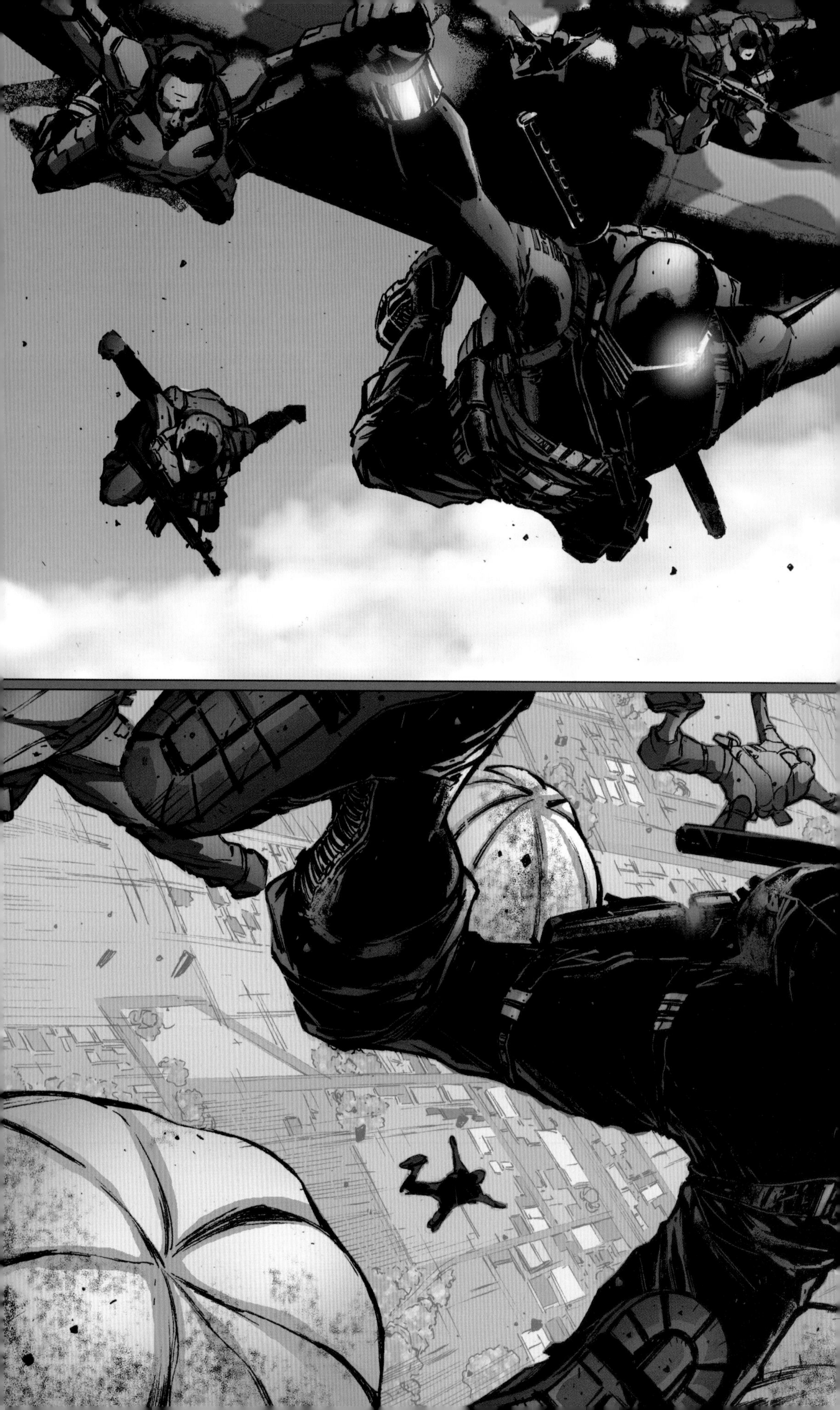

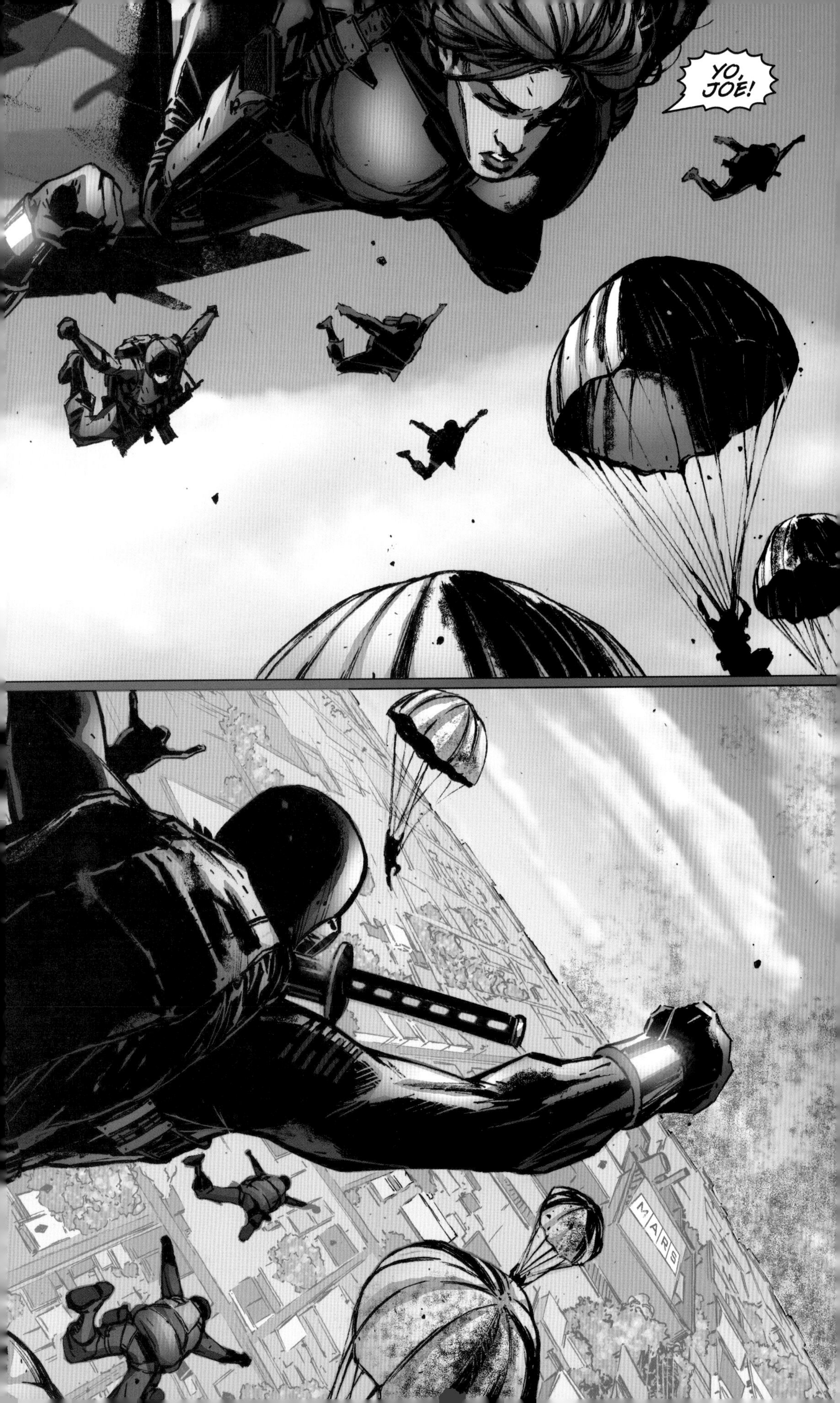
YO, JOE!
MARS

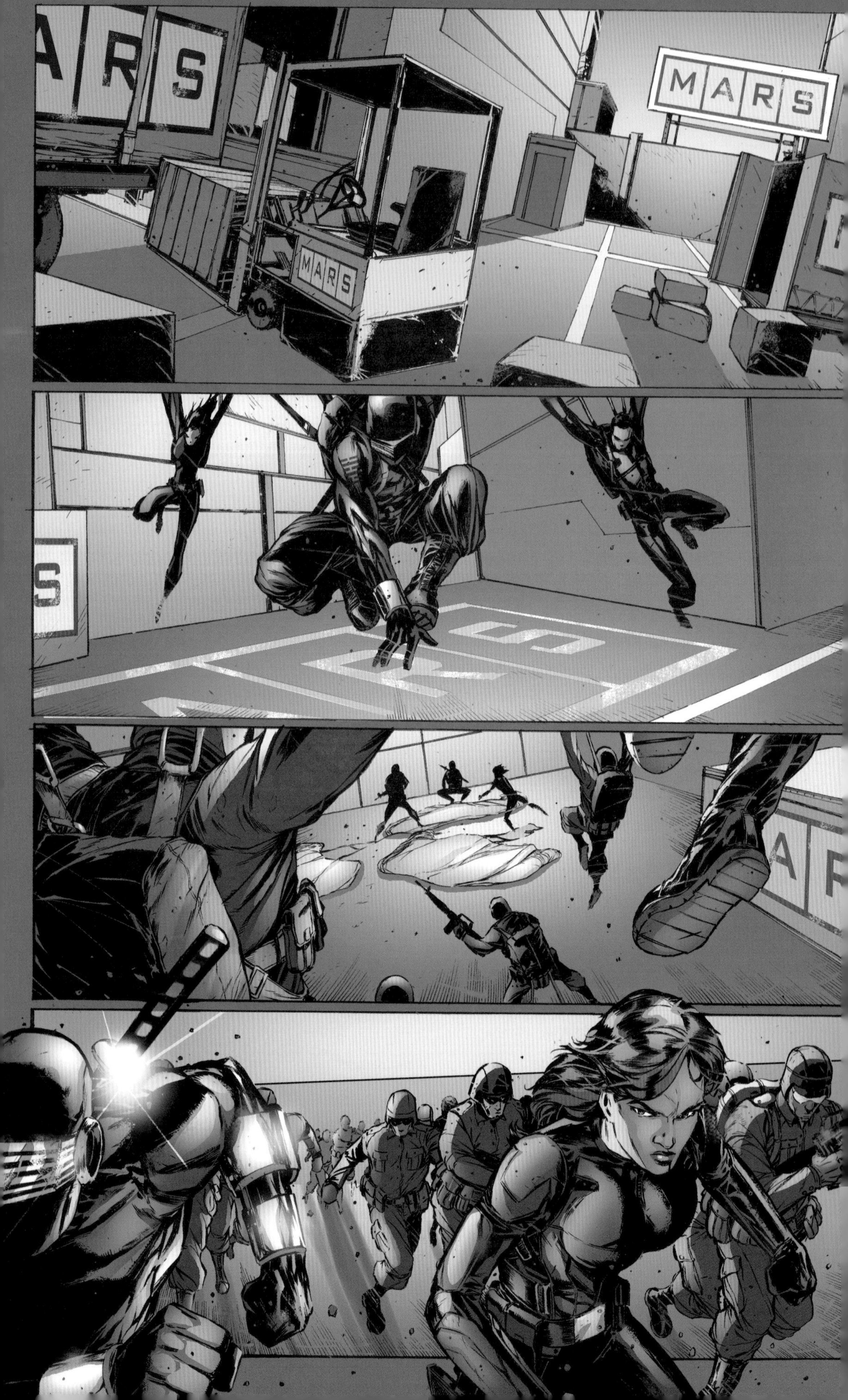
MARS
MARS

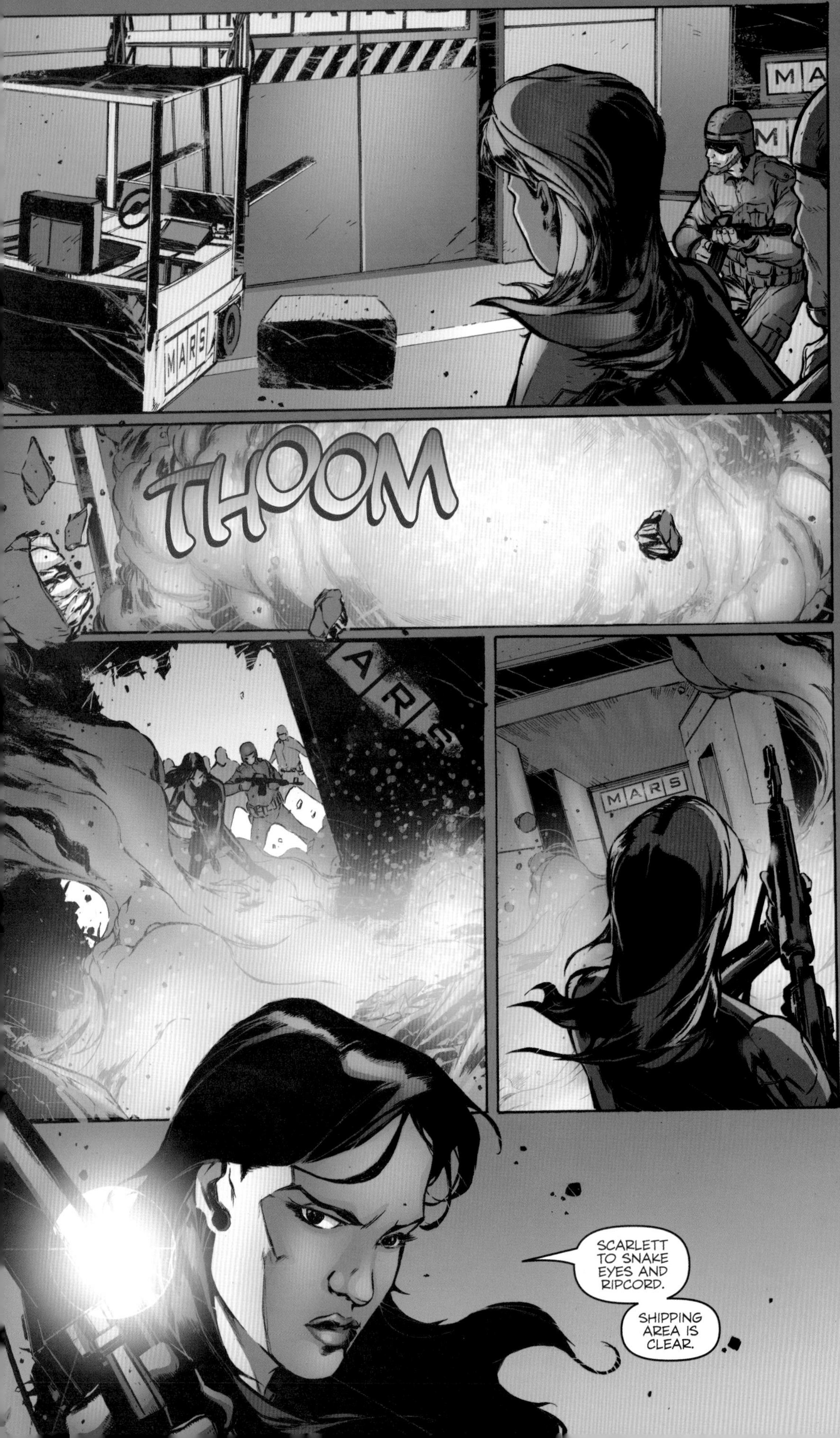
MARS
THOOM
SCARLETT TO SNAKE EYES AND RIPCORD.
SHIPPING AREA IS CLEAR.

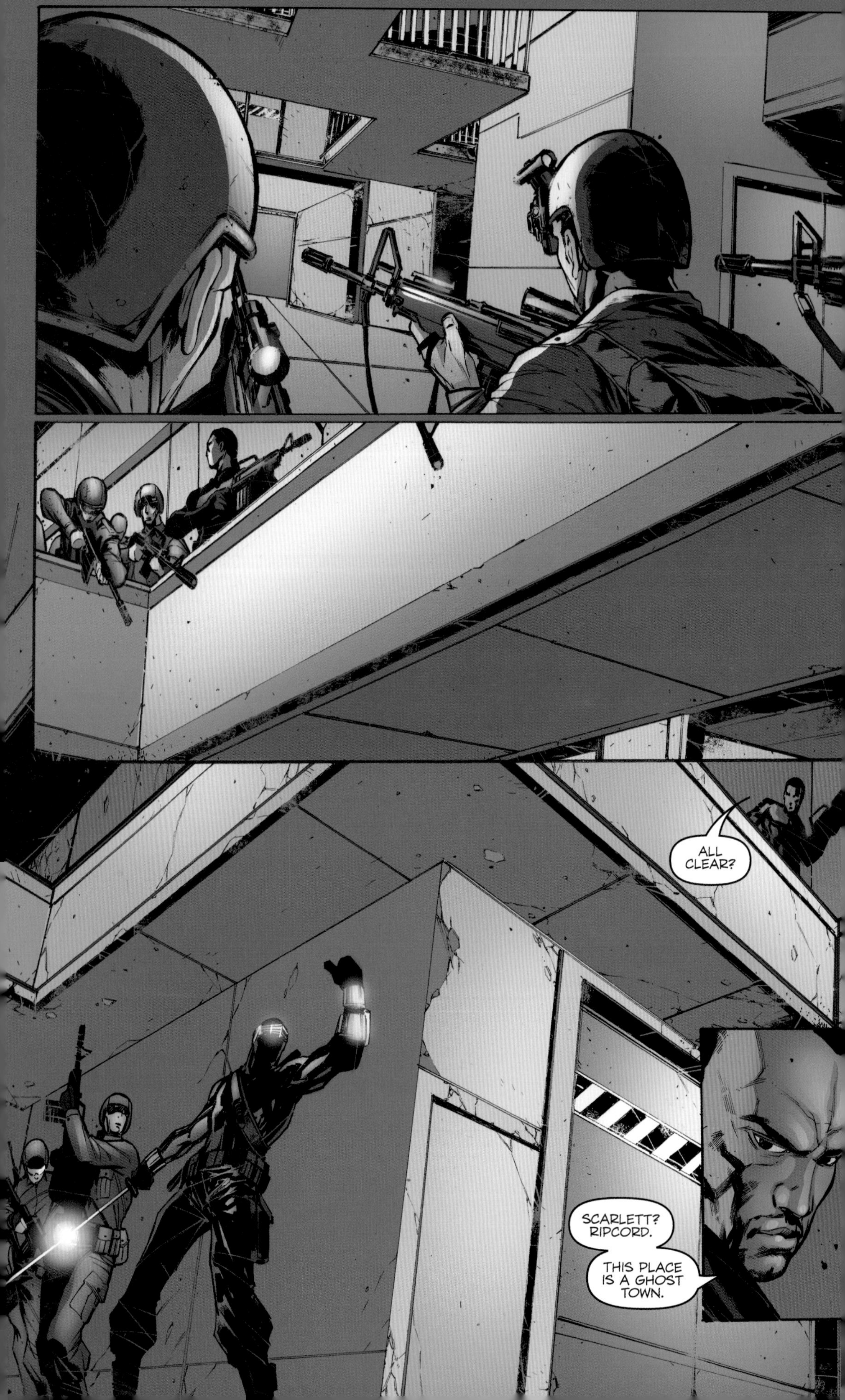
ALL CLEAR?
SCARLETT? RIPCORD.
THIS PLACE IS A GHOST TOWN.

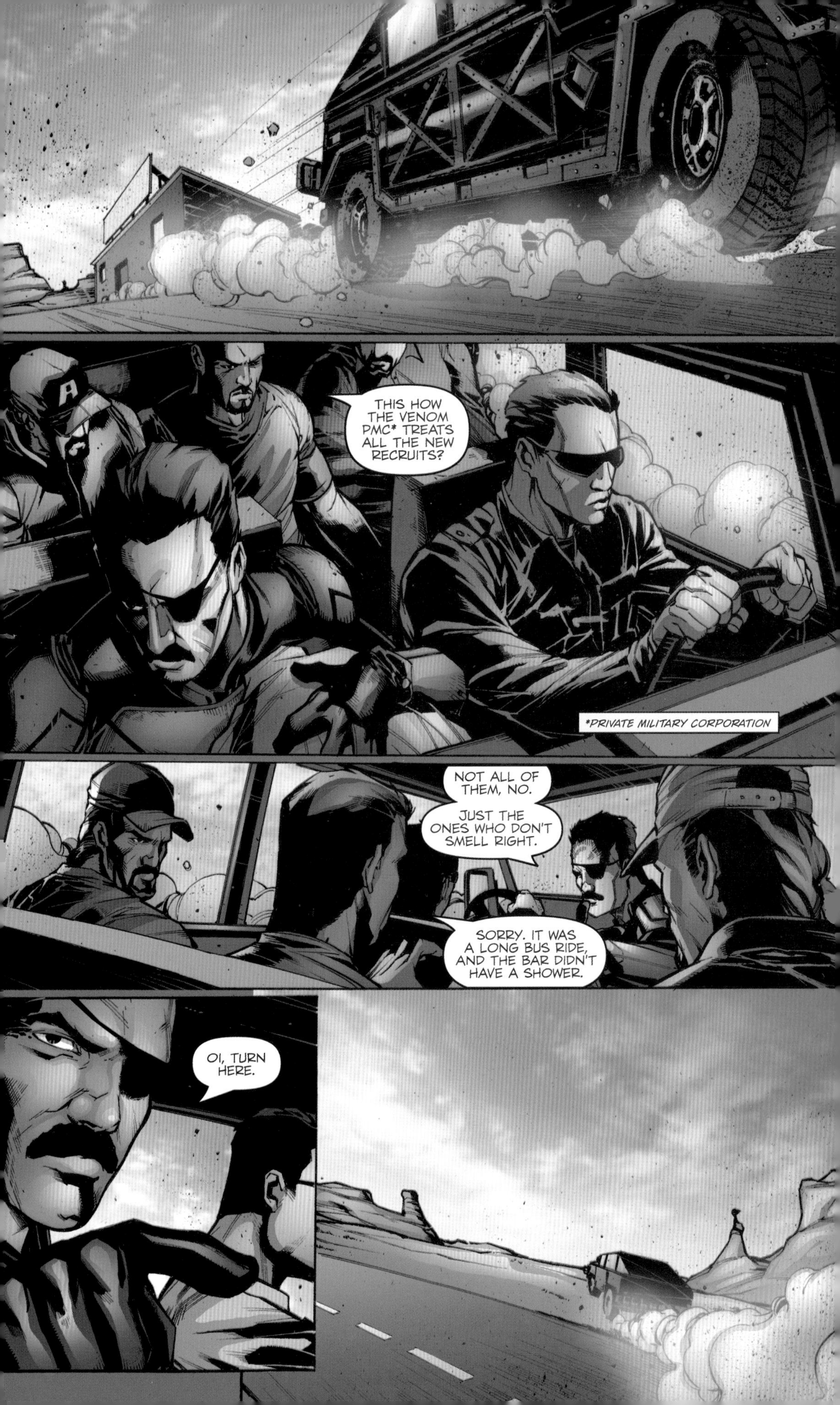
THIS HOW THE VENOM PMC* TREATS ALL THE NEW RECRUITS?
*PRIVATE MILITARY CORPORATION
NOT ALL OF THEM, NO.
JUST THE ONES WHO DON'T SMELL RIGHT.
SORRY. IT WAS A LONG BUS RIDE, AND THE BAR DIDN'T HAVE A SHOWER.
OI, TURN HERE.

DAVID, WHY DO YOU WANT TO JOIN VENOM?

I'D HEARD YOUR COMPANY WAS THE BEST THERE IS.

OH, WE ARE, MATE.

BUT WE HAVE TO BE CAREFUL WITH WHOM WE LET IN THE DOOR NOW, DON'T WE?

SO... ...MY BACKGROUND CHECK DIDN'T WORK OUT?

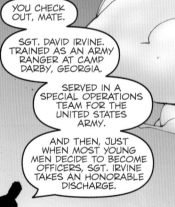

YOU CHECK OUT, MATE.

SGT. DAVID IRVINE. TRAINED AS AN ARMY RANGER AT CAMP DARBY, GEORGIA.

SERVED IN A SPECIAL OPERATIONS TEAM FOR THE UNITED STATES ARMY.

AND THEN, JUST WHEN MOST YOUNG MEN DECIDE TO BECOME OFFICERS, SGT. IRVINE TAKES AN HONORABLE DISCHARGE.

SIX MONTHS LATER, YOU'RE KNOCKING ON MY DOOR.

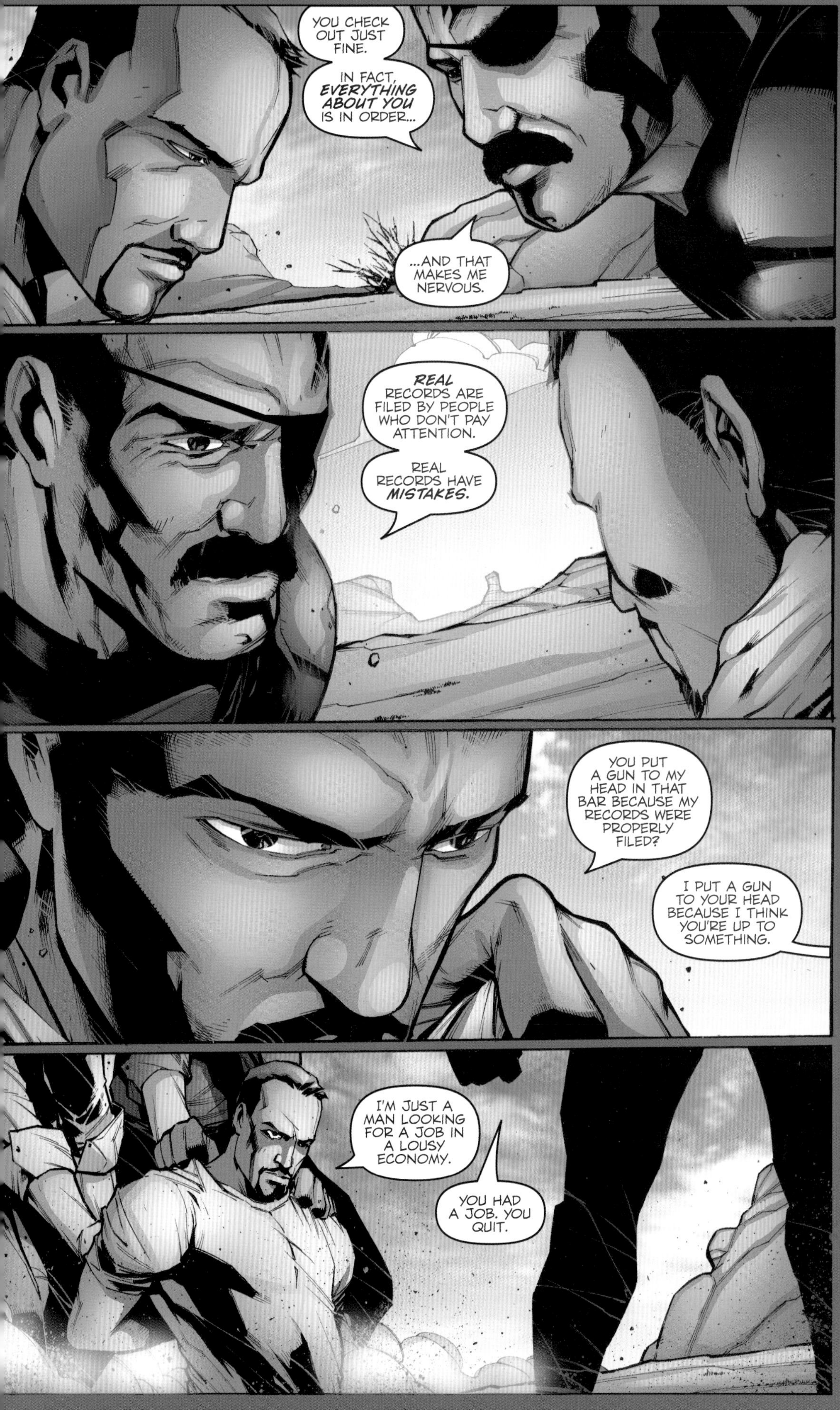
YOU CHECK OUT JUST FINE.
IN FACT, EVERYTHING ABOUT YOU IS IN ORDER...
...AND THAT MAKES ME NERVOUS.
REAL RECORDS ARE FILED BY PEOPLE WHO DON'T PAY ATTENTION.
REAL RECORDS HAVE MISTAKES.
YOU PUT A GUN TO MY HEAD IN THAT BAR BECAUSE MY RECORDS WERE PROPERLY FILED?
I PUT A GUN TO YOUR HEAD BECAUSE I THINK YOU'RE UP TO SOMETHING.
I'M JUST A MAN LOOKING FOR A JOB IN A LOUSY ECONOMY.
YOU HAD A JOB. YOU QUIT.

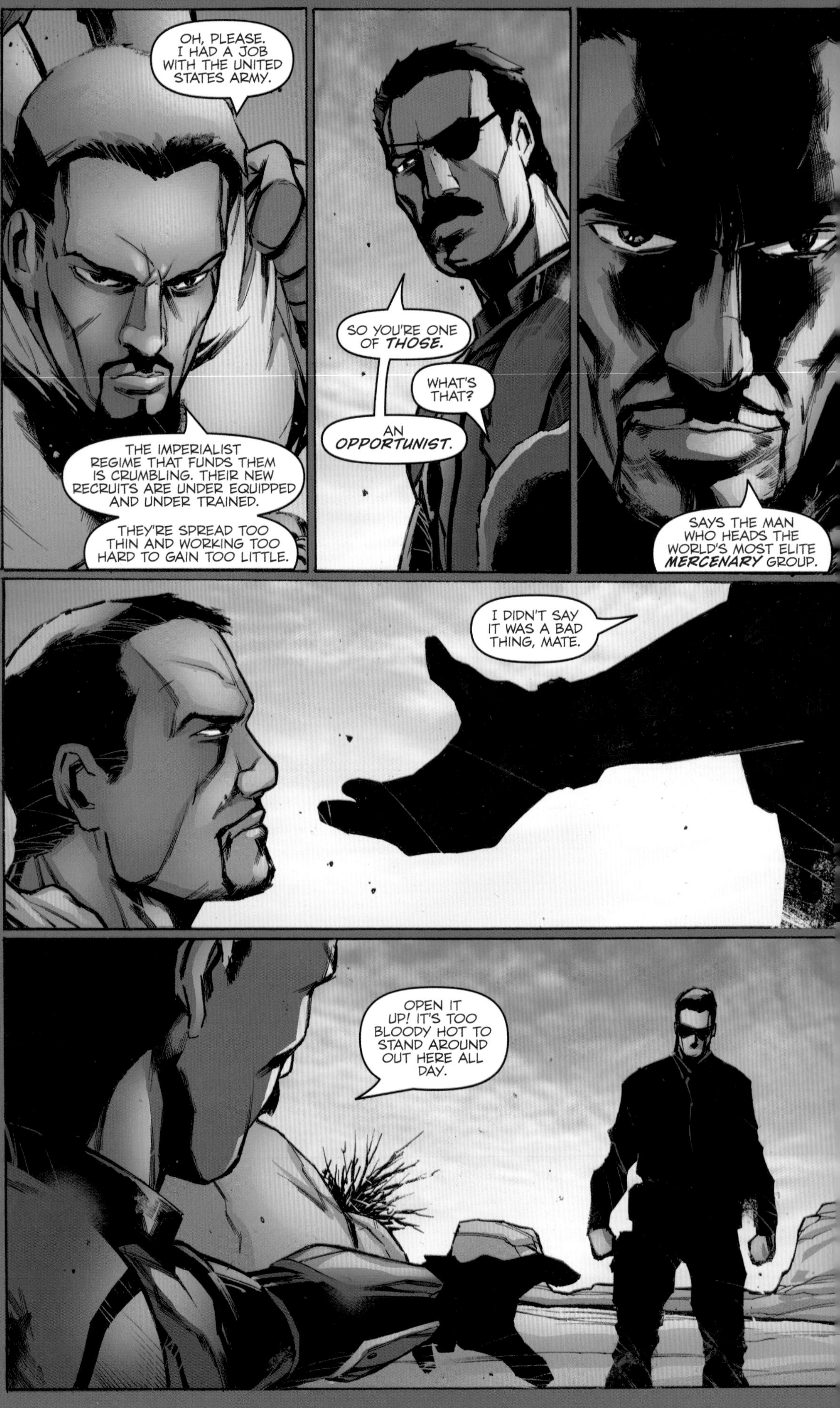
OH, PLEASE. I HAD A JOB WITH THE UNITED STATES ARMY.
THE IMPERIALIST REGIME THAT FUNDS THEM IS CRUMBLING. THEIR NEW RECRUITS ARE UNDER EQUIPPED AND UNDER TRAINED.
THEY'RE SPREAD TOO THIN AND WORKING TOO HARD TO GAIN TOO LITTLE.
SO YOU'RE ONE OF *THOSE.*
WHAT'S THAT?
AN *OPPORTUNIST.*
SAYS THE MAN WHO HEADS THE WORLD'S MOST ELITE *MERCENARY* GROUP.
I DIDN'T SAY IT WAS A BAD THING, MATE.
OPEN IT UP! IT'S TOO BLOODY HOT TO STAND AROUND OUT HERE ALL DAY.

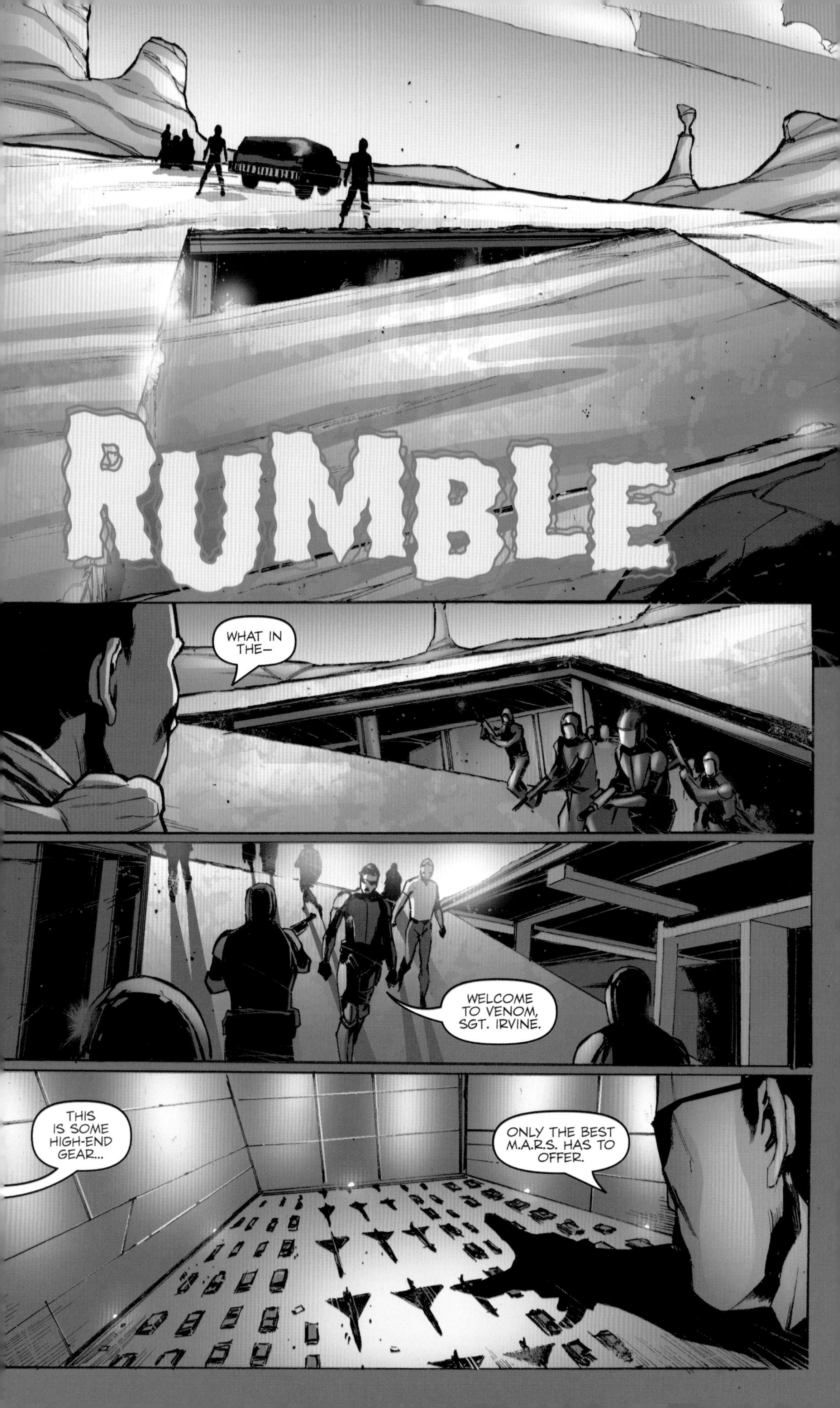
RUMBLE
WHAT IN THE—
WELCOME TO VENOM, SGT. IRVINE.
THIS IS SOME HIGH-END GEAR...
ONLY THE BEST M.A.R.S. HAS TO OFFER.

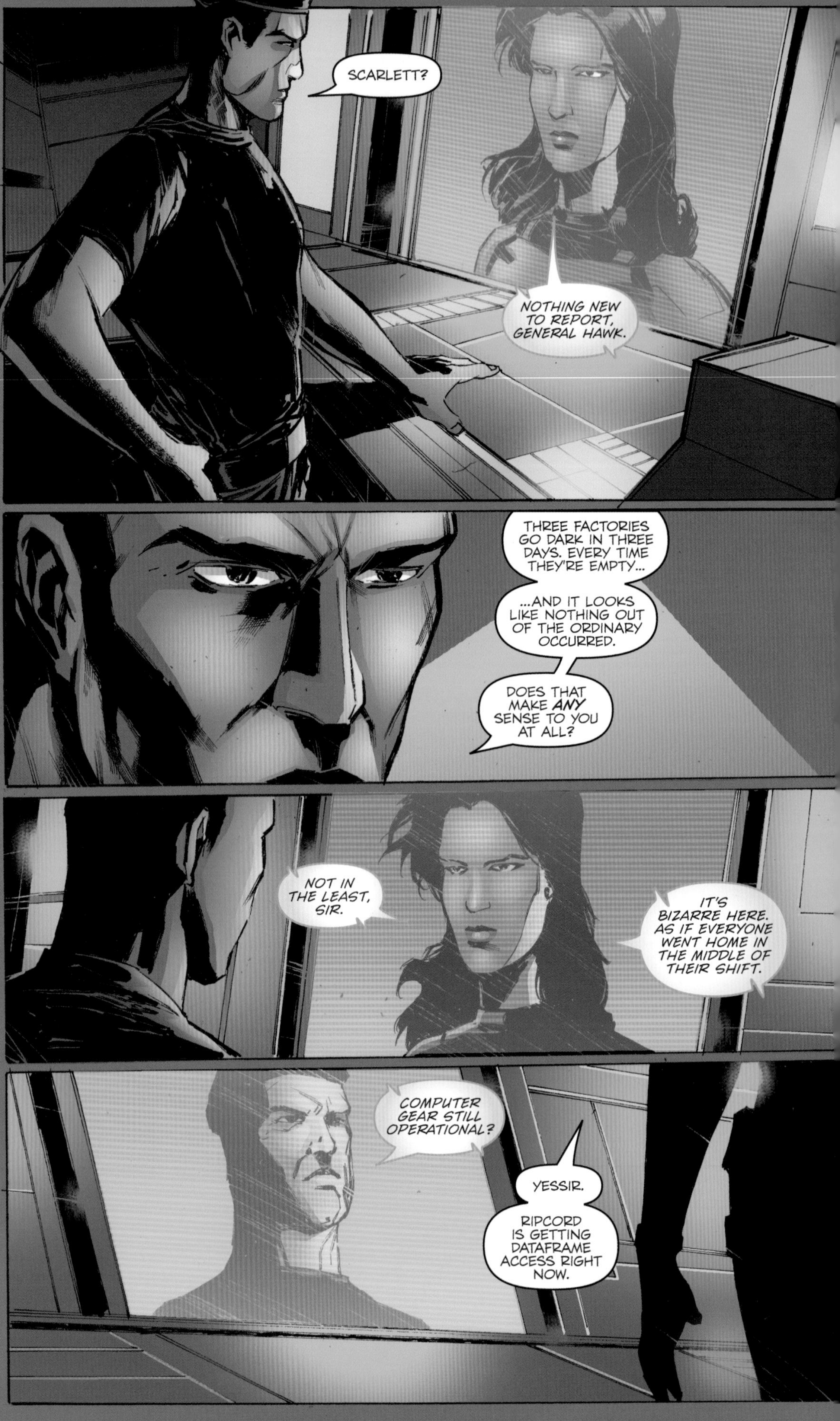
SCARLETT?
NOTHING NEW TO REPORT, GENERAL HAWK.
THREE FACTORIES GO DARK IN THREE DAYS. EVERY TIME THEY'RE EMPTY...
...AND IT LOOKS LIKE NOTHING OUT OF THE ORDINARY OCCURRED.
DOES THAT MAKE ANY SENSE TO YOU AT ALL?
NOT IN THE LEAST, SIR.
IT'S BIZARRE HERE. AS IF EVERYONE WENT HOME IN THE MIDDLE OF THEIR SHIFT.
COMPUTER GEAR STILL OPERATIONAL?
YESSIR.
RIPCORD IS GETTING DATAFRAME ACCESS RIGHT NOW.

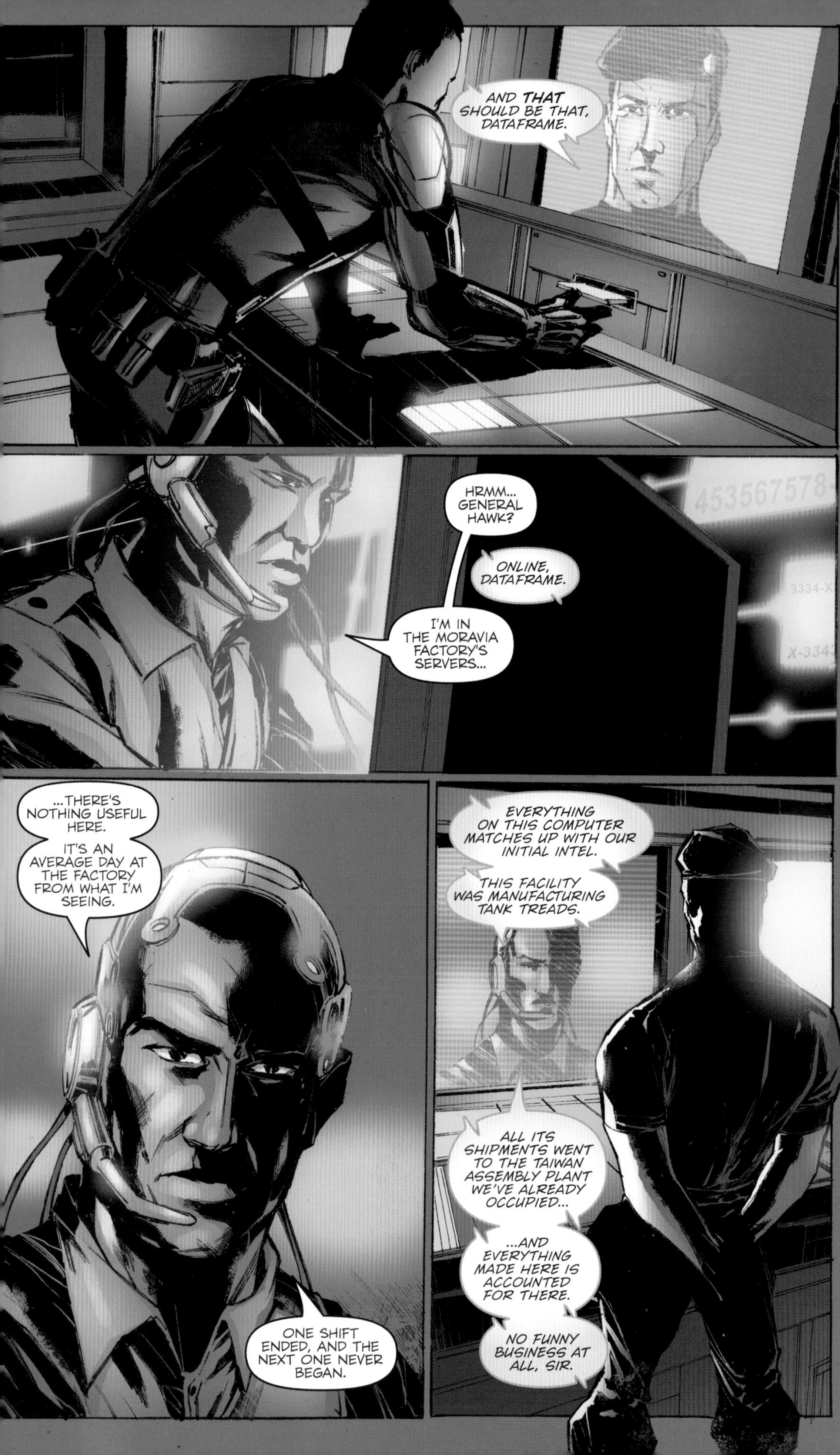
AND THAT SHOULD BE THAT, DATAFRAME.
HRMM... GENERAL HAWK?
ONLINE, DATAFRAME.
I'M IN THE MORAVIA FACTORY'S SERVERS...
453567578
3334-X
X-3343
...THERE'S NOTHING USEFUL HERE.
IT'S AN AVERAGE DAY AT THE FACTORY FROM WHAT I'M SEEING.
ONE SHIFT ENDED, AND THE NEXT ONE NEVER BEGAN.
EVERYTHING ON THIS COMPUTER MATCHES UP WITH OUR INITIAL INTEL.
THIS FACILITY WAS MANUFACTURING TANK TREADS.
ALL ITS SHIPMENTS WENT TO THE TAIWAN ASSEMBLY PLANT WE'VE ALREADY OCCUPIED...
...AND EVERYTHING MADE HERE IS ACCOUNTED FOR THERE.
NO FUNNY BUSINESS AT ALL, SIR.

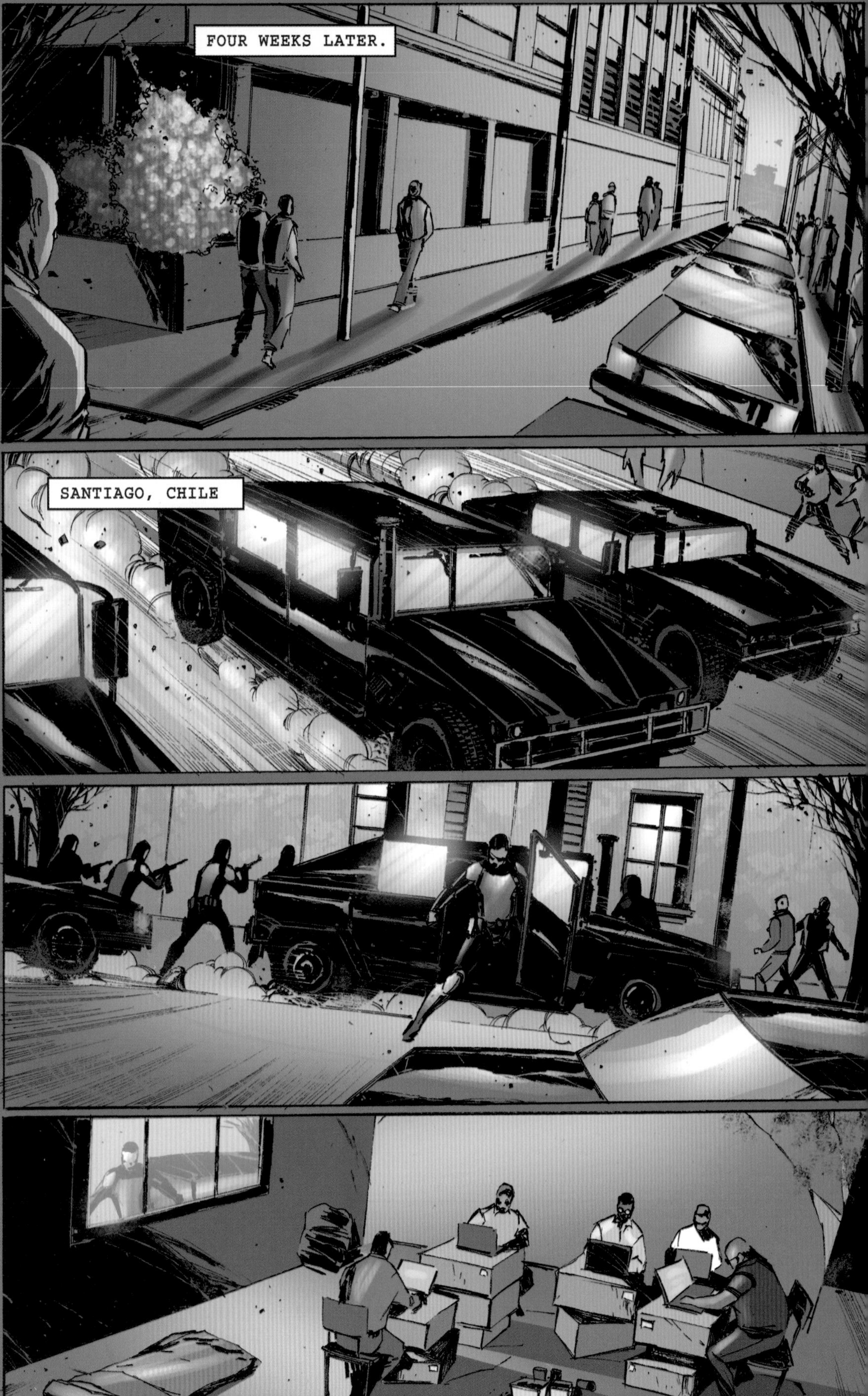
FOUR WEEKS LATER.
SANTIAGO, CHILE

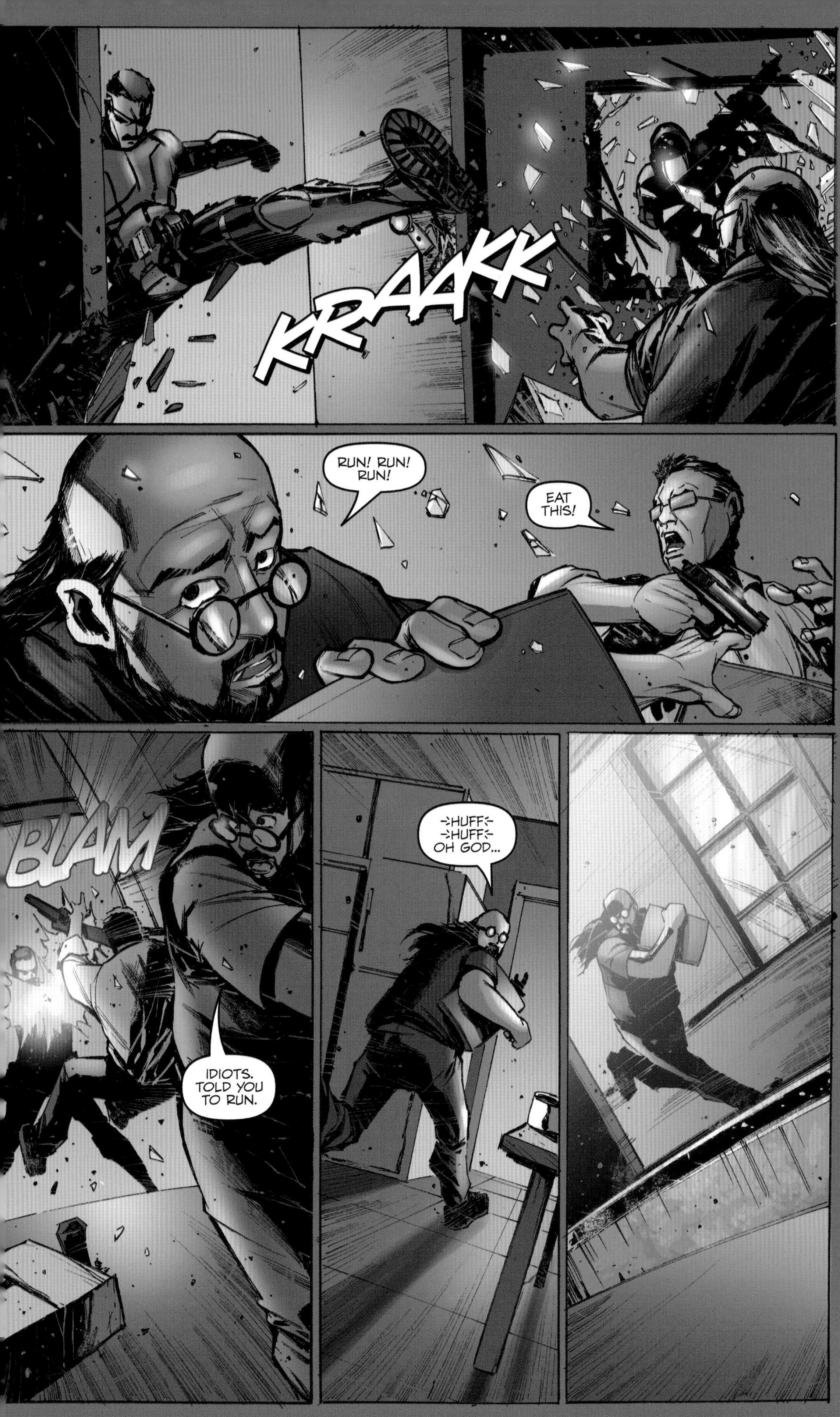
KRAAKK
RUN! RUN! RUN!
EAT THIS!
BLAM
IDIOTS. TOLD YOU TO RUN.
-HUFF- -HUFF- OH GOD...

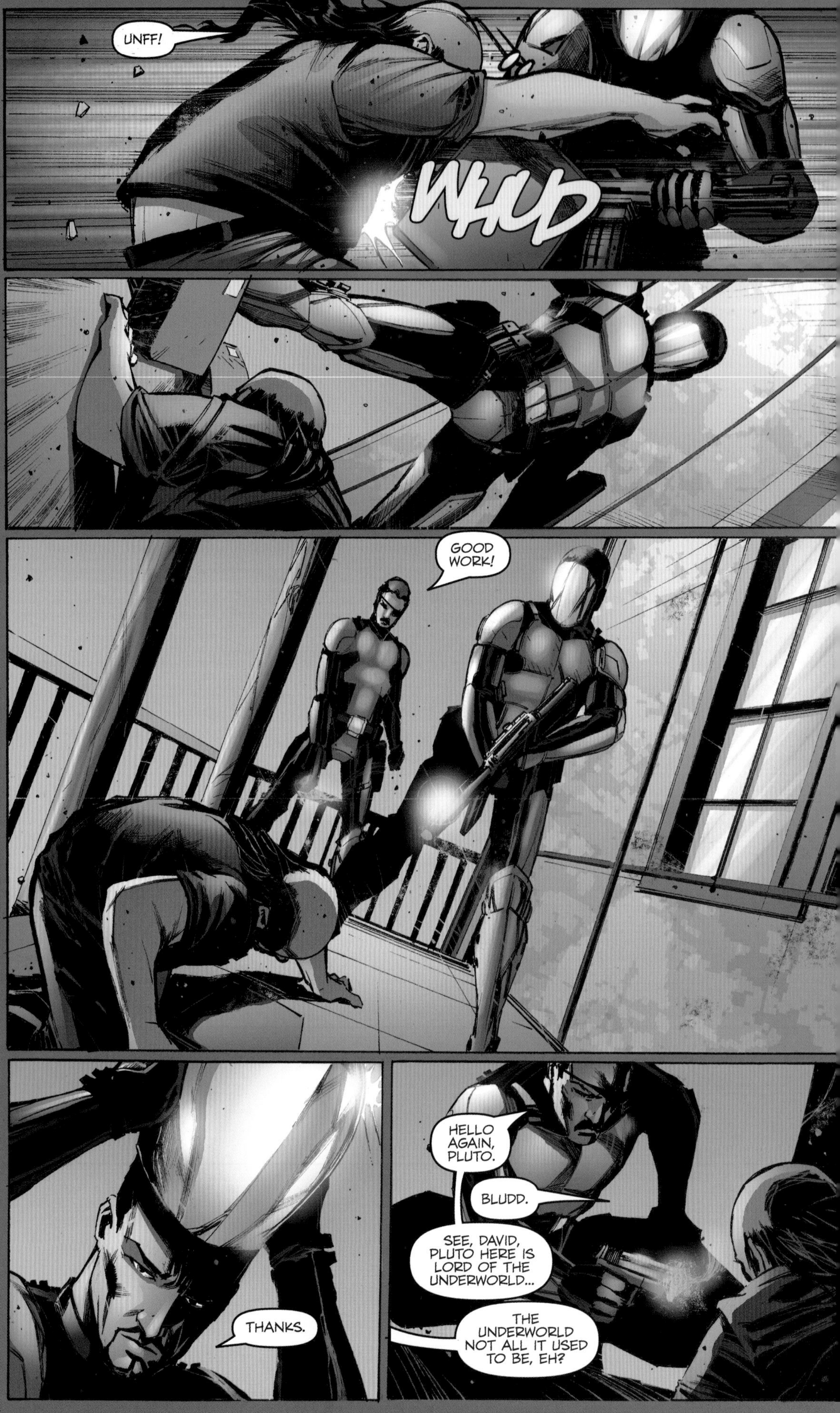
UNFF!
WHUD
GOOD WORK!
THANKS.
HELLO AGAIN, PLUTO.
BLUDD.
SEE, DAVID, PLUTO HERE IS LORD OF THE UNDERWORLD...
THE UNDERWORLD NOT ALL IT USED TO BE, EH?

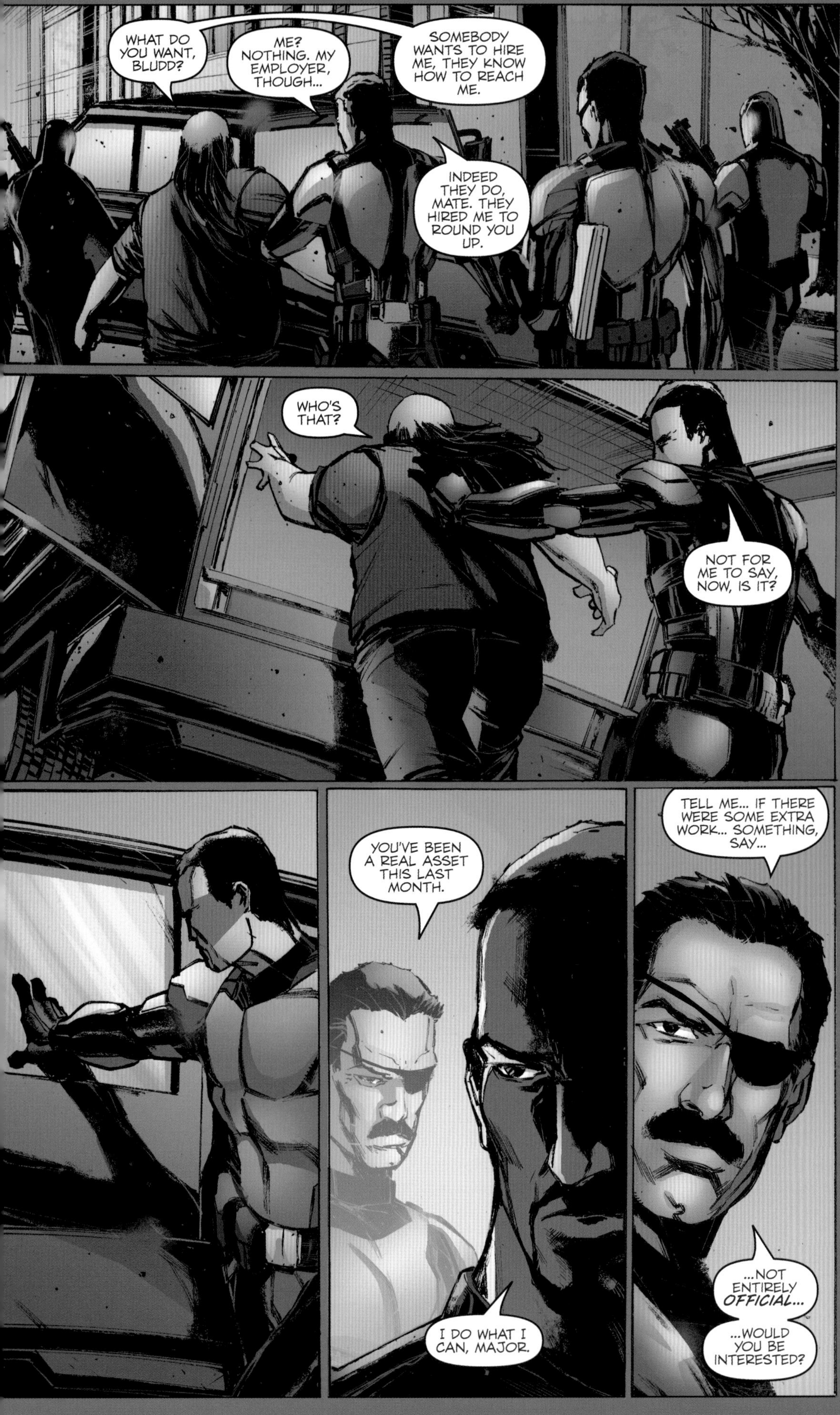
WHAT DO YOU WANT, BLUDD?
ME? NOTHING. MY EMPLOYER, THOUGH...
SOMEBODY WANTS TO HIRE ME, THEY KNOW HOW TO REACH ME.
INDEED THEY DO, MATE. THEY HIRED ME TO ROUND YOU UP.
WHO'S THAT?
NOT FOR ME TO SAY, NOW, IS IT?
YOU'VE BEEN A REAL ASSET THIS LAST MONTH.
I DO WHAT I CAN, MAJOR.
TELL ME... IF THERE WERE SOME EXTRA WORK... SOMETHING, SAY...
...NOT ENTIRELY *OFFICIAL*...
...WOULD YOU BE INTERESTED?

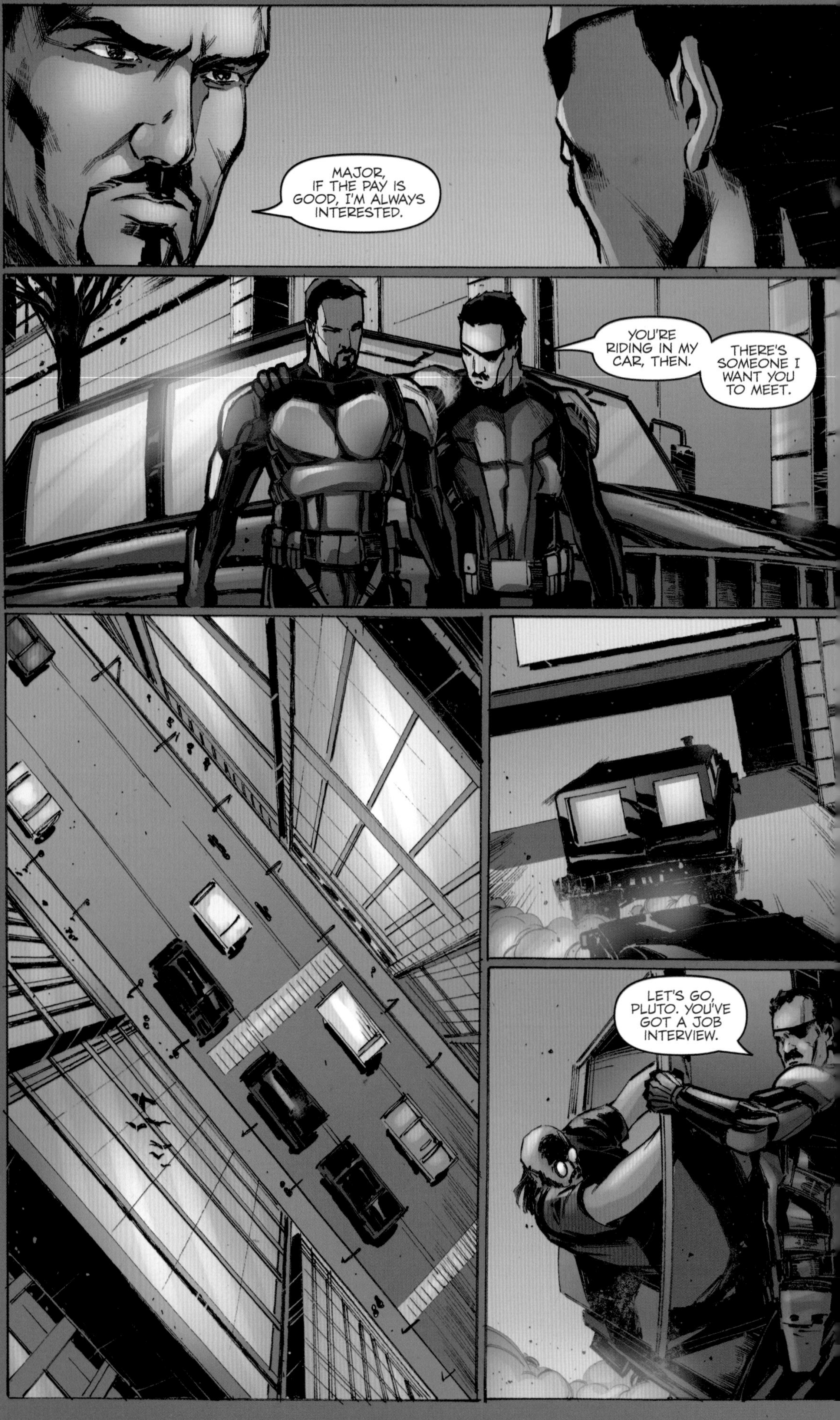
MAJOR, IF THE PAY IS GOOD, I'M ALWAYS INTERESTED.
YOU'RE RIDING IN MY CAR, THEN.
THERE'S SOMEONE I WANT YOU TO MEET.
LET'S GO, PLUTO. YOU'VE GOT A JOB INTERVIEW.

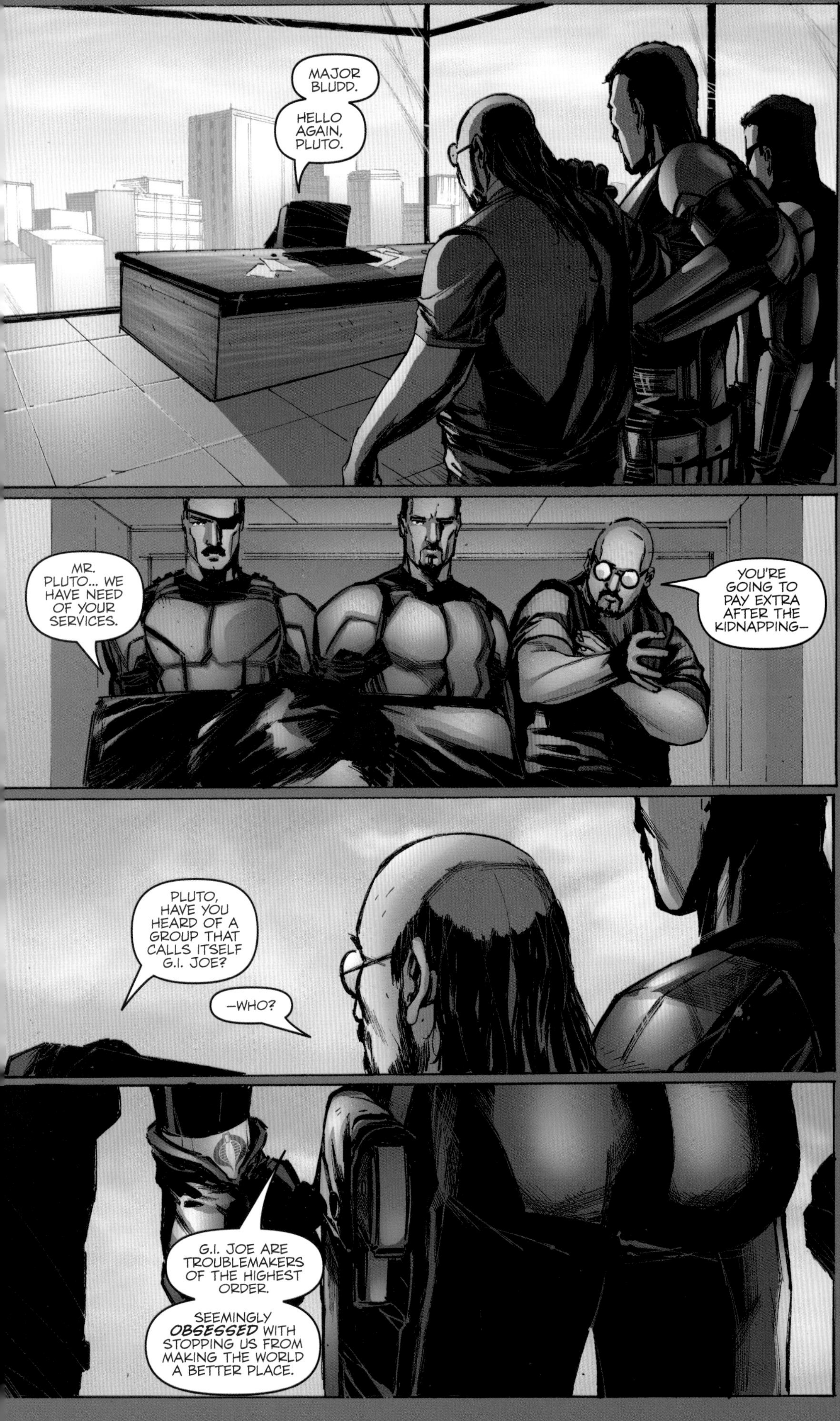
MAJOR BLUDD.
HELLO AGAIN, PLUTO.
MR. PLUTO... WE HAVE NEED OF YOUR SERVICES.
YOU'RE GOING TO PAY EXTRA AFTER THE KIDNAPPING—
PLUTO, HAVE YOU HEARD OF A GROUP THAT CALLS ITSELF G.I. JOE?
—WHO?
G.I. JOE ARE TROUBLEMAKERS OF THE HIGHEST ORDER.
SEEMINGLY ***OBSESSED*** WITH STOPPING US FROM MAKING THE WORLD A BETTER PLACE.

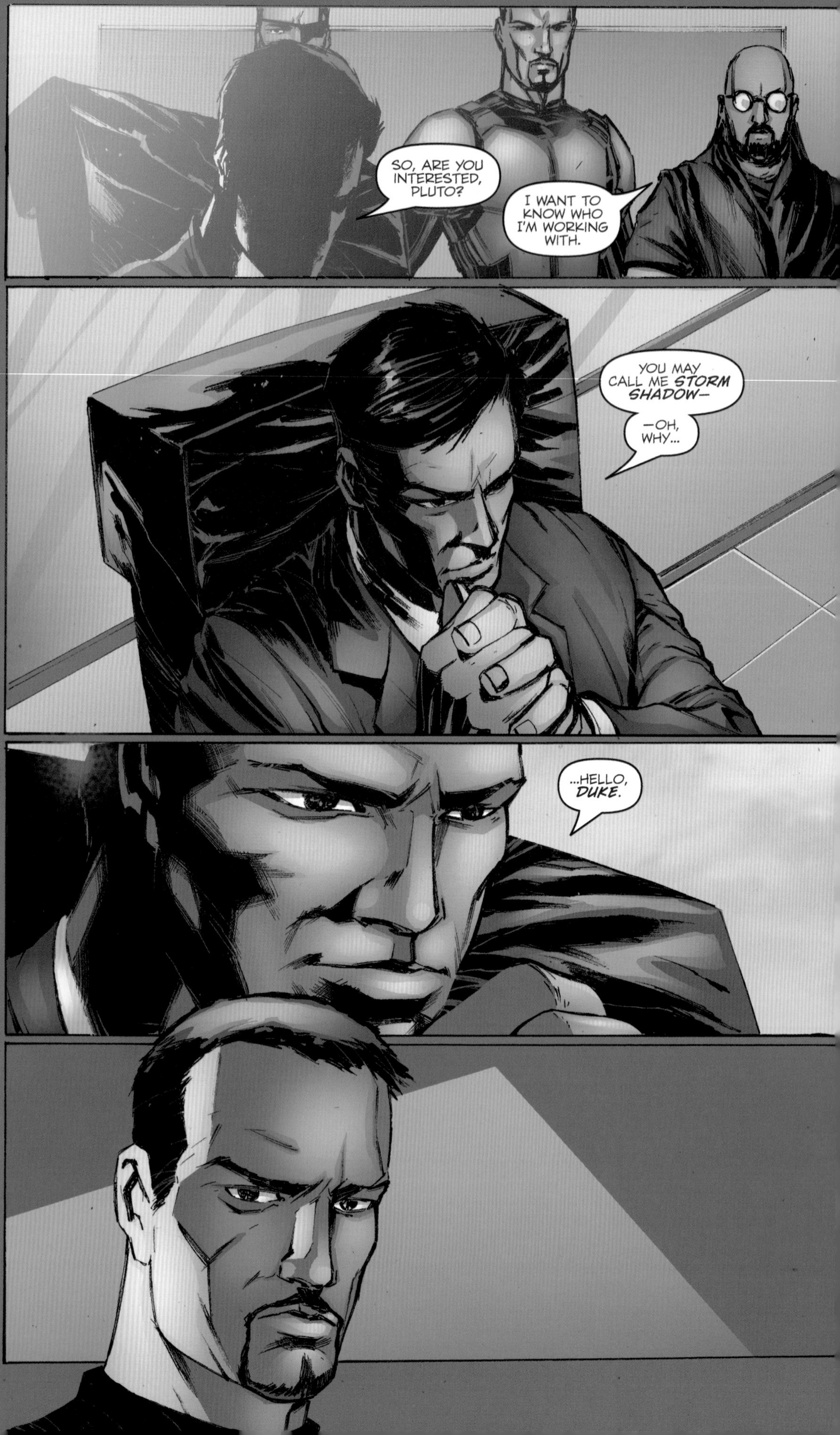

SO, ARE YOU INTERESTED, PLUTO?
I WANT TO KNOW WHO I'M WORKING WITH.
YOU MAY CALL ME STORM SHADOW—
—OH, WHY...
...HELLO, DUKE.

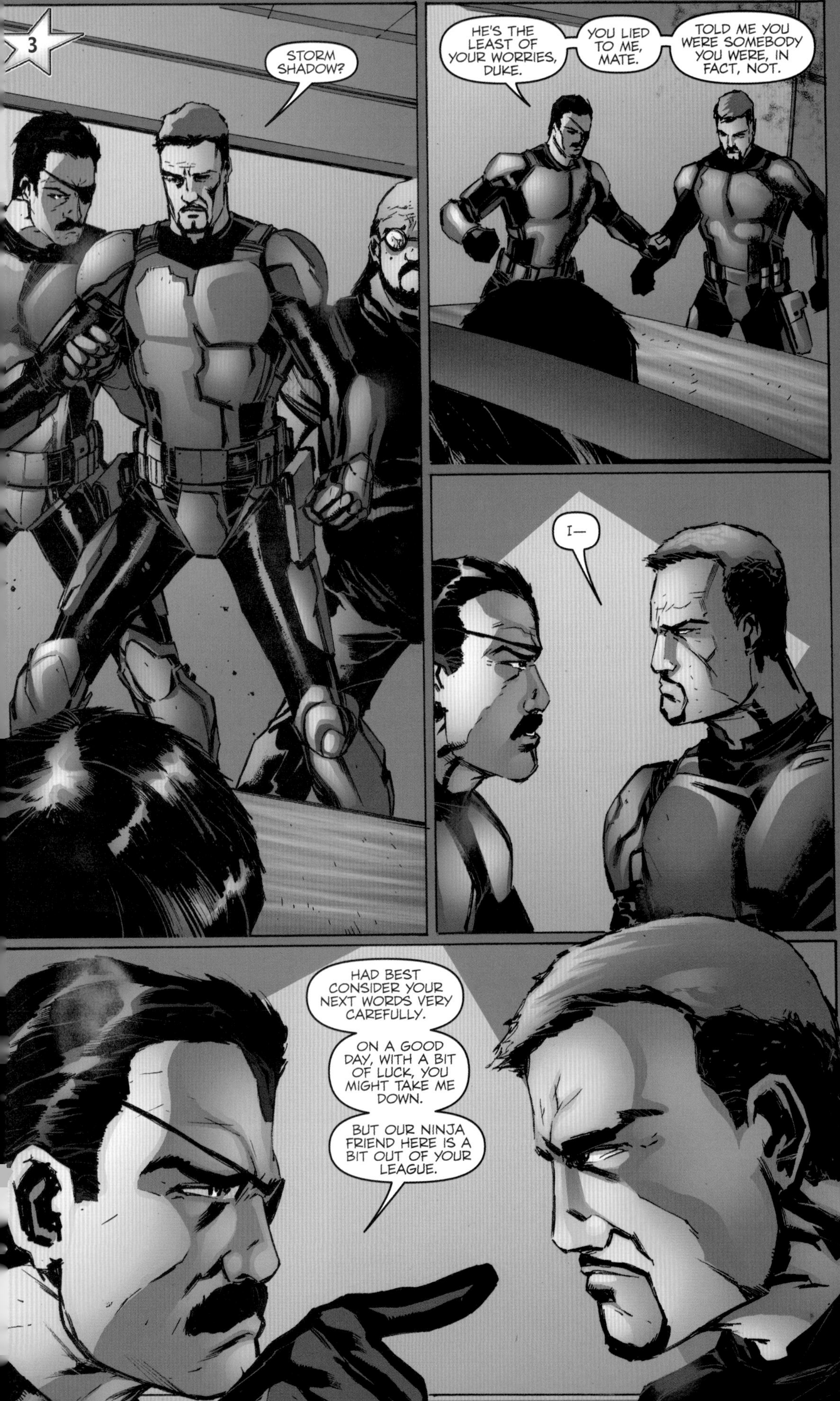
3
STORM SHADOW?
HE'S THE LEAST OF YOUR WORRIES, DUKE.
YOU LIED TO ME, MATE.
TOLD ME YOU WERE SOMEBODY YOU WERE, IN FACT, NOT.
I—
HAD BEST CONSIDER YOUR NEXT WORDS VERY CAREFULLY.
ON A GOOD DAY, WITH A BIT OF LUCK, YOU MIGHT TAKE ME DOWN.
BUT OUR NINJA FRIEND HERE IS A BIT OUT OF YOUR LEAGUE.

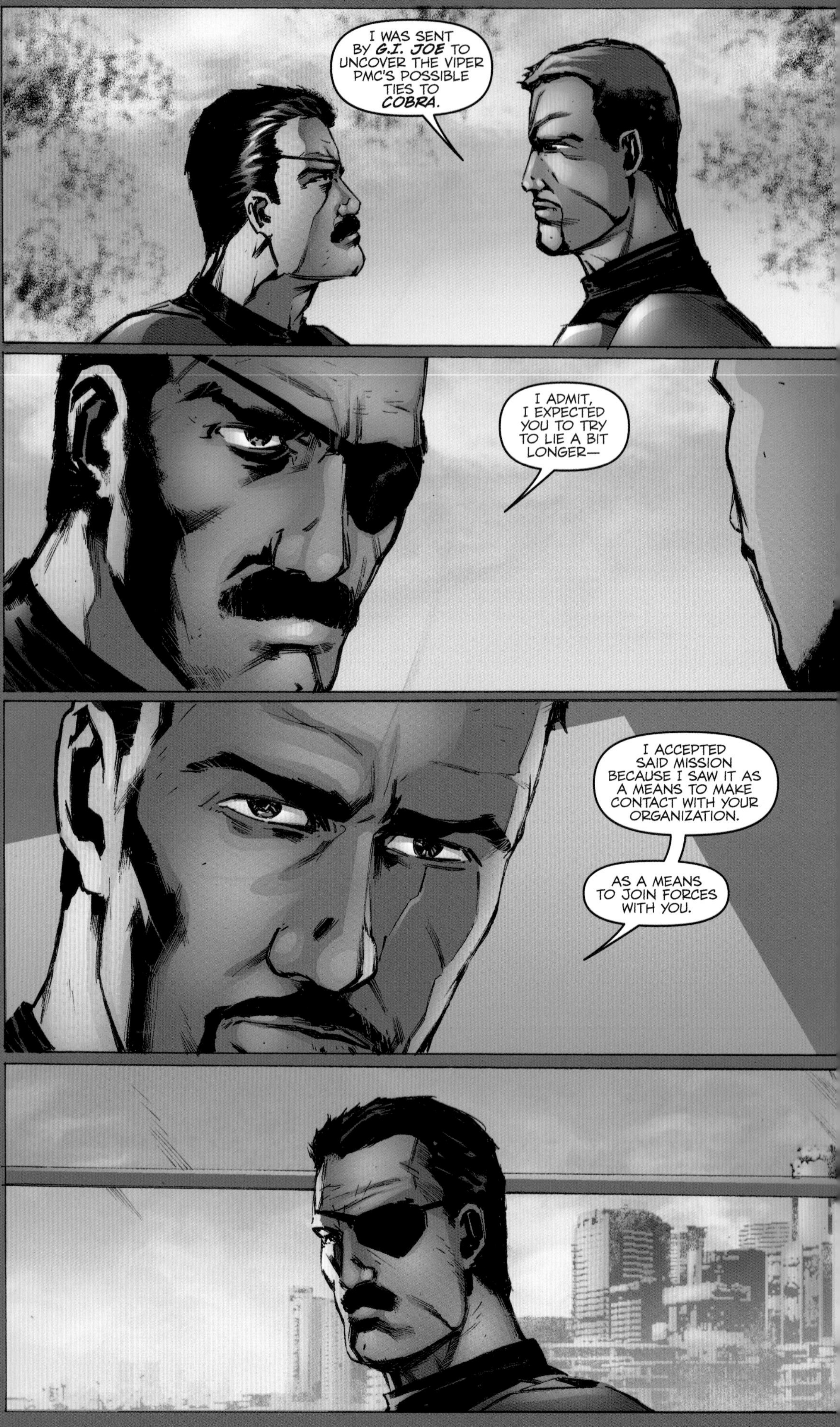
I WAS SENT BY G.I. JOE TO UNCOVER THE VIPER PMC'S POSSIBLE TIES TO COBRA.
I ADMIT, I EXPECTED YOU TO TRY TO LIE A BIT LONGER—
I ACCEPTED SAID MISSION BECAUSE I SAW IT AS A MEANS TO MAKE CONTACT WITH YOUR ORGANIZATION.
AS A MEANS TO JOIN FORCES WITH YOU.

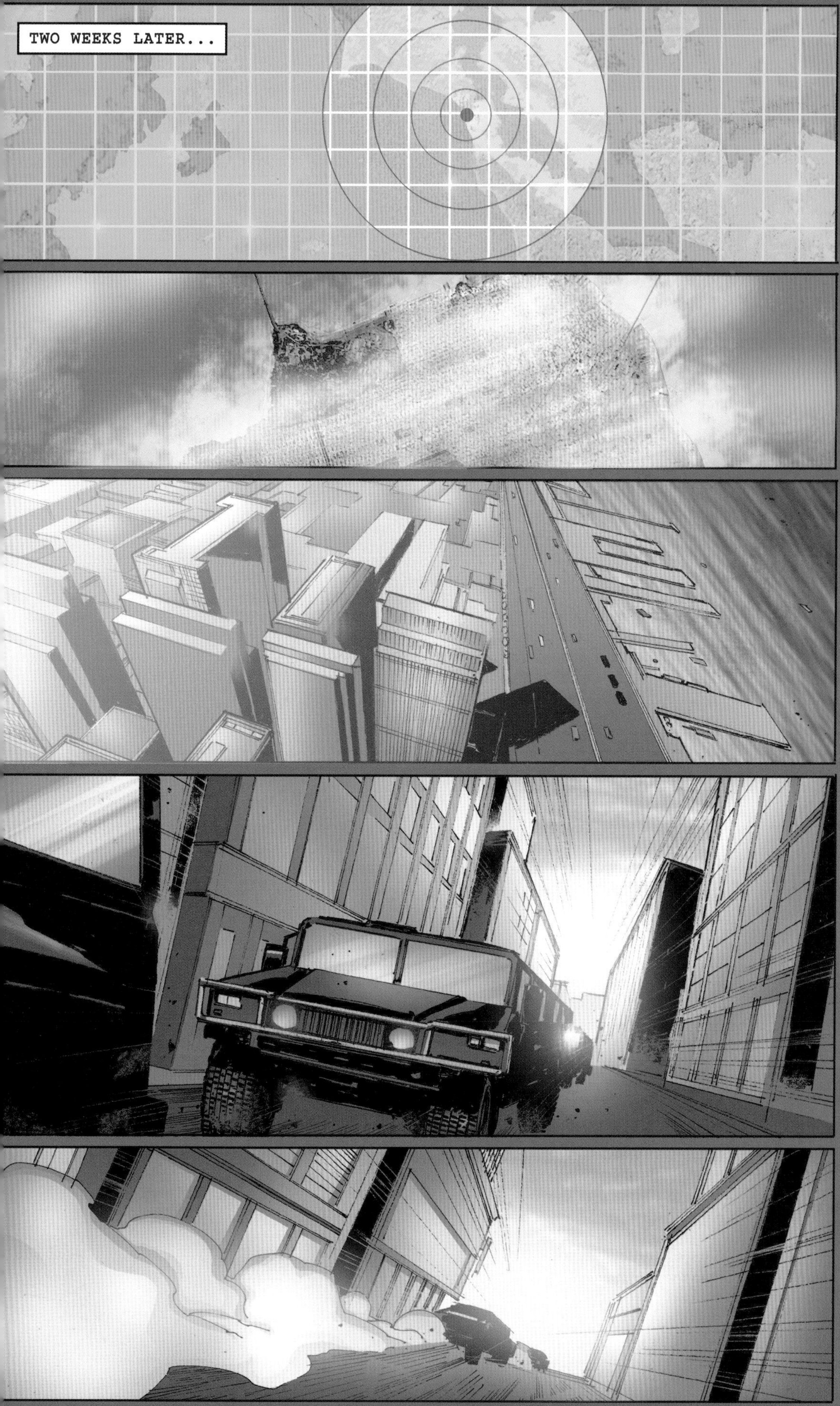
TWO WEEKS LATER...

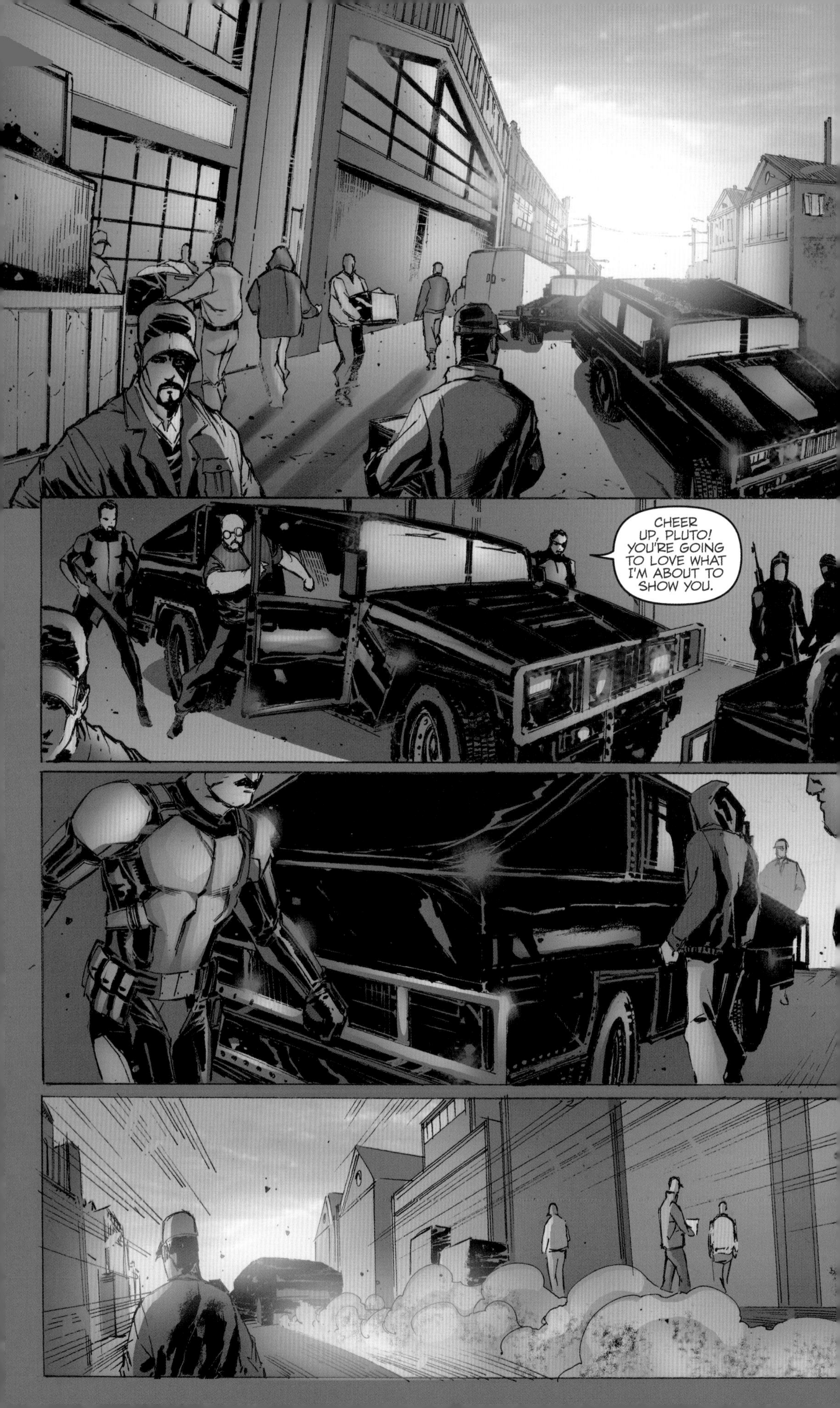
CHEER UP, PLUTO! YOU'RE GOING TO LOVE WHAT I'M ABOUT TO SHOW YOU.

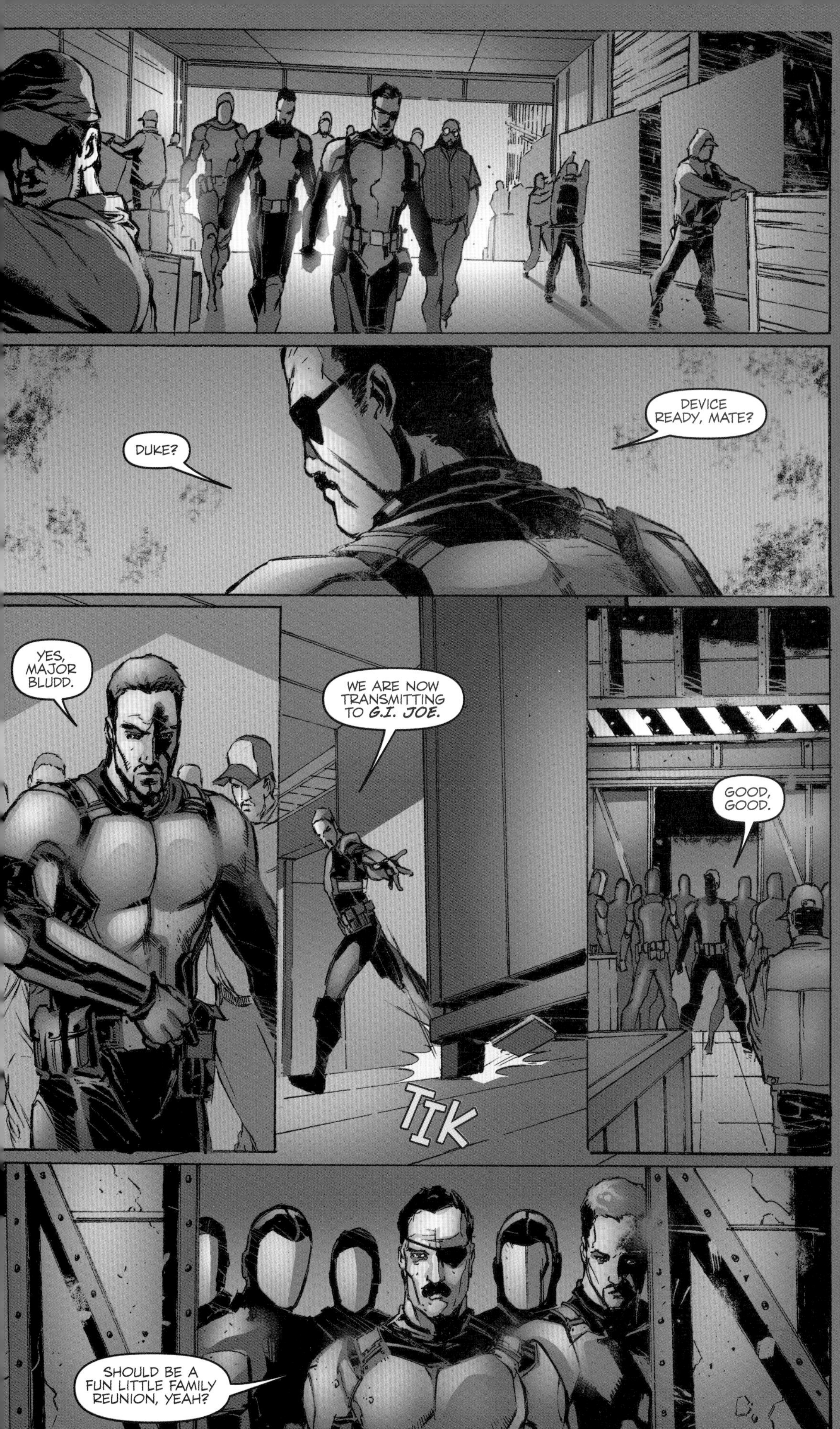
DUKE?
DEVICE READY, MATE?
YES, MAJOR BLUDD.
WE ARE NOW TRANSMITTING TO *G.I. JOE.*
TIK
GOOD, GOOD.
SHOULD BE A FUN LITTLE FAMILY REUNION, YEAH?

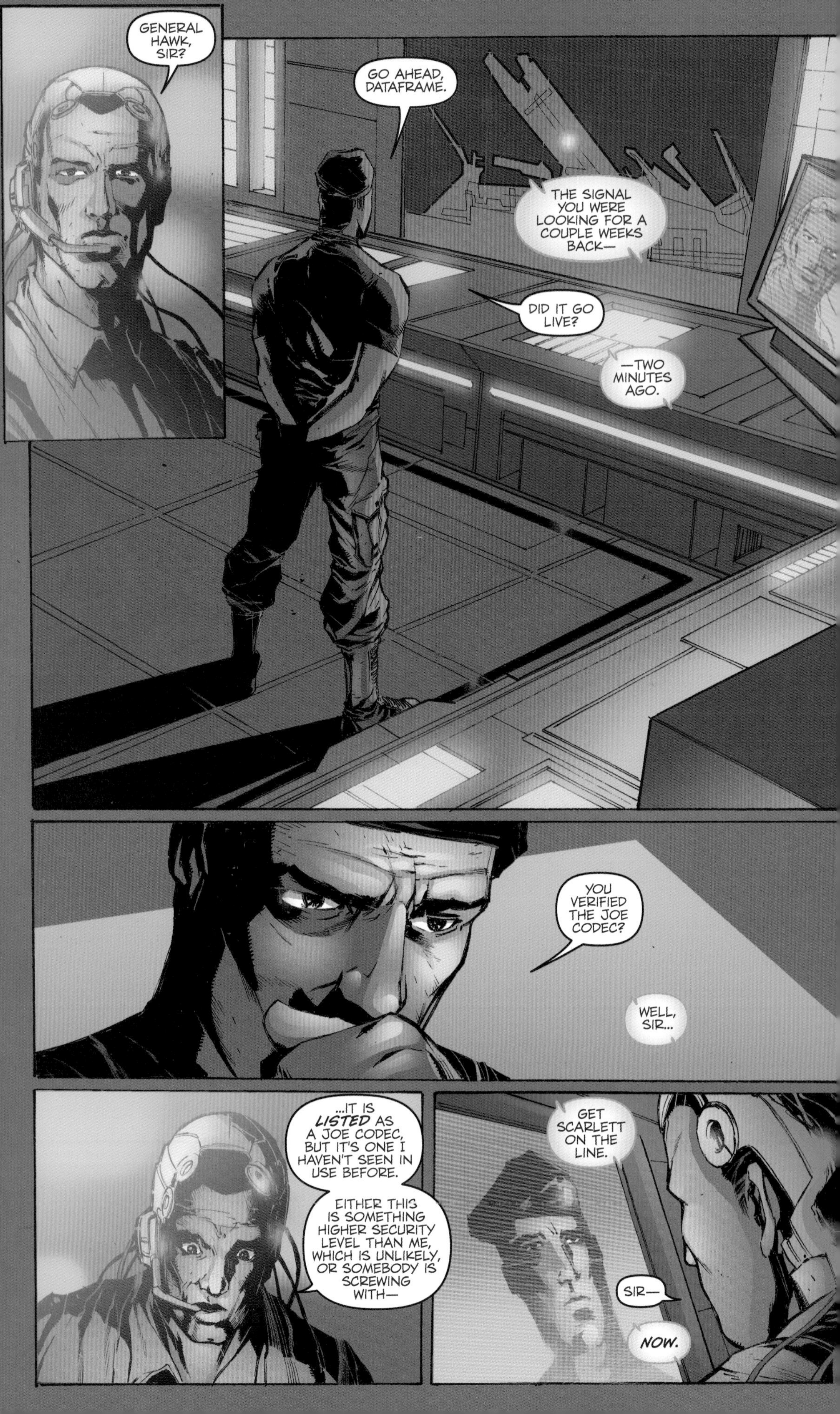
GENERAL HAWK, SIR?
GO AHEAD, DATAFRAME.
THE SIGNAL YOU WERE LOOKING FOR A COUPLE WEEKS BACK—
DID IT GO LIVE?
—TWO MINUTES AGO.
YOU VERIFIED THE JOE CODEC?
WELL, SIR...
...IT IS *LISTED* AS A JOE CODEC, BUT IT'S ONE I HAVEN'T SEEN IN USE BEFORE.
EITHER THIS IS SOMETHING HIGHER SECURITY LEVEL THAN ME, WHICH IS UNLIKELY, OR SOMEBODY IS SCREWING WITH—
GET SCARLETT ON THE LINE.
SIR—
NOW.

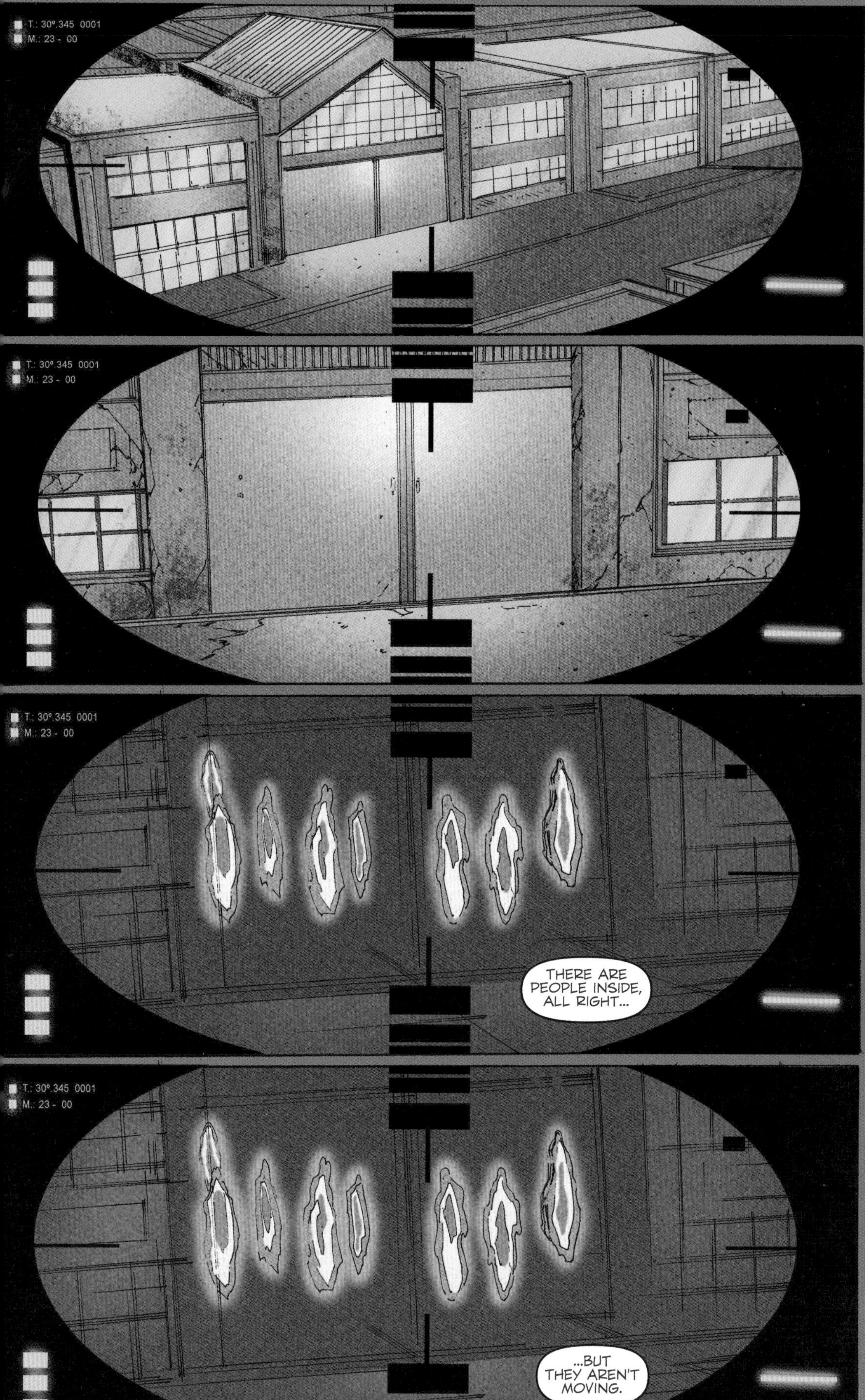
T.: 30º.345 0001
M.: 23 - 00
T.: 30º.345 0001
M.: 23 - 00
T.: 30º.345 0001
M.: 23 - 00
THERE ARE PEOPLE INSIDE, ALL RIGHT...
T.: 30º.345 0001
M.: 23 - 00
...BUT THEY AREN'T MOVING.

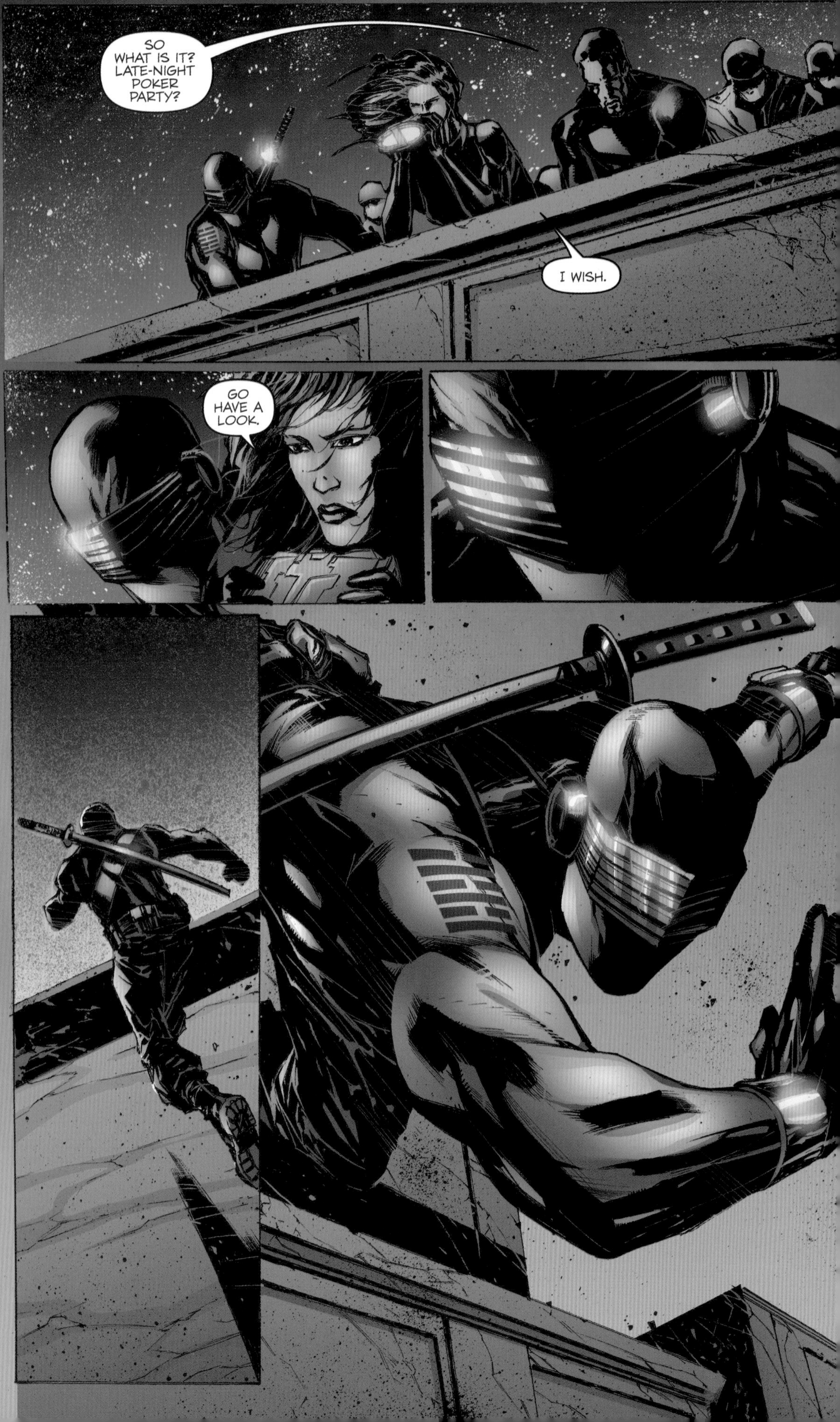
SO WHAT IS IT? LATE-NIGHT POKER PARTY?
I WISH.
GO HAVE A LOOK.

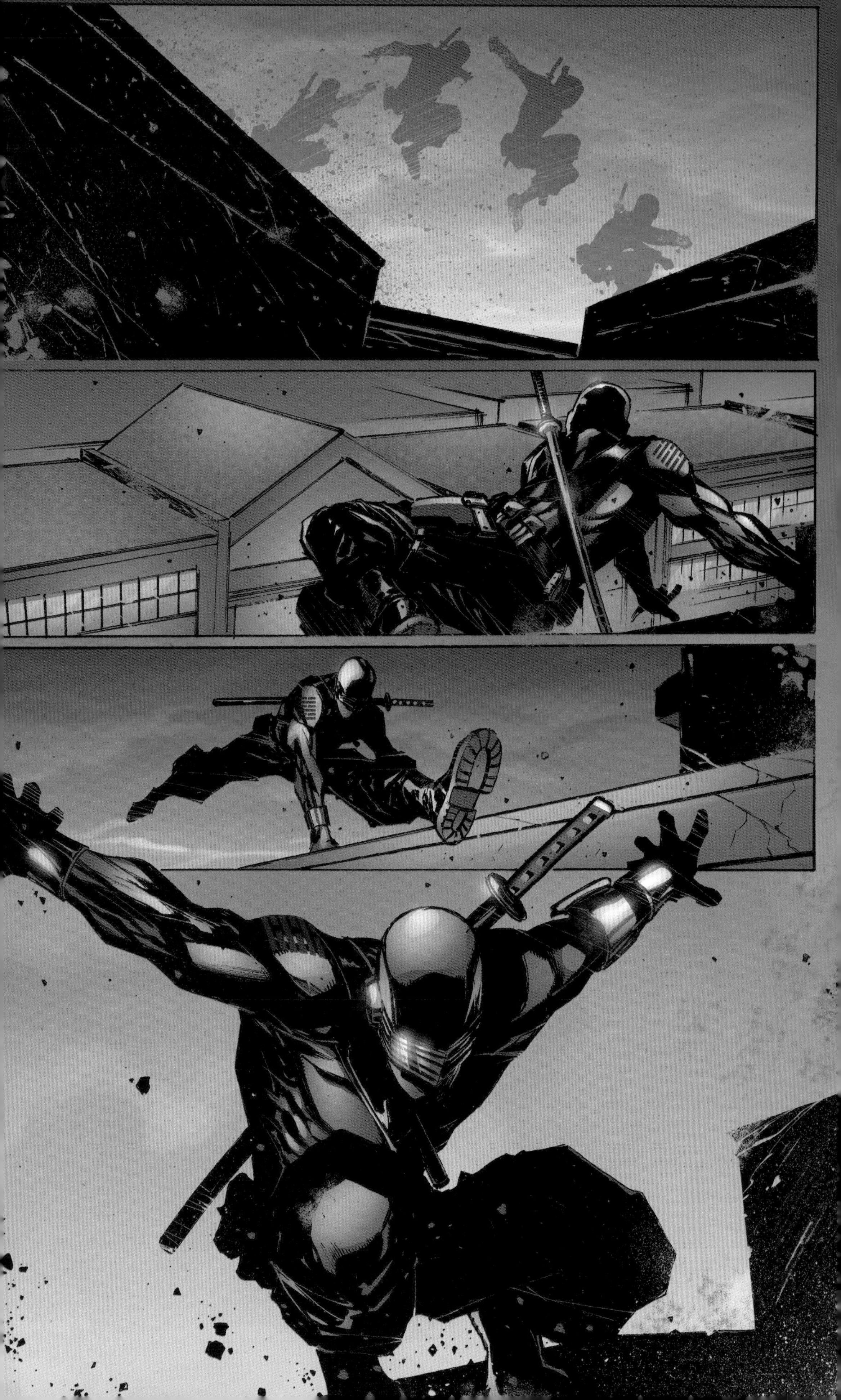

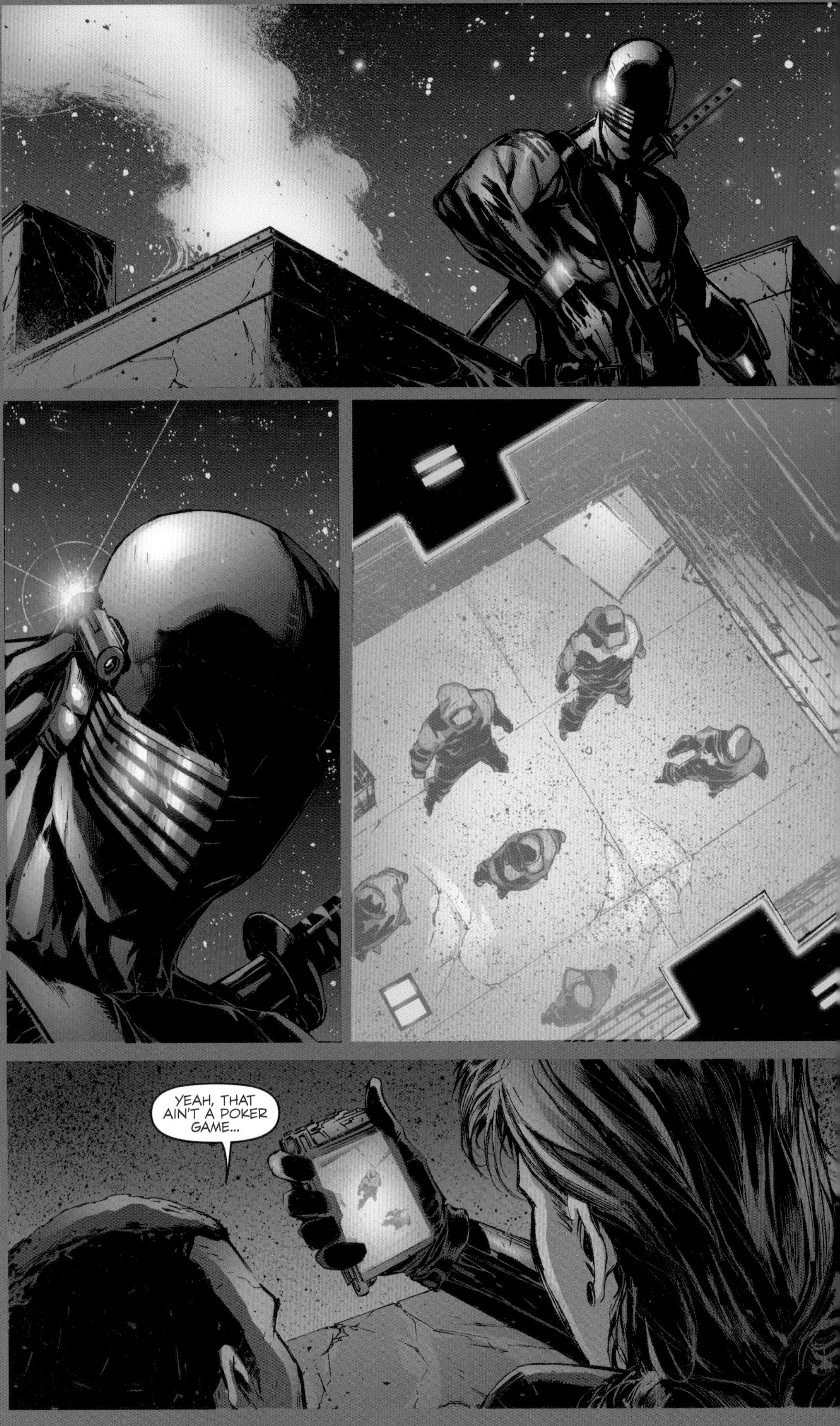
YEAH, THAT AIN'T A POKER GAME...

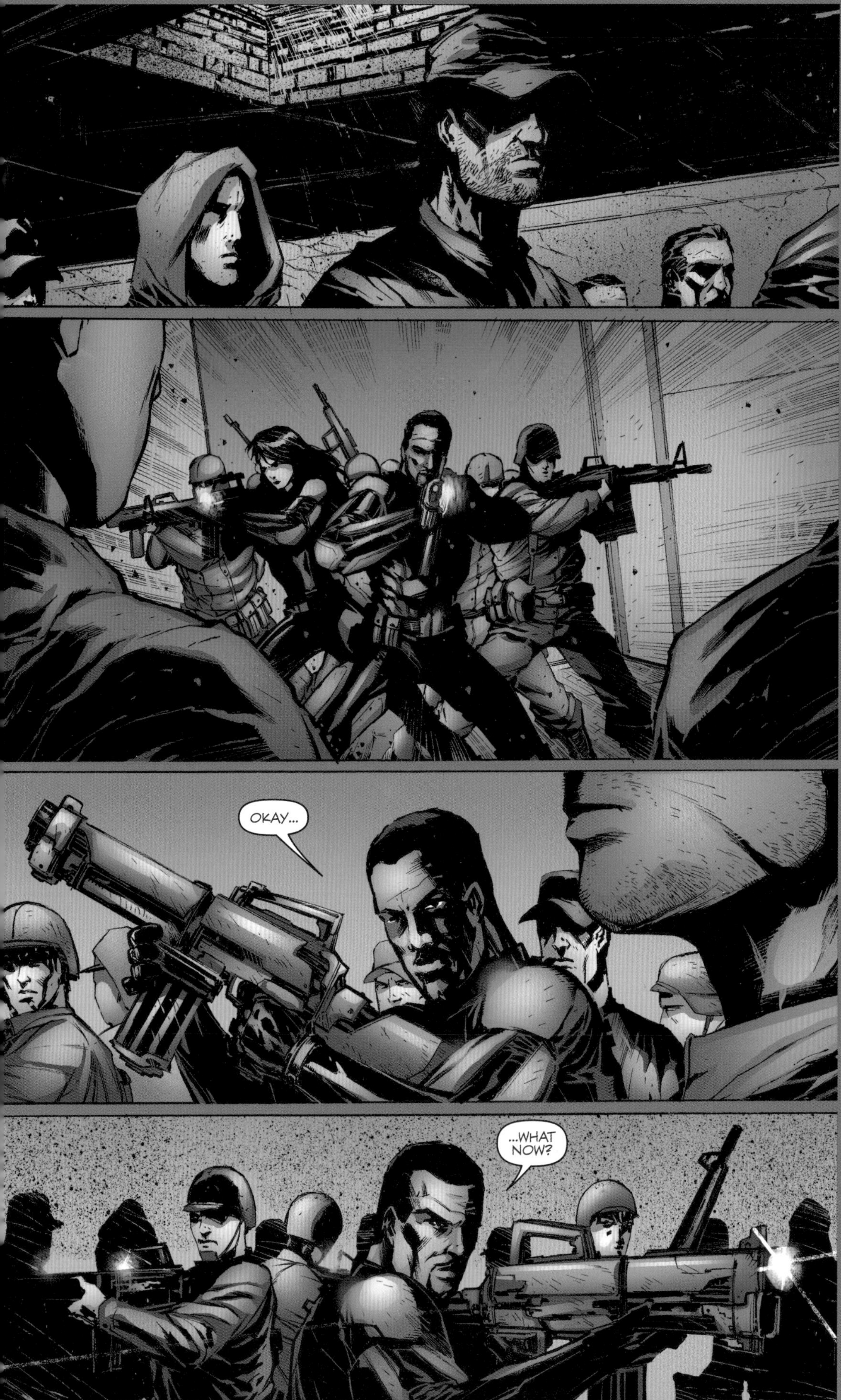
OKAY...
...WHAT NOW?

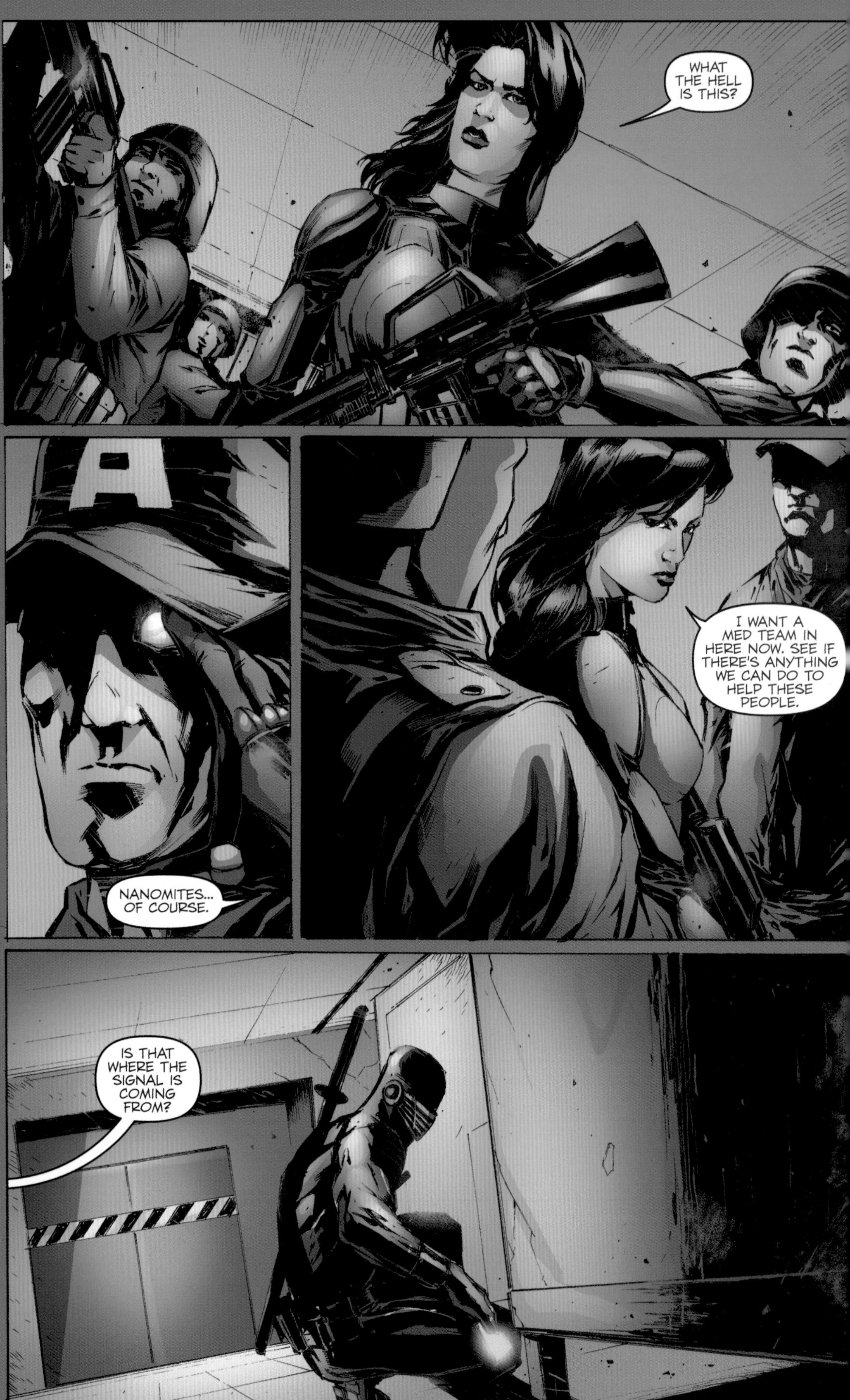
WHAT THE HELL IS THIS?
NANOMITES... OF COURSE.
I WANT A MED TEAM IN HERE NOW. SEE IF THERE'S ANYTHING WE CAN DO TO HELP THESE PEOPLE.
IS THAT WHERE THE SIGNAL IS COMING FROM?

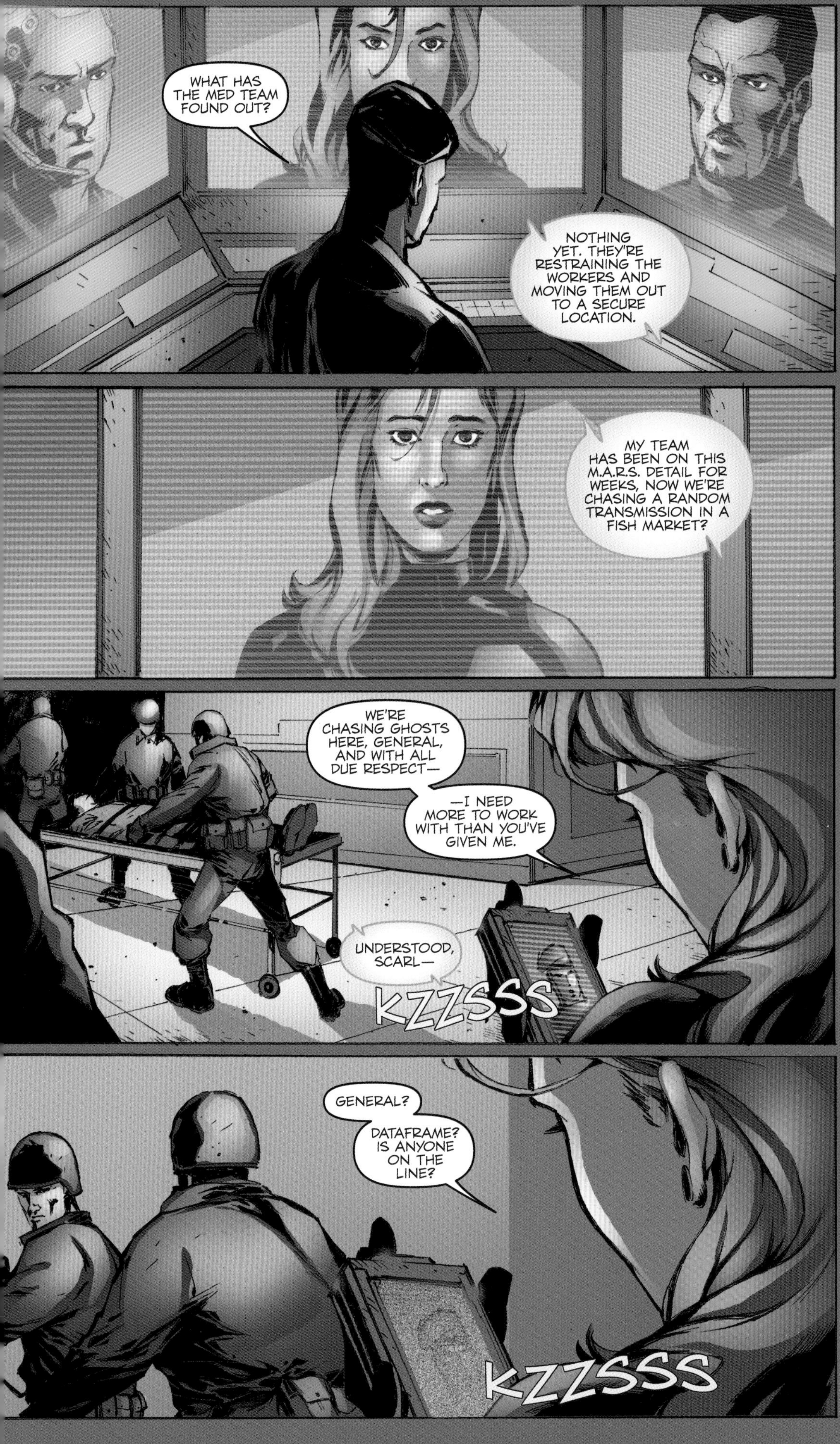
WHAT HAS THE MED TEAM FOUND OUT?
NOTHING YET. THEY'RE RESTRAINING THE WORKERS AND MOVING THEM OUT TO A SECURE LOCATION.
MY TEAM HAS BEEN ON THIS M.A.R.S. DETAIL FOR WEEKS, NOW WE'RE CHASING A RANDOM TRANSMISSION IN A FISH MARKET?
WE'RE CHASING GHOSTS HERE, GENERAL, AND WITH ALL DUE RESPECT—
—I NEED MORE TO WORK WITH THAN YOU'VE GIVEN ME.
UNDERSTOOD, SCARL—
KZZSSS
GENERAL?
DATAFRAME? IS ANYONE ON THE LINE?
KZZSSS

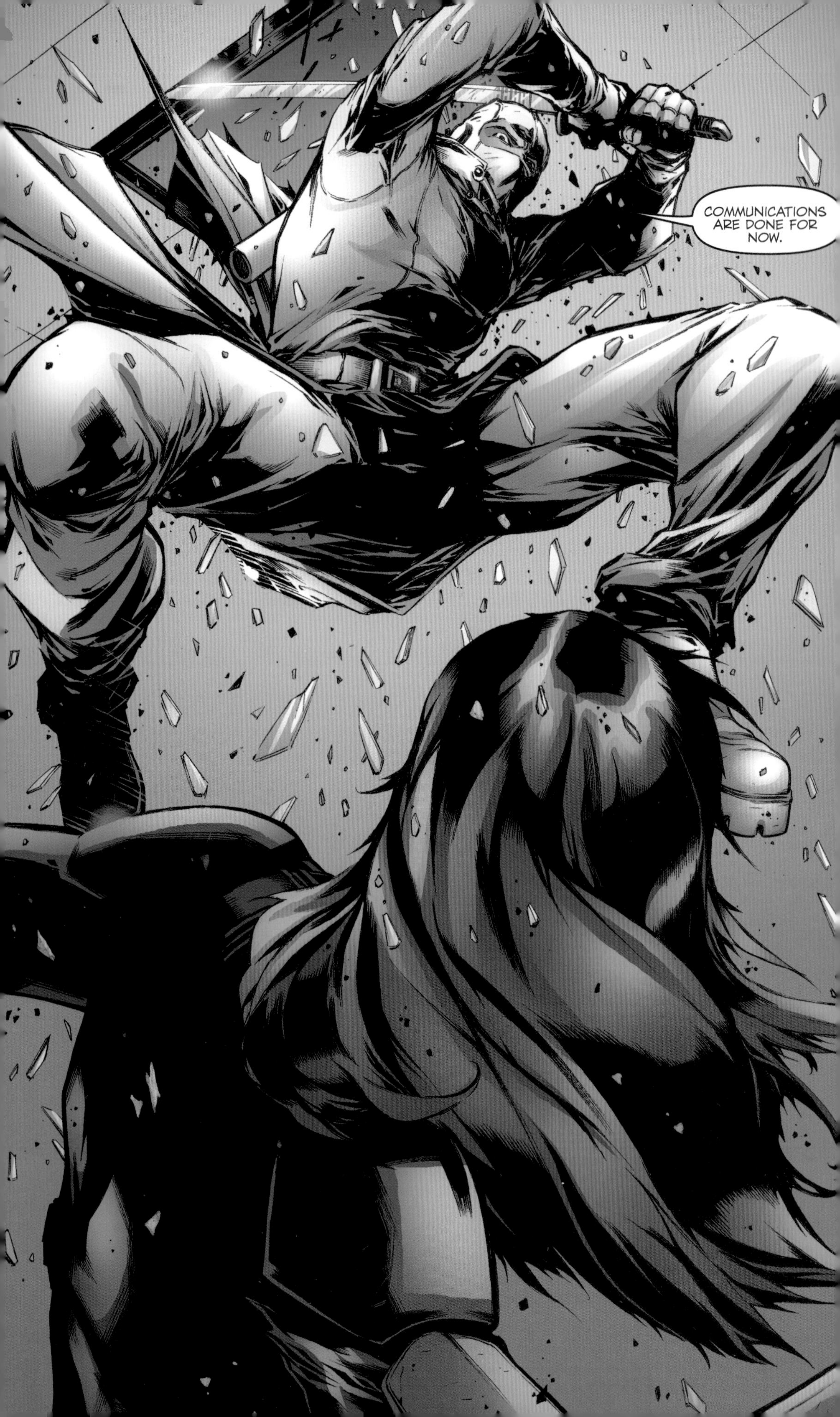
COMMUNICATIONS ARE DONE FOR NOW.

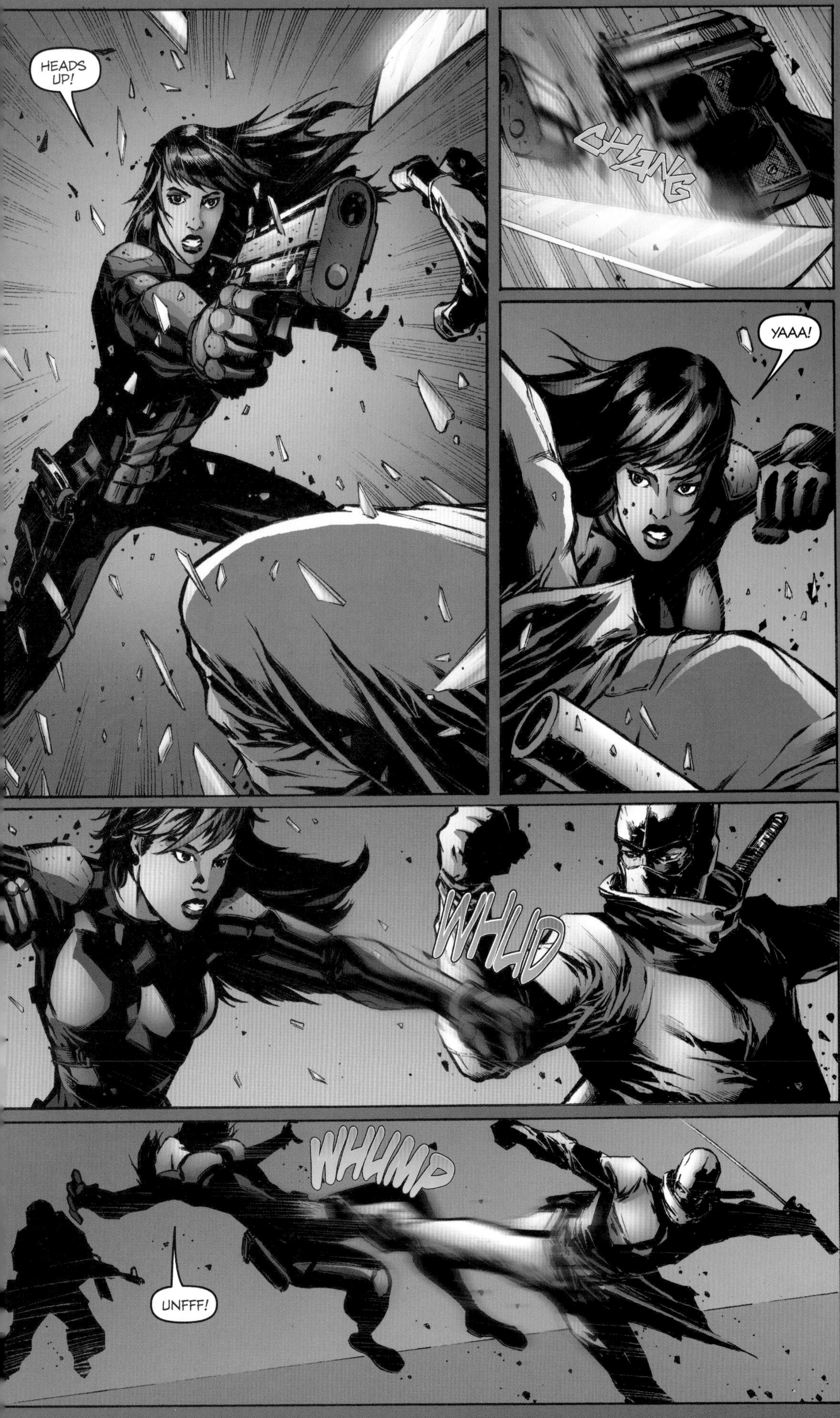
HEADS UP!
CHANG
YAAA!
WHUD
WHUMP
UNFFF!

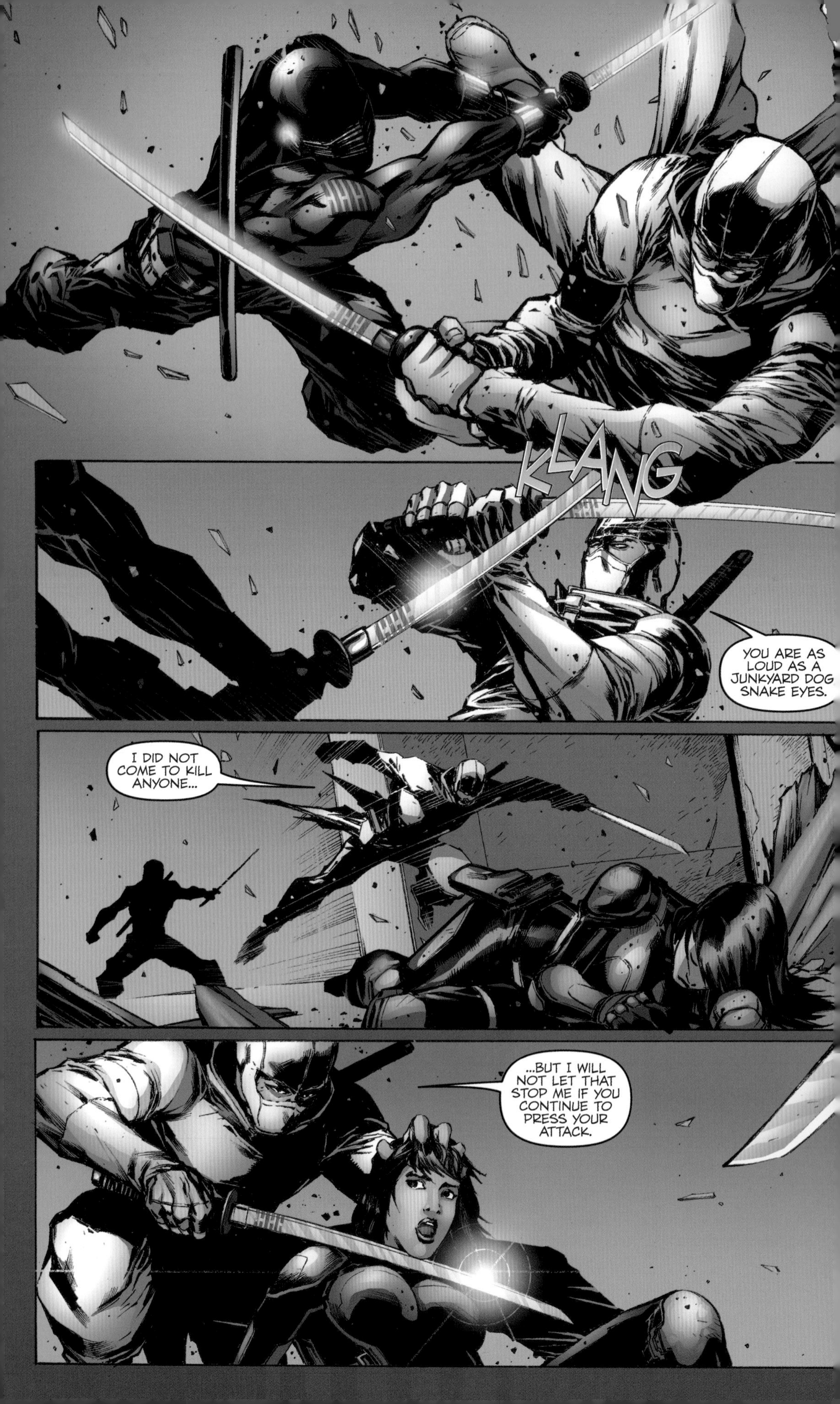
KLANG
YOU ARE AS LOUD AS A JUNKYARD DOG SNAKE EYES.
I DID NOT COME TO KILL ANYONE...
...BUT I WILL NOT LET THAT STOP ME IF YOU CONTINUE TO PRESS YOUR ATTACK.

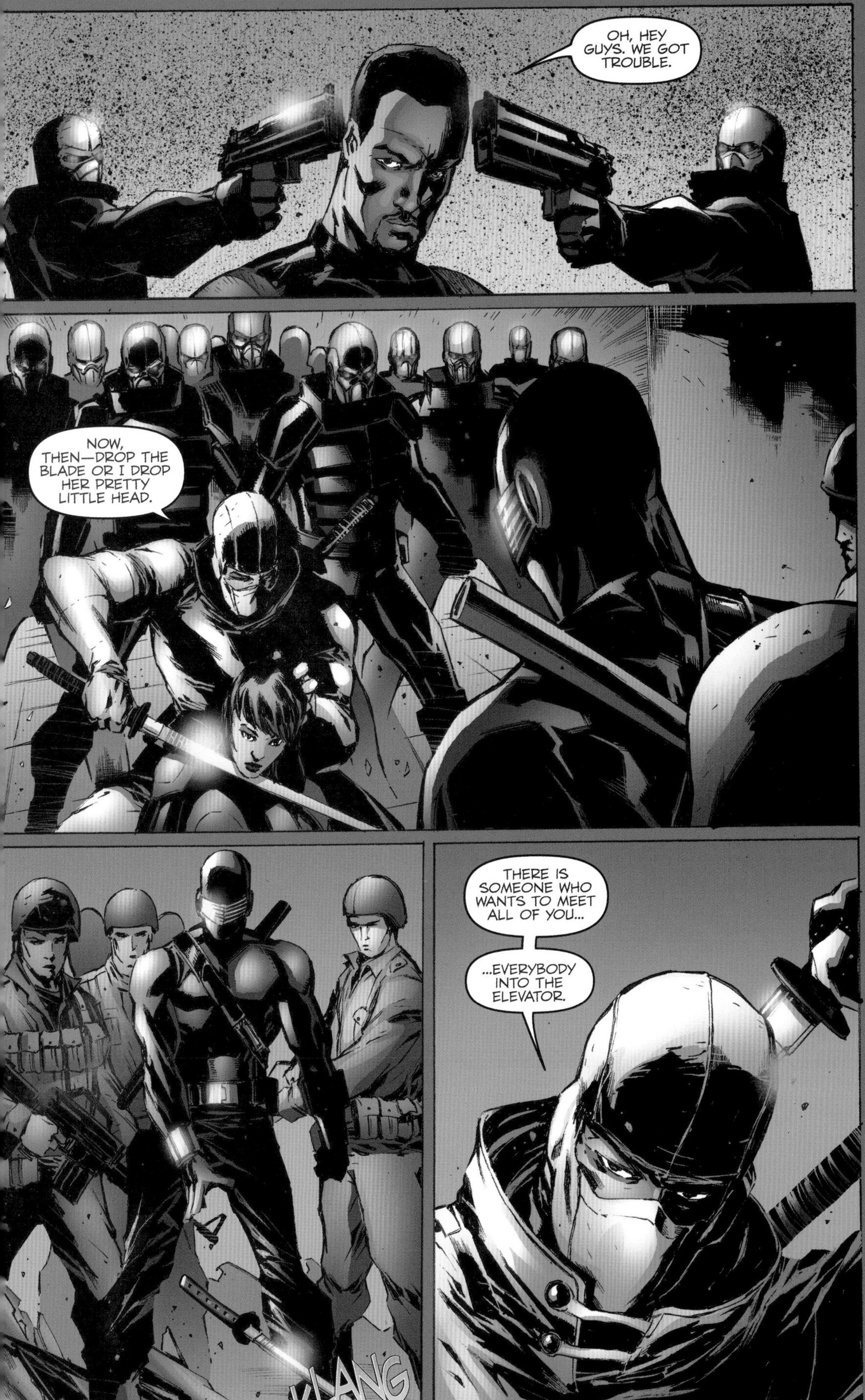
OH, HEY GUYS. WE GOT TROUBLE.
NOW, THEN—DROP THE BLADE OR I DROP HER PRETTY LITTLE HEAD.
KLANG
THERE IS SOMEONE WHO WANTS TO MEET ALL OF YOU...
...EVERYBODY INTO THE ELEVATOR.

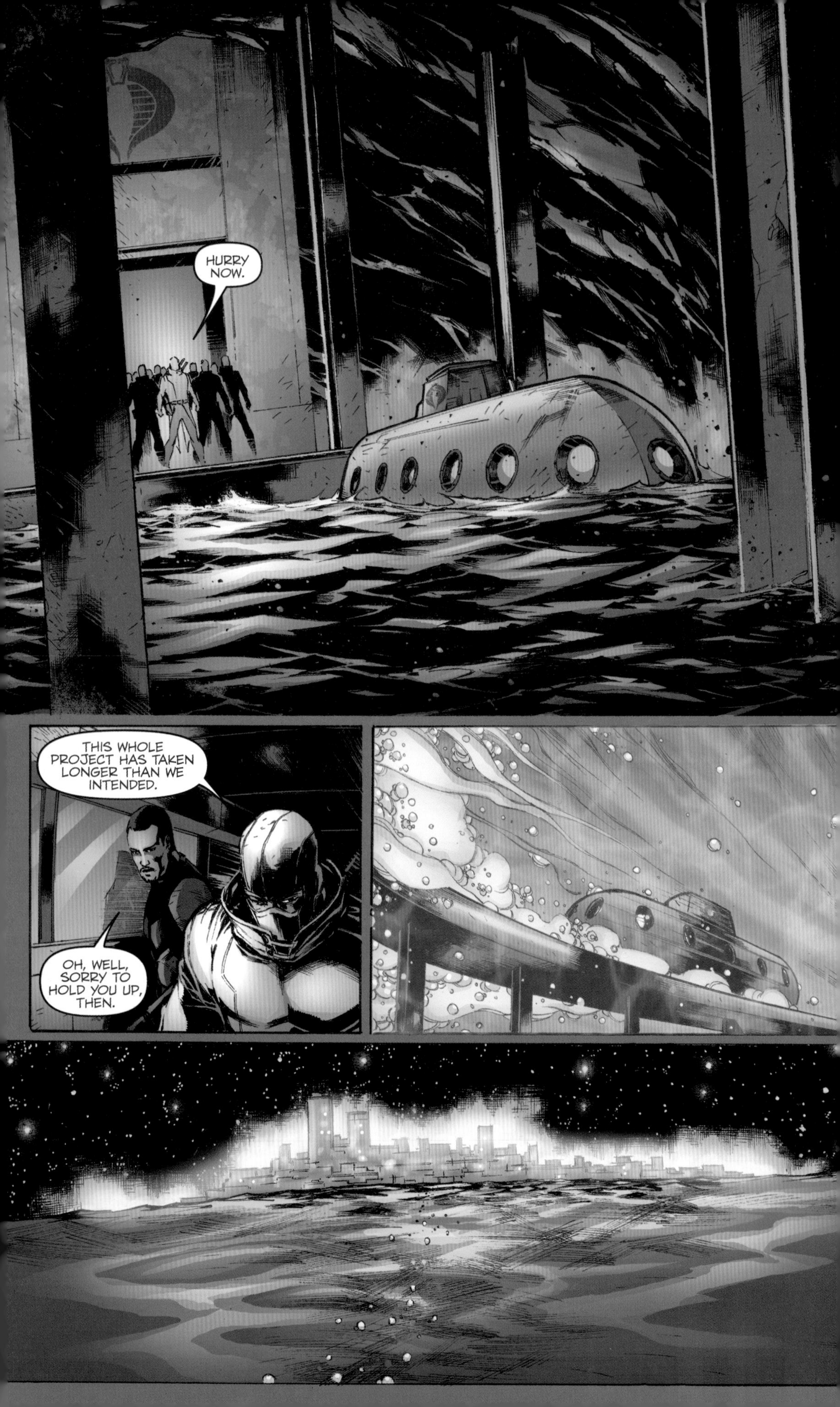
HURRY NOW.
THIS WHOLE PROJECT HAS TAKEN LONGER THAN WE INTENDED.
OH, WELL, SORRY TO HOLD YOU UP, THEN.

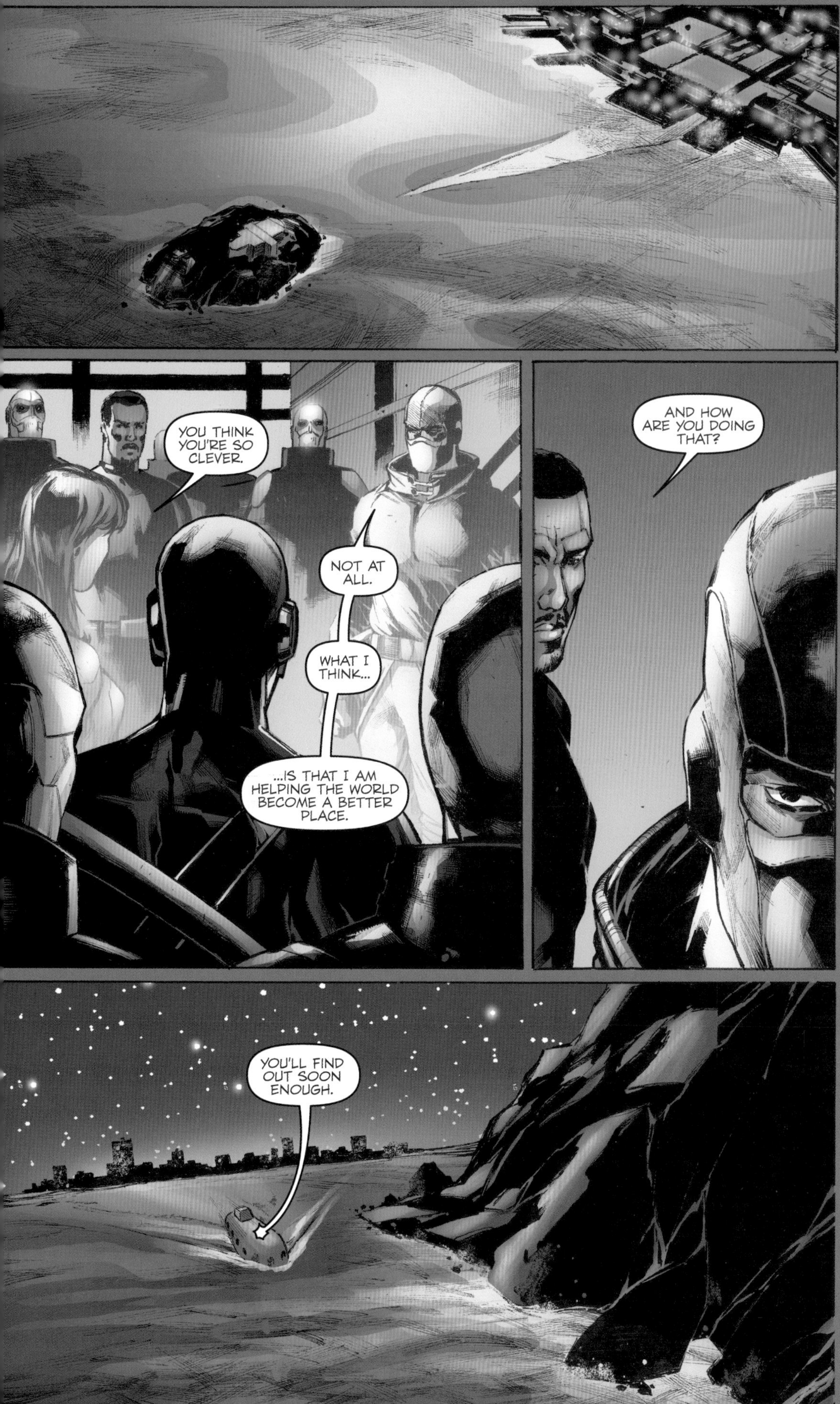
YOU THINK YOU'RE SO CLEVER.
NOT AT ALL.
WHAT I THINK...
...IS THAT I AM HELPING THE WORLD BECOME A BETTER PLACE.
AND HOW ARE YOU DOING THAT?
YOU'LL FIND OUT SOON ENOUGH.

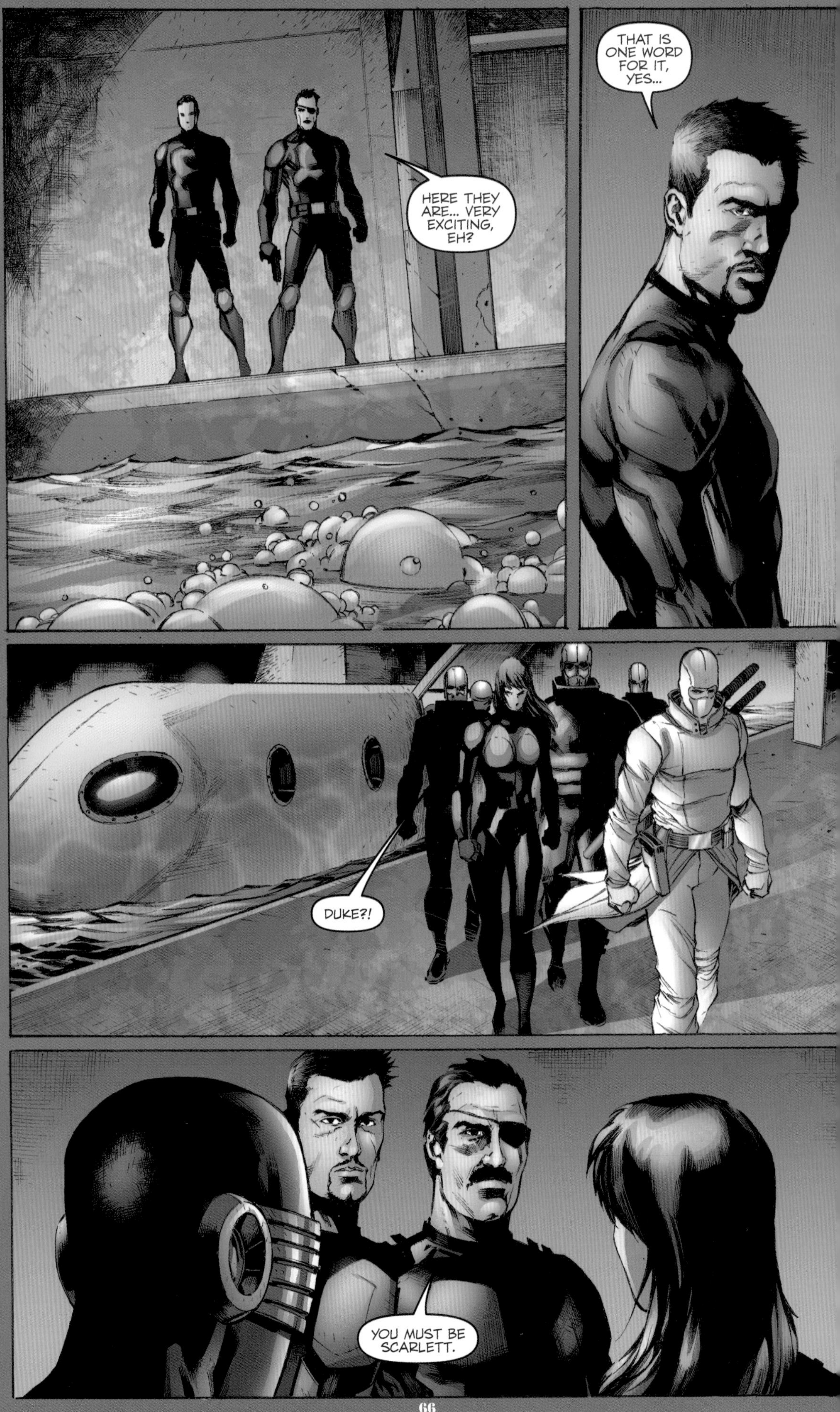
HERE THEY ARE... VERY EXCITING, EH?
THAT IS ONE WORD FOR IT, YES...
DUKE?!
YOU MUST BE SCARLETT.

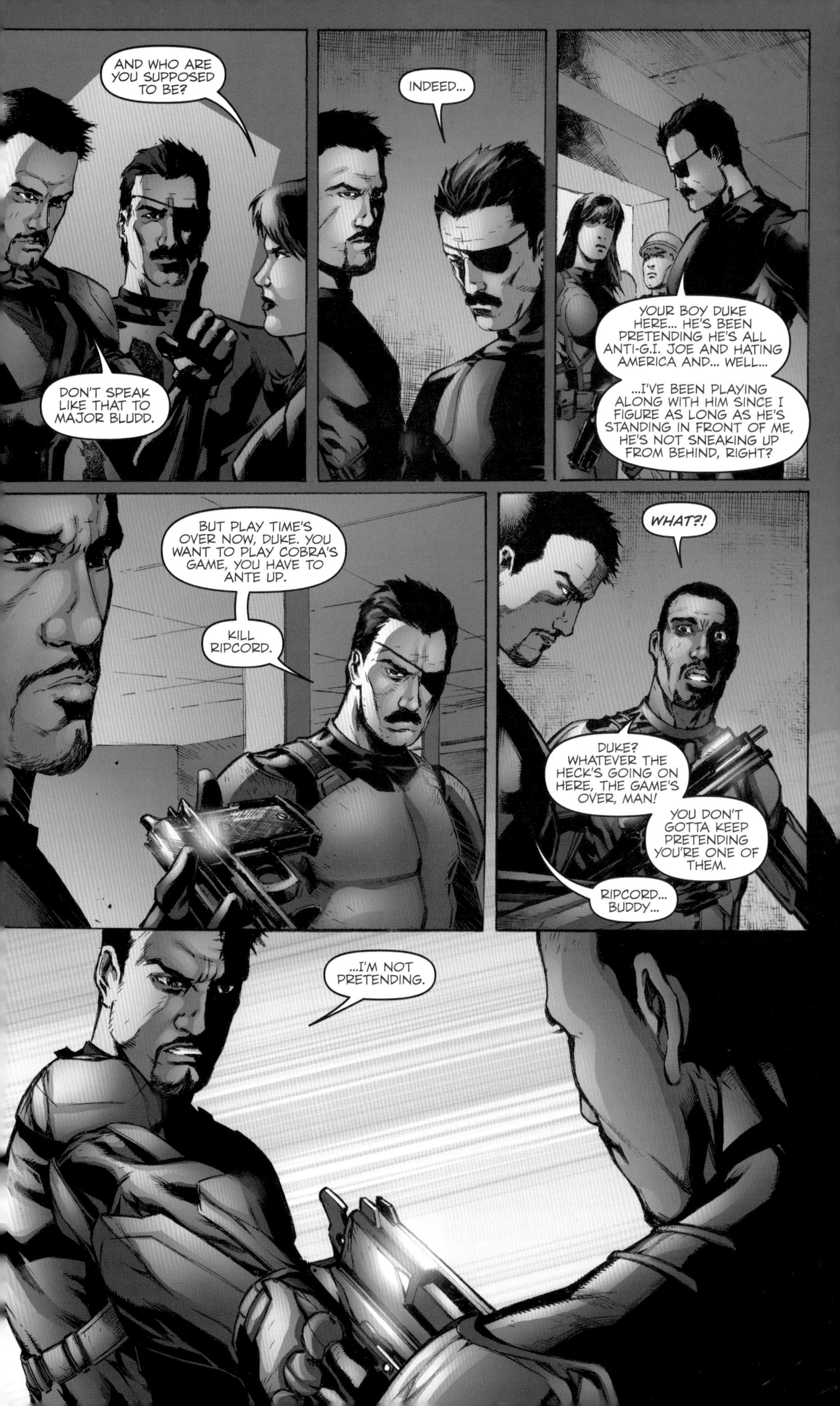
AND WHO ARE YOU SUPPOSED TO BE?
DON'T SPEAK LIKE THAT TO MAJOR BLUDD.
INDEED...
YOUR BOY DUKE HERE... HE'S BEEN PRETENDING HE'S ALL ANTI-G.I. JOE AND HATING AMERICA AND... WELL...
...I'VE BEEN PLAYING ALONG WITH HIM SINCE I FIGURE AS LONG AS HE'S STANDING IN FRONT OF ME, HE'S NOT SNEAKING UP FROM BEHIND, RIGHT?
BUT PLAY TIME'S OVER NOW, DUKE. YOU WANT TO PLAY COBRA'S GAME, YOU HAVE TO ANTE UP.
KILL RIPCORD.
WHAT?!
DUKE? WHATEVER THE HECK'S GOING ON HERE, THE GAME'S OVER, MAN!
YOU DON'T GOTTA KEEP PRETENDING YOU'RE ONE OF THEM.
RIPCORD... BUDDY...
...I'M NOT PRETENDING.

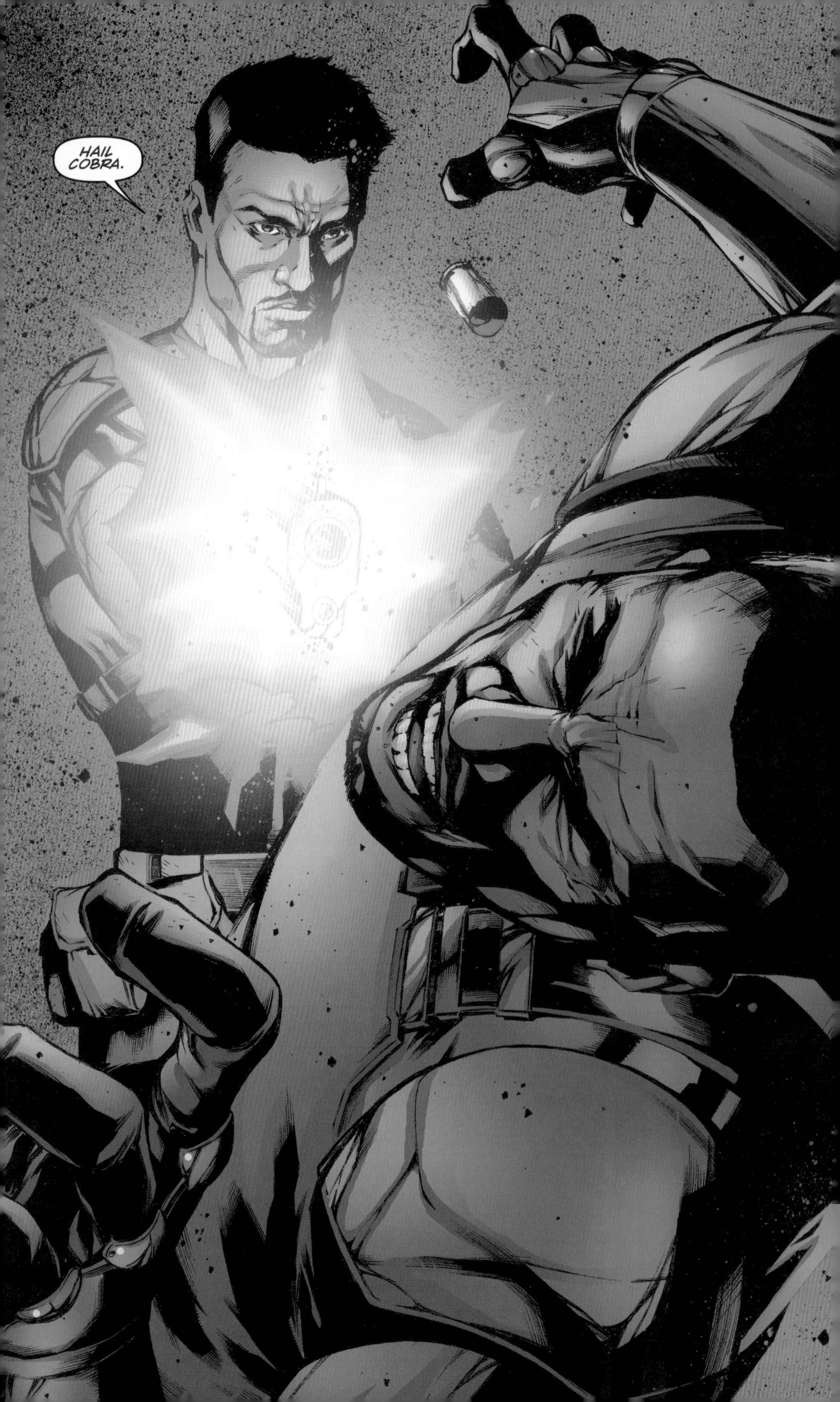
HAIL COBRA.

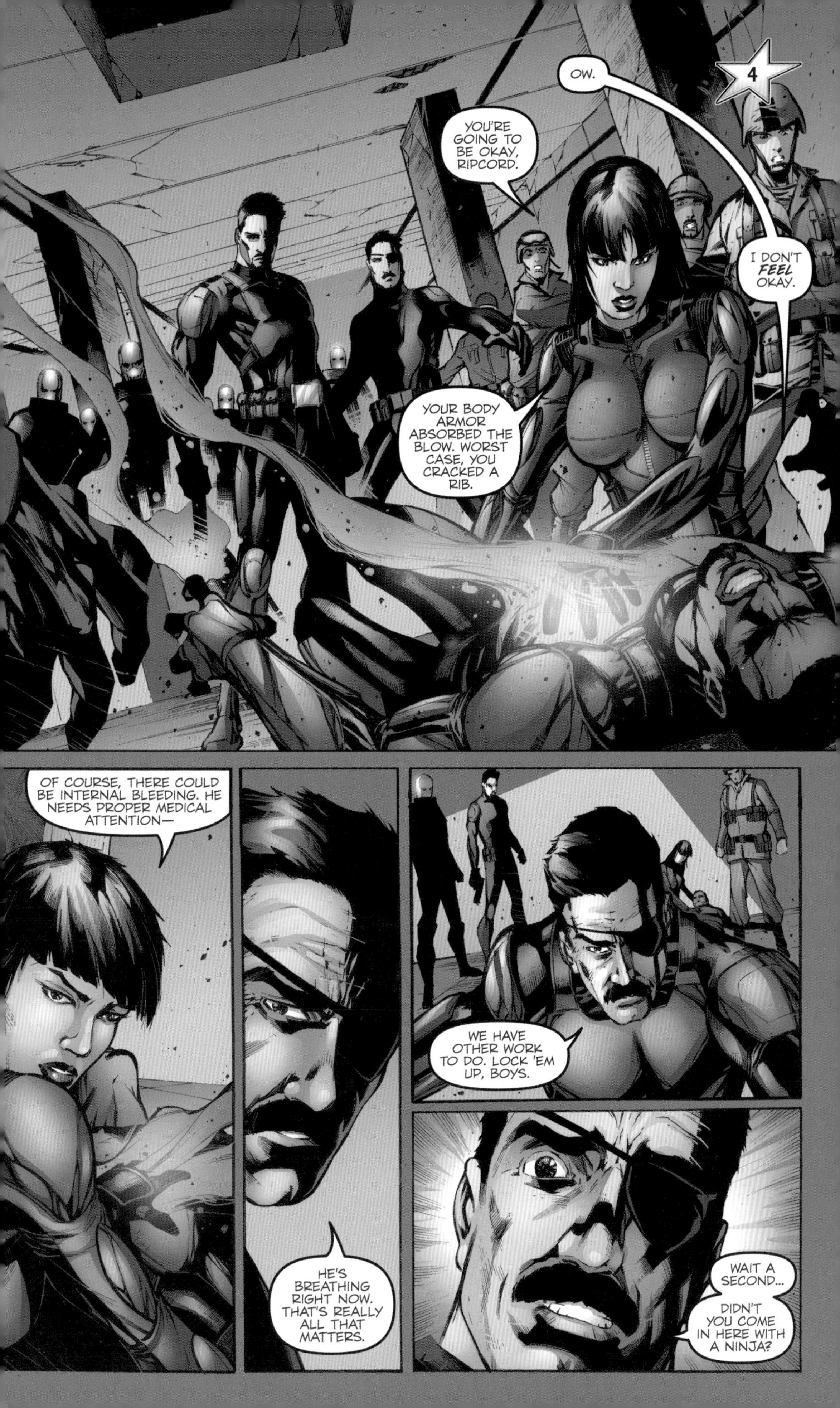
4
YOU'RE GOING TO BE OKAY, RIPCORD.
OW.
I DON'T FEEL OKAY.
YOUR BODY ARMOR ABSORBED THE BLOW. WORST CASE, YOU CRACKED A RIB.
OF COURSE, THERE COULD BE INTERNAL BLEEDING. HE NEEDS PROPER MEDICAL ATTENTION—
HE'S BREATHING RIGHT NOW. THAT'S REALLY ALL THAT MATTERS.
WE HAVE OTHER WORK TO DO. LOCK 'EM UP, BOYS.
WAIT A SECOND...
DIDN'T YOU COME IN HERE WITH A NINJA?

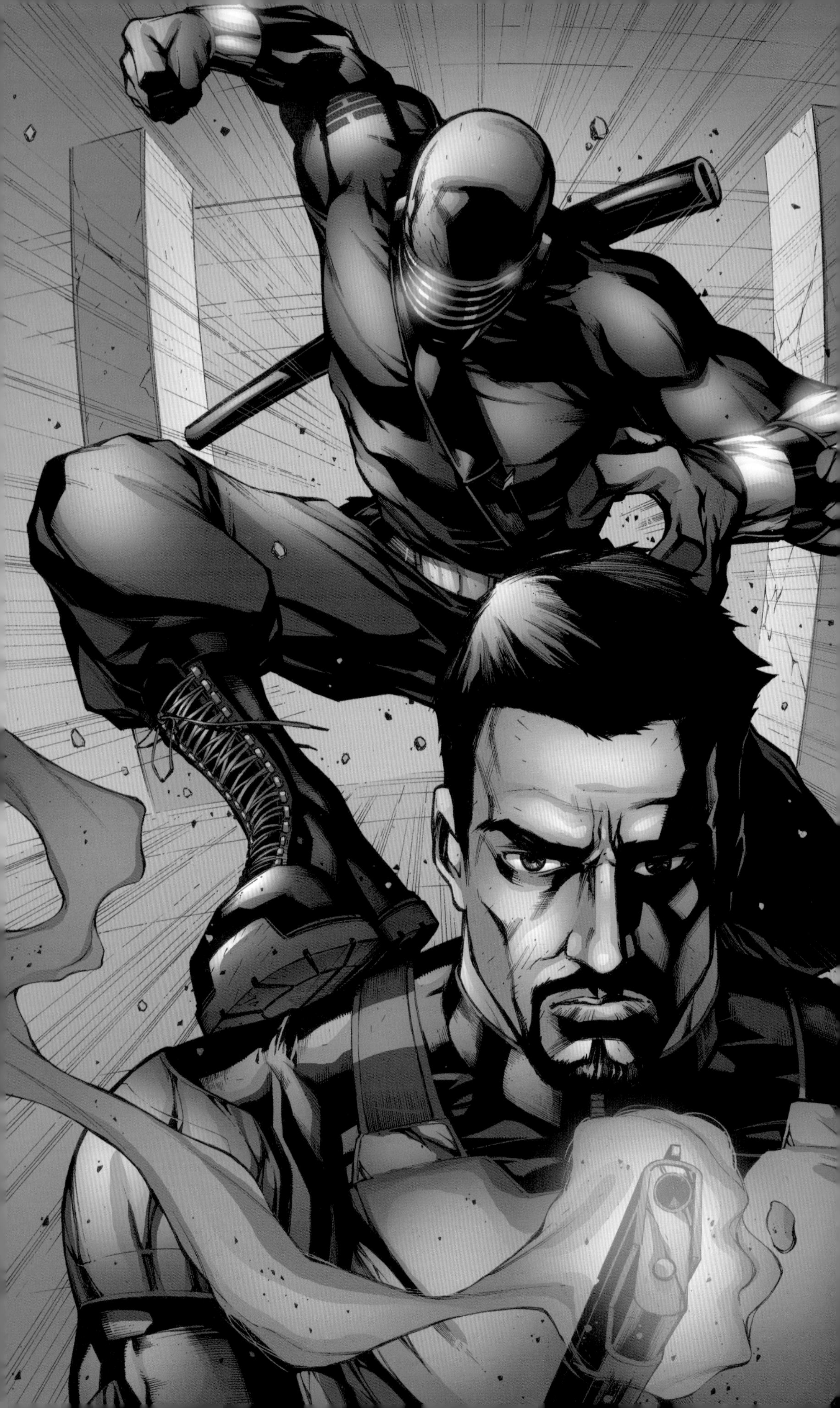

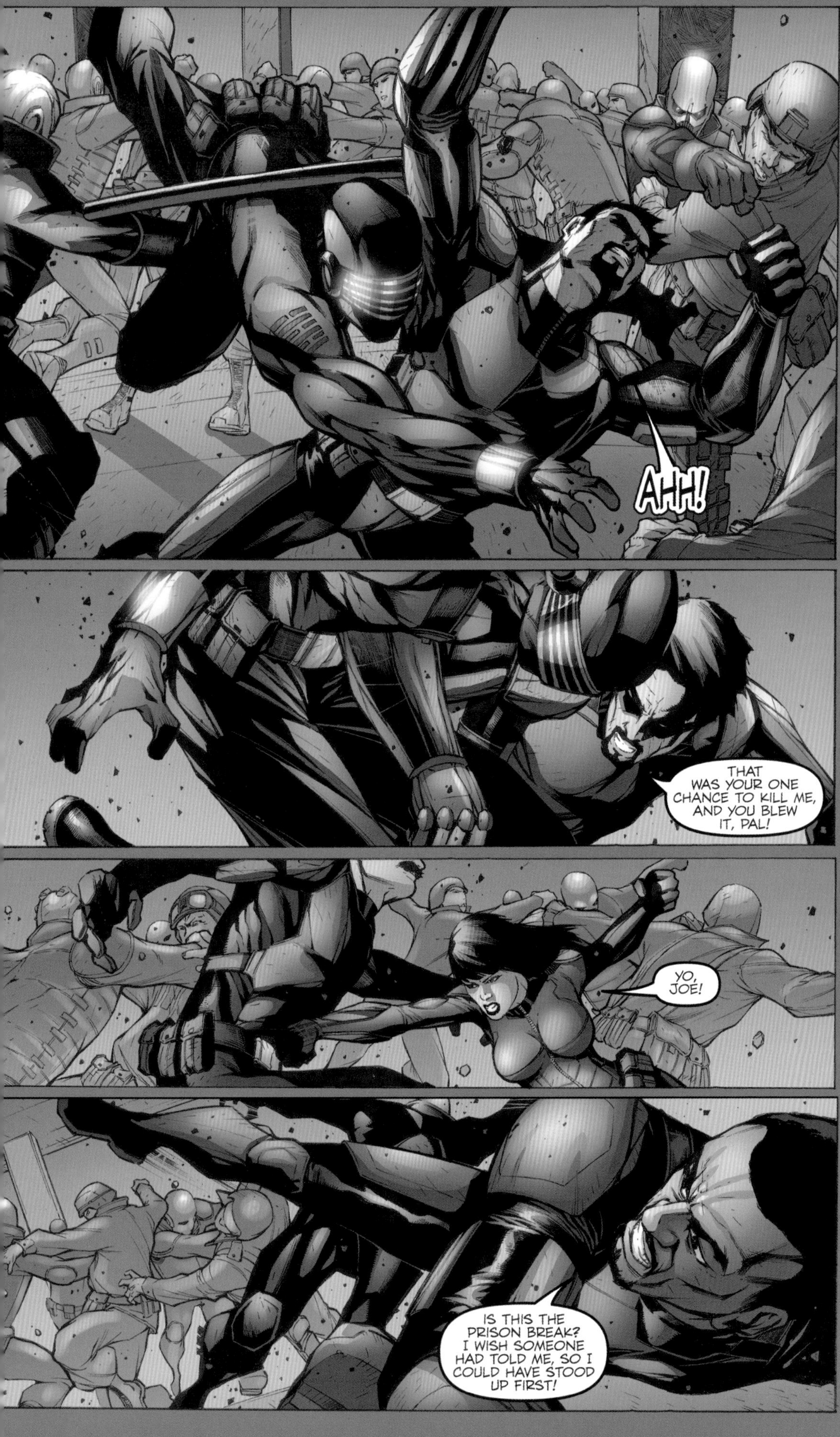
AHH!
THAT WAS YOUR ONE CHANCE TO KILL ME, AND YOU BLEW IT, PAL!
YO, JOE!
IS THIS THE PRISON BREAK? I WISH SOMEONE HAD TOLD ME, SO I COULD HAVE STOOD UP FIRST!

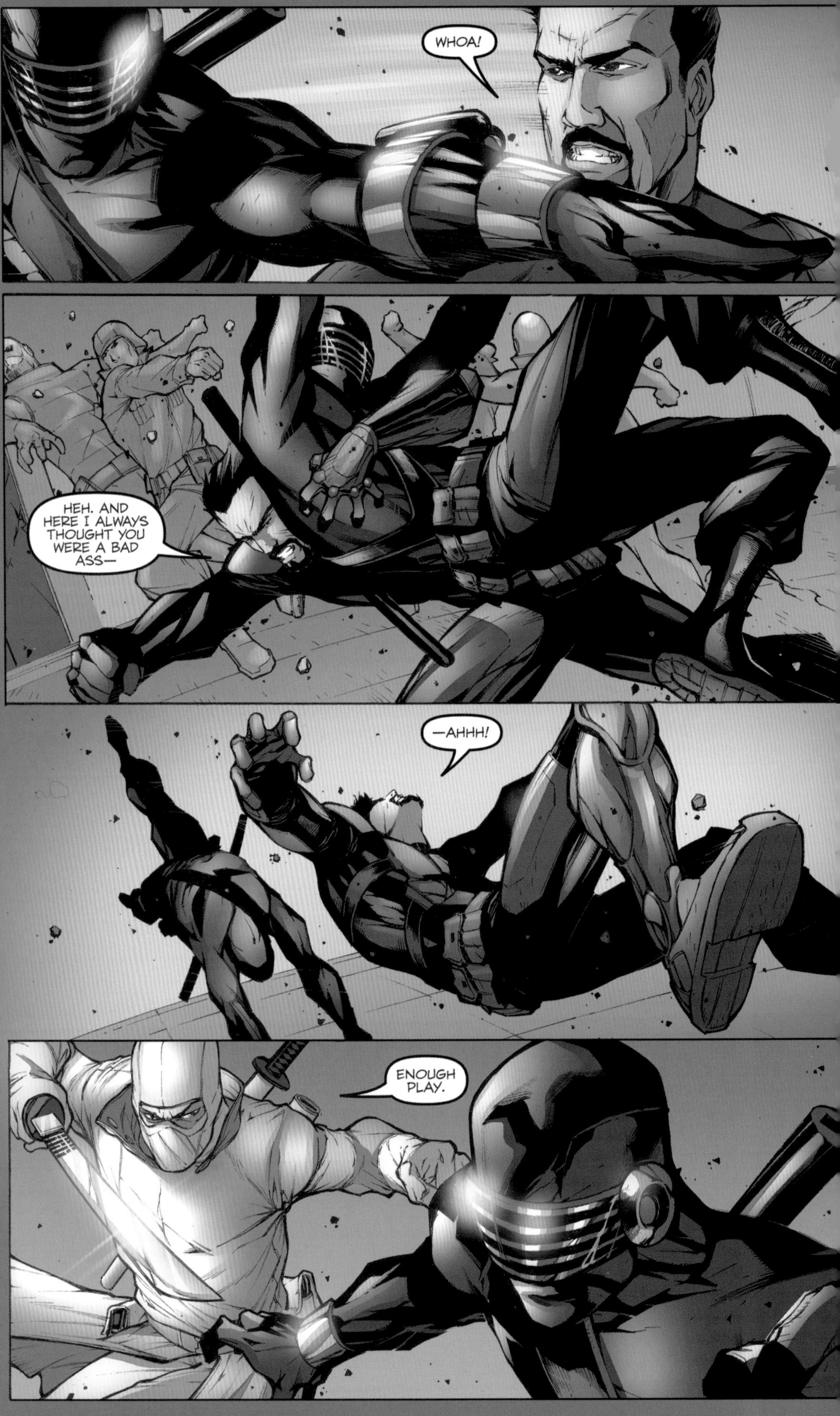
WHOA!
HEH. AND HERE I ALWAYS THOUGHT YOU WERE A BAD ASS—
—AHHH!
ENOUGH PLAY.

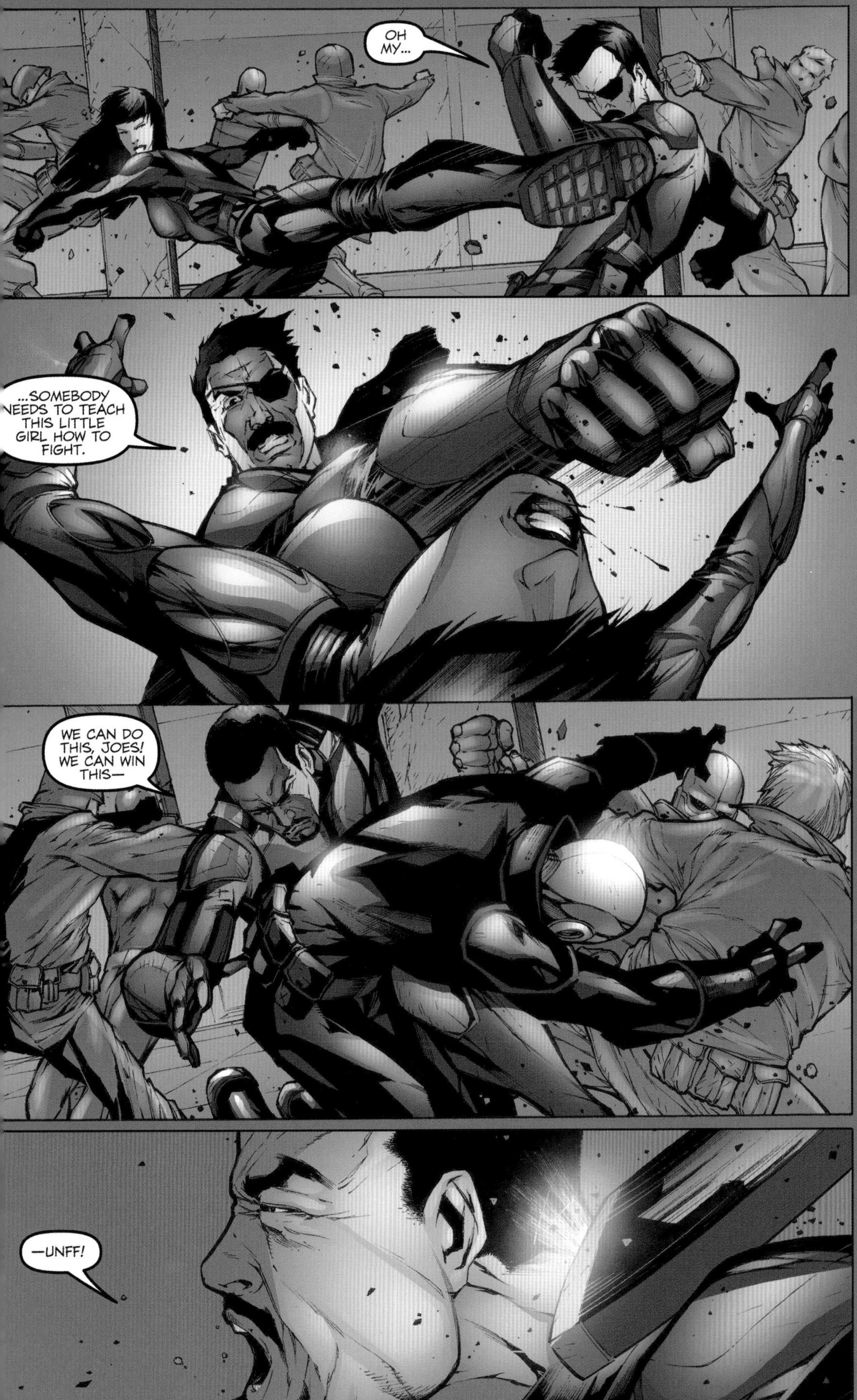
OH MY...
...SOMEBODY NEEDS TO TEACH THIS LITTLE GIRL HOW TO FIGHT.
WE CAN DO THIS, JOES! WE CAN WIN THIS—
—UNFF!

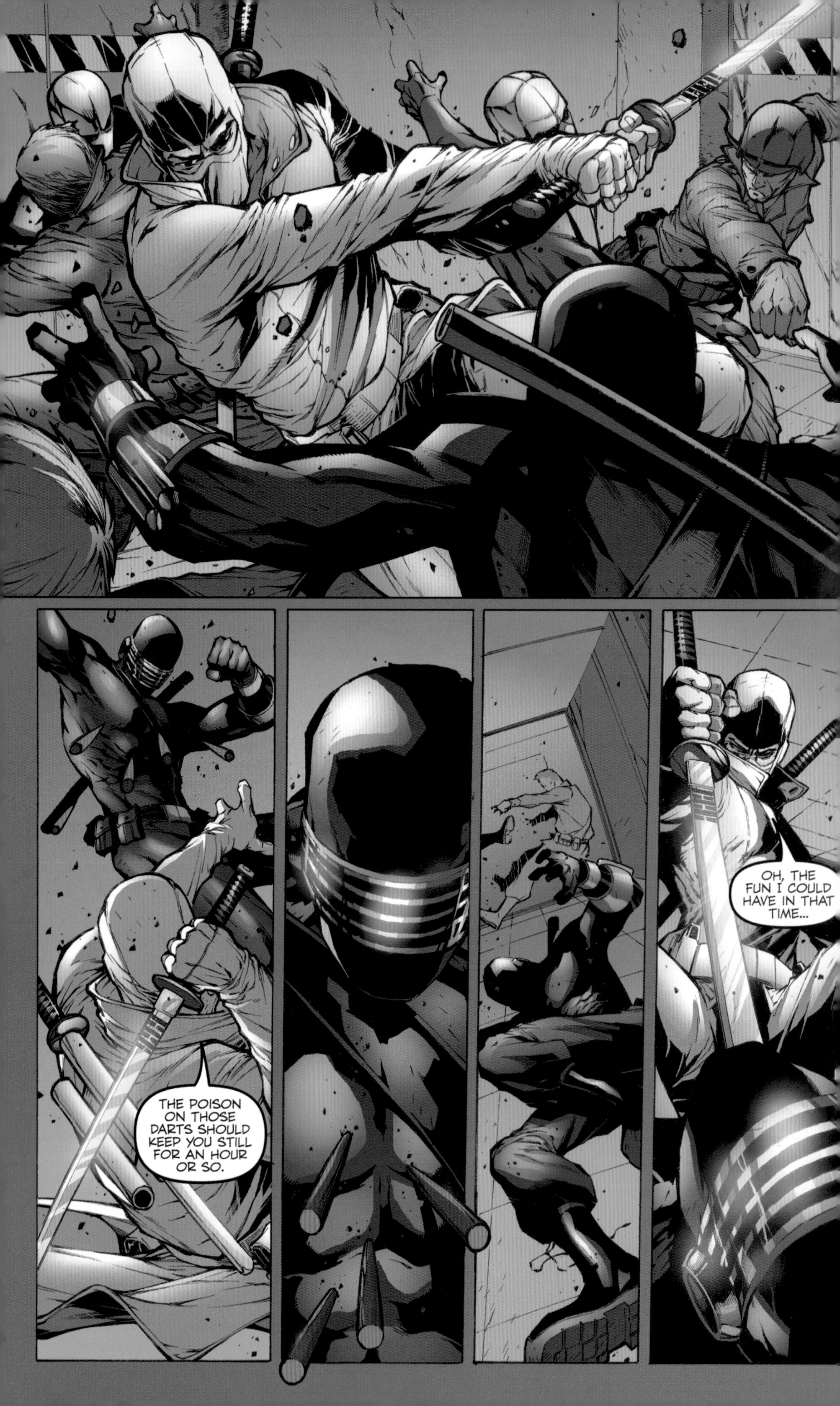
THE POISON ON THOSE DARTS SHOULD KEEP YOU STILL FOR AN HOUR OR SO.
OH, THE FUN I COULD HAVE IN THAT TIME...

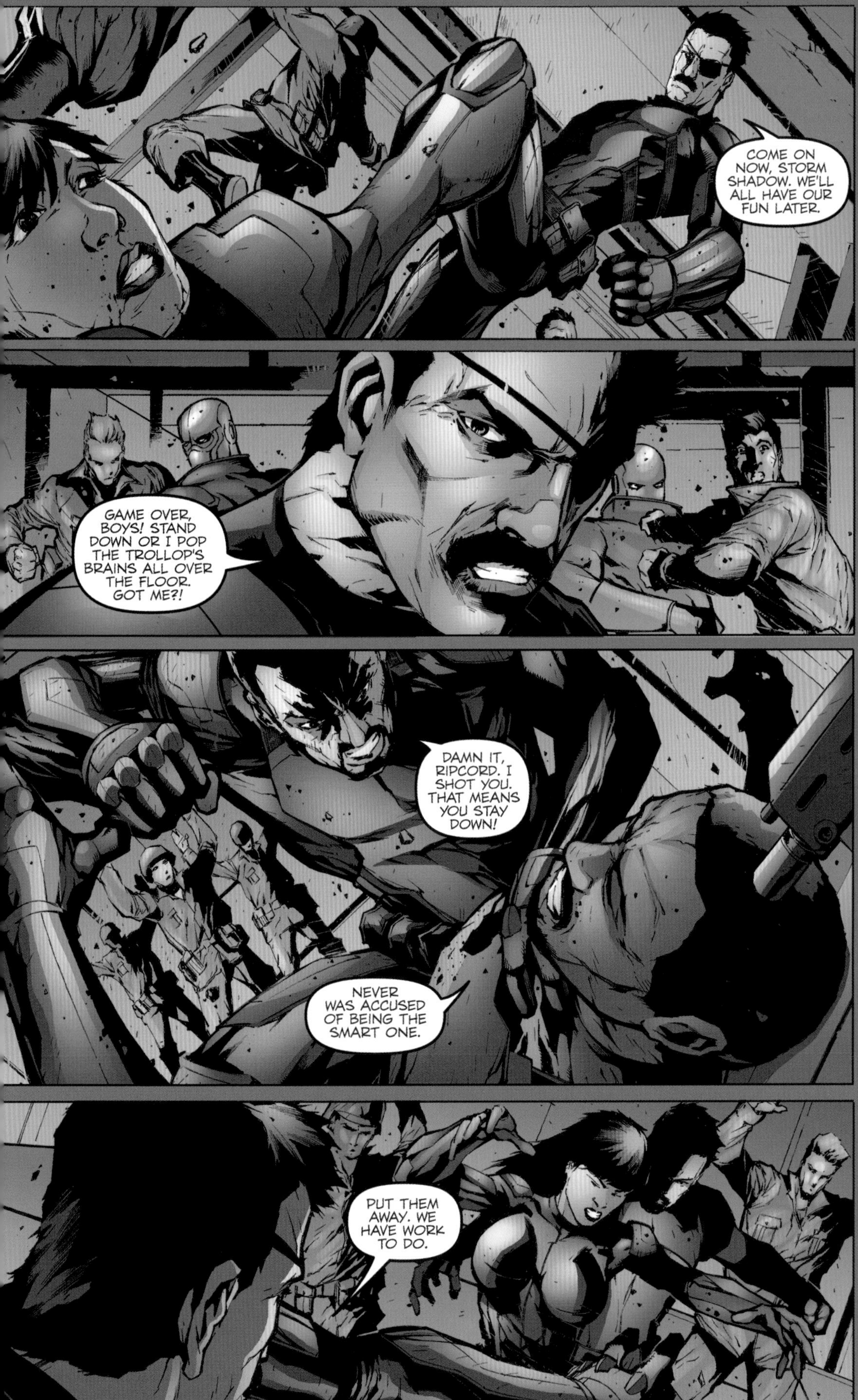
COME ON NOW, STORM SHADOW. WE'LL ALL HAVE OUR FUN LATER.
GAME OVER, BOYS! STAND DOWN OR I POP THE TROLLOP'S BRAINS ALL OVER THE FLOOR. GOT ME?!
DAMN IT, RIPCORD. I SHOT YOU. THAT MEANS YOU STAY DOWN!
NEVER WAS ACCUSED OF BEING THE SMART ONE.
PUT THEM AWAY. WE HAVE WORK TO DO.

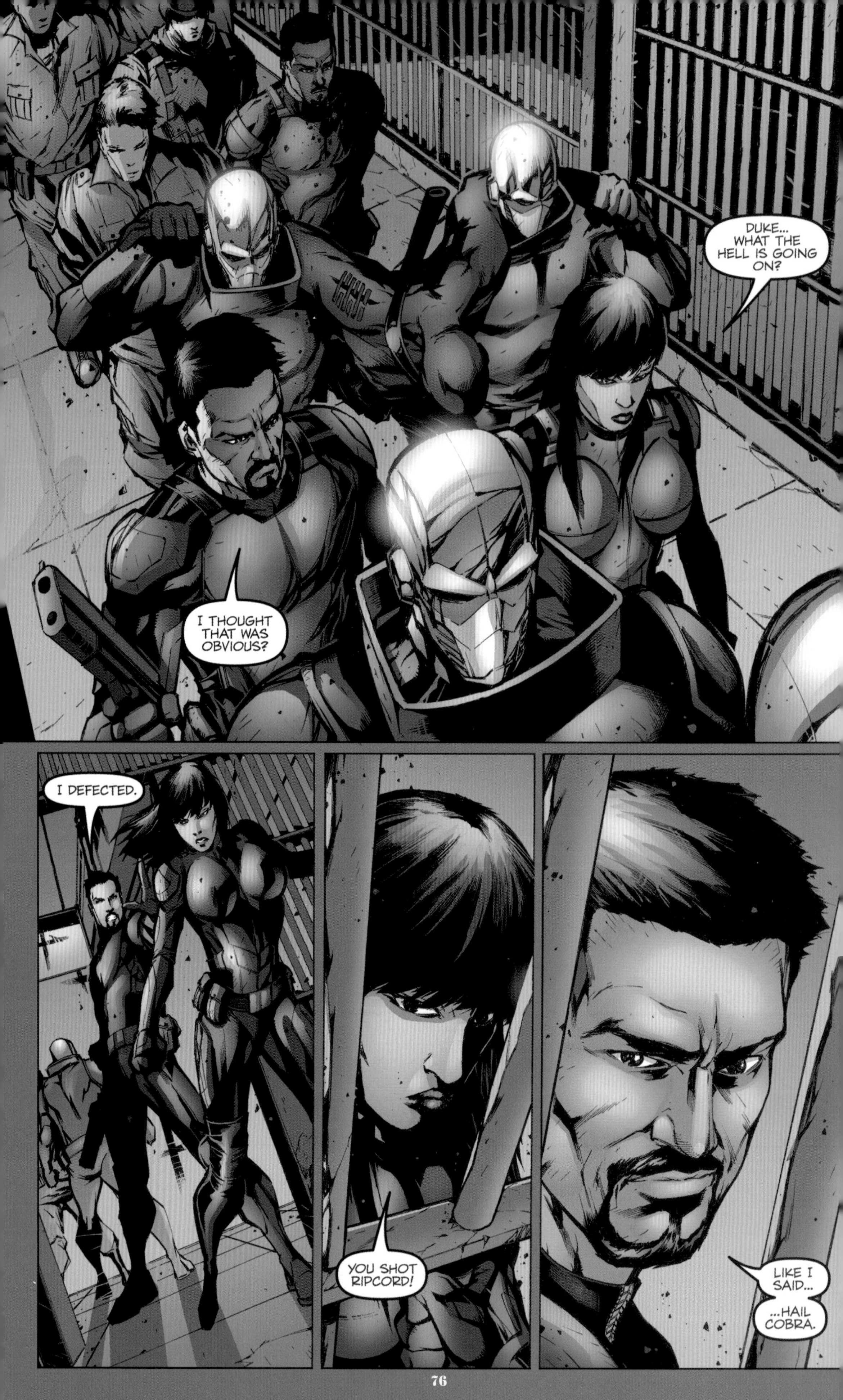
DUKE... WHAT THE HELL IS GOING ON?
I THOUGHT THAT WAS OBVIOUS?
I DEFECTED.
YOU SHOT RIPCORD!
LIKE I SAID...
...HAIL COBRA.

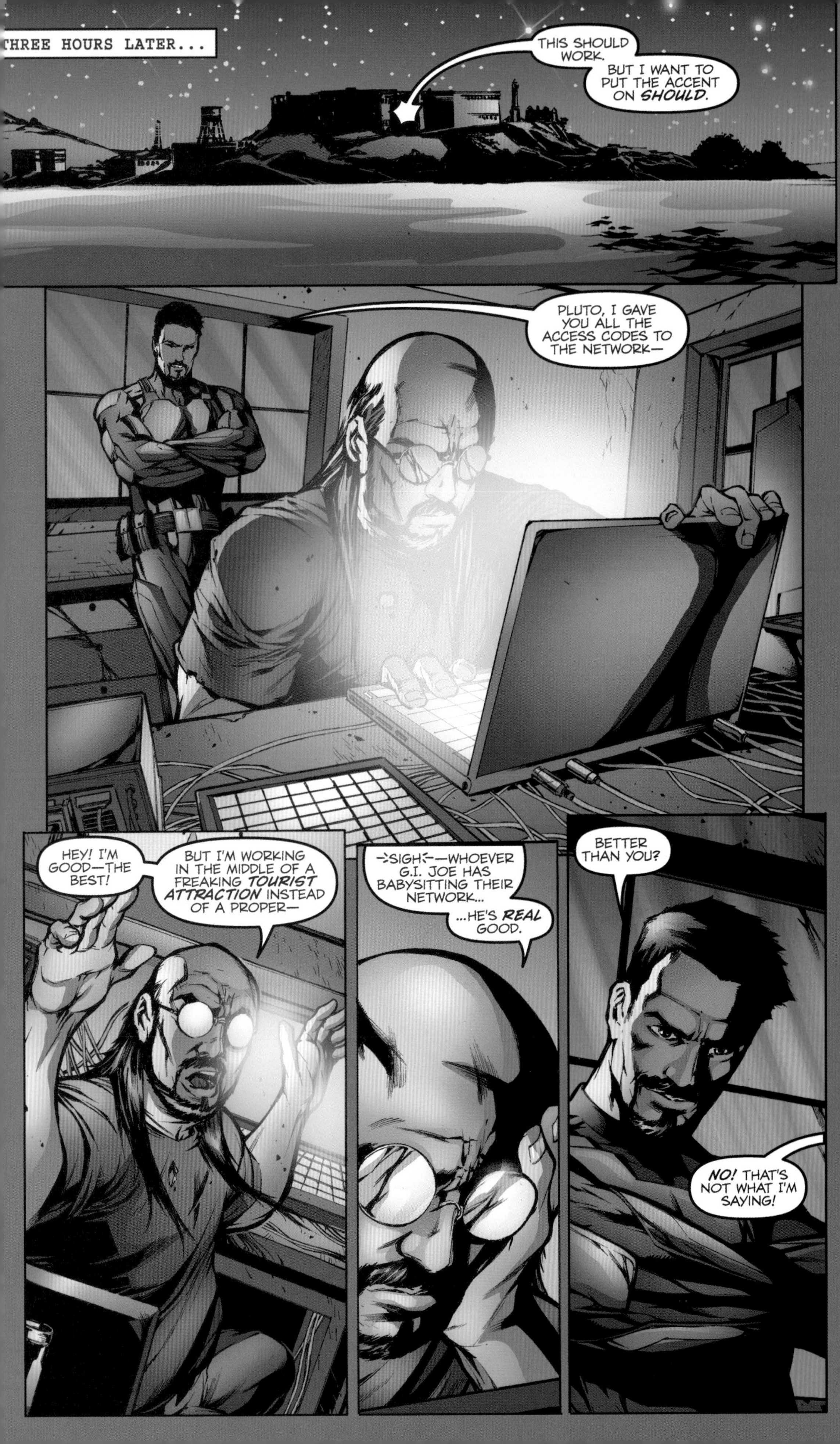
THREE HOURS LATER...
THIS SHOULD WORK.
BUT I WANT TO PUT THE ACCENT ON SHOULD.
PLUTO, I GAVE YOU ALL THE ACCESS CODES TO THE NETWORK—
HEY! I'M GOOD—THE BEST!
BUT I'M WORKING IN THE MIDDLE OF A FREAKING TOURIST ATTRACTION INSTEAD OF A PROPER—
-SIGH-—WHOEVER G.I. JOE HAS BABYSITTING THEIR NETWORK...
...HE'S REAL GOOD.
BETTER THAN YOU?
NO! THAT'S NOT WHAT I'M SAYING!

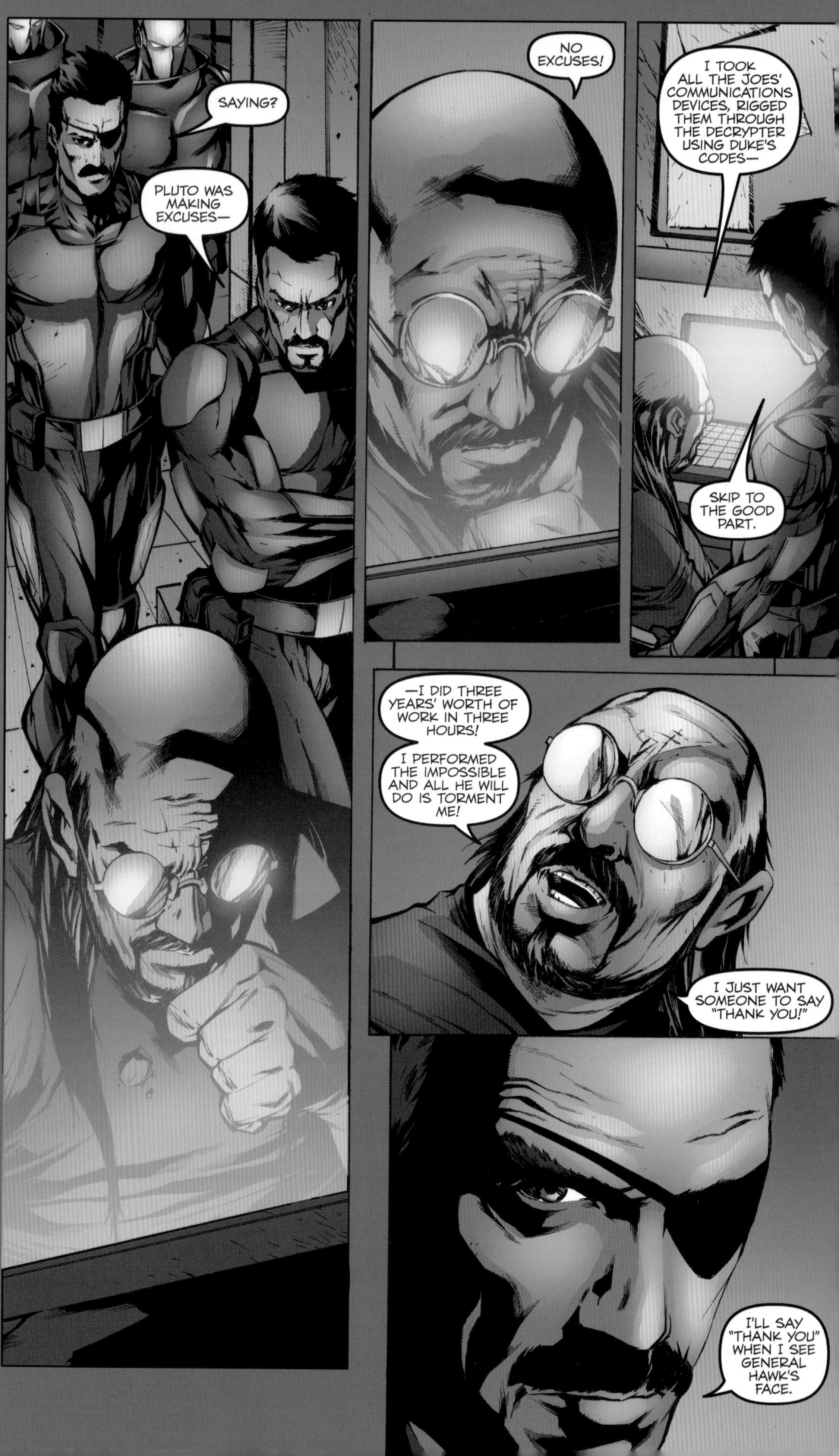
SAYING?
PLUTO WAS MAKING EXCUSES—
NO EXCUSES!
I TOOK ALL THE JOES' COMMUNICATIONS DEVICES, RIGGED THEM THROUGH THE DECRYPTER USING DUKE'S CODES—
SKIP TO THE GOOD PART.
—I DID THREE YEARS' WORTH OF WORK IN THREE HOURS!
I PERFORMED THE IMPOSSIBLE AND ALL HE WILL DO IS TORMENT ME!
I JUST WANT SOMEONE TO SAY "THANK YOU!"
I'LL SAY "THANK YOU" WHEN I SEE GENERAL HAWK'S FACE.

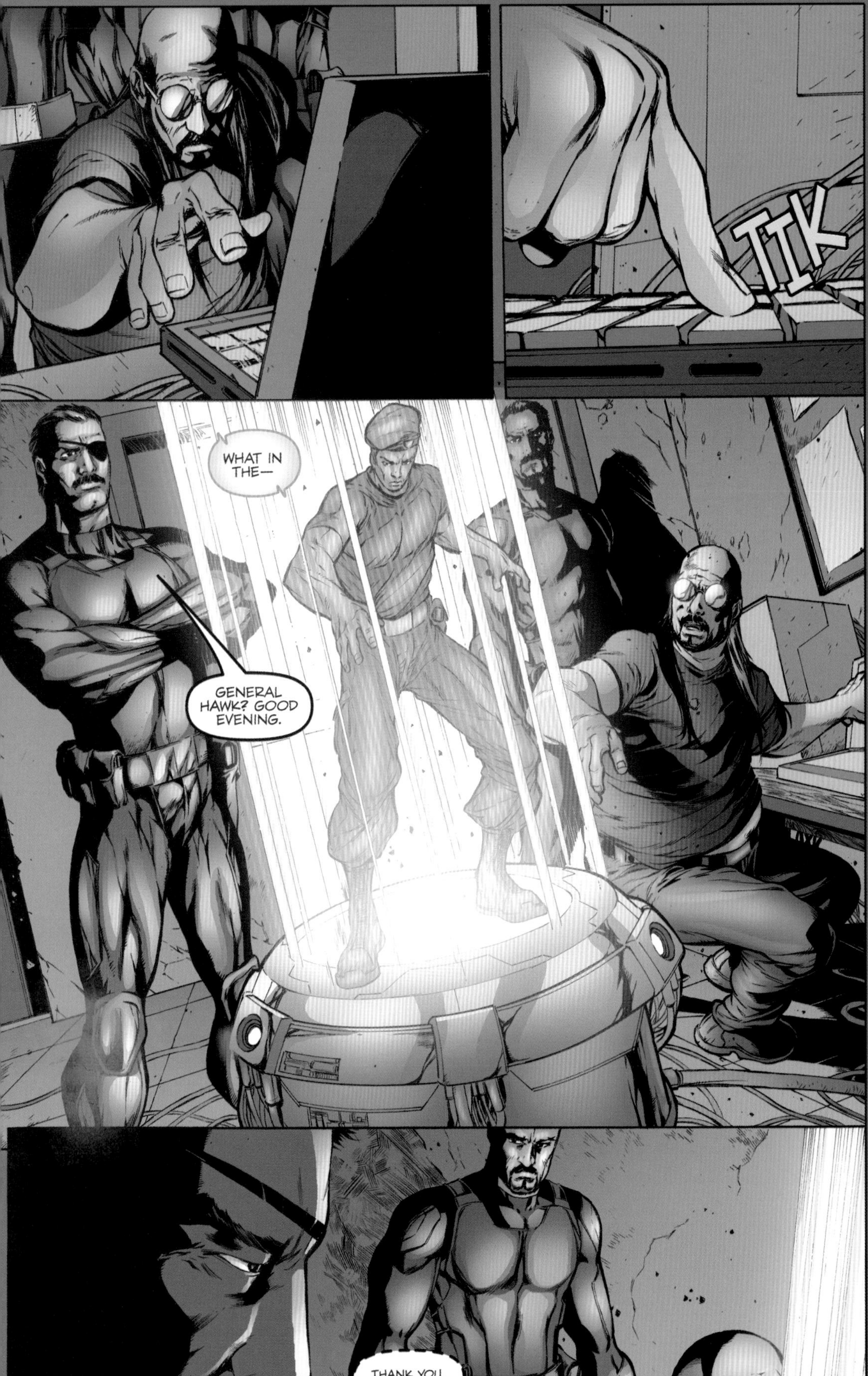
TIK
WHAT IN THE—
GENERAL HAWK? GOOD EVENING.
THANK YOU, PLUTO.

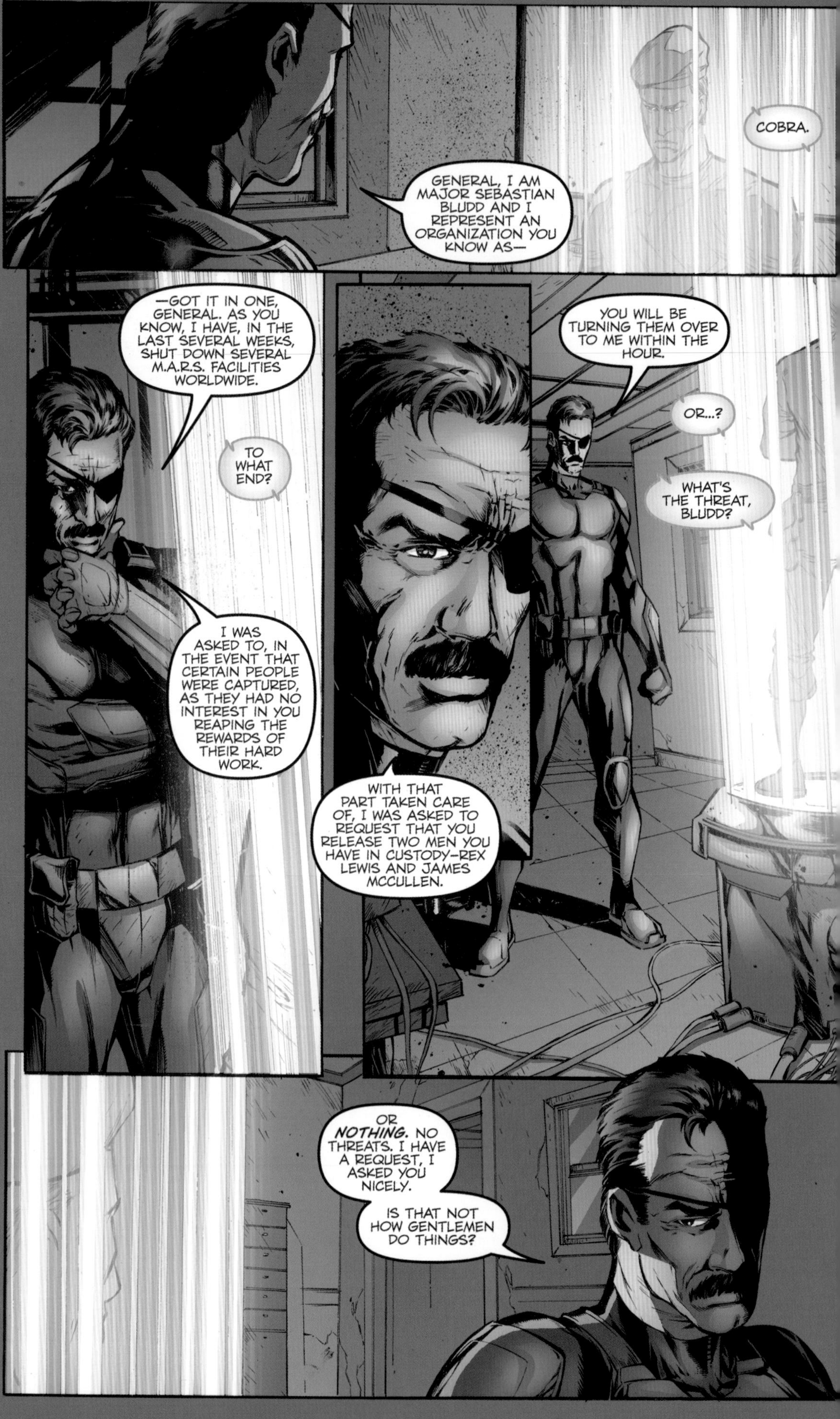

GENERAL, I AM MAJOR SEBASTIAN BLUDD AND I REPRESENT AN ORGANIZATION YOU KNOW AS—
COBRA.
—GOT IT IN ONE, GENERAL. AS YOU KNOW, I HAVE, IN THE LAST SEVERAL WEEKS, SHUT DOWN SEVERAL M.A.R.S. FACILITIES WORLDWIDE.
TO WHAT END?
I WAS ASKED TO, IN THE EVENT THAT CERTAIN PEOPLE WERE CAPTURED, AS THEY HAD NO INTEREST IN YOU REAPING THE REWARDS OF THEIR HARD WORK.
WITH THAT PART TAKEN CARE OF, I WAS ASKED TO REQUEST THAT YOU RELEASE TWO MEN YOU HAVE IN CUSTODY—REX LEWIS AND JAMES MCCULLEN.
YOU WILL BE TURNING THEM OVER TO ME WITHIN THE HOUR.
OR...?
WHAT'S THE THREAT, BLUDD?
OR *NOTHING*. NO THREATS. I HAVE A REQUEST, I ASKED YOU NICELY.
IS THAT NOT HOW GENTLEMEN DO THINGS?

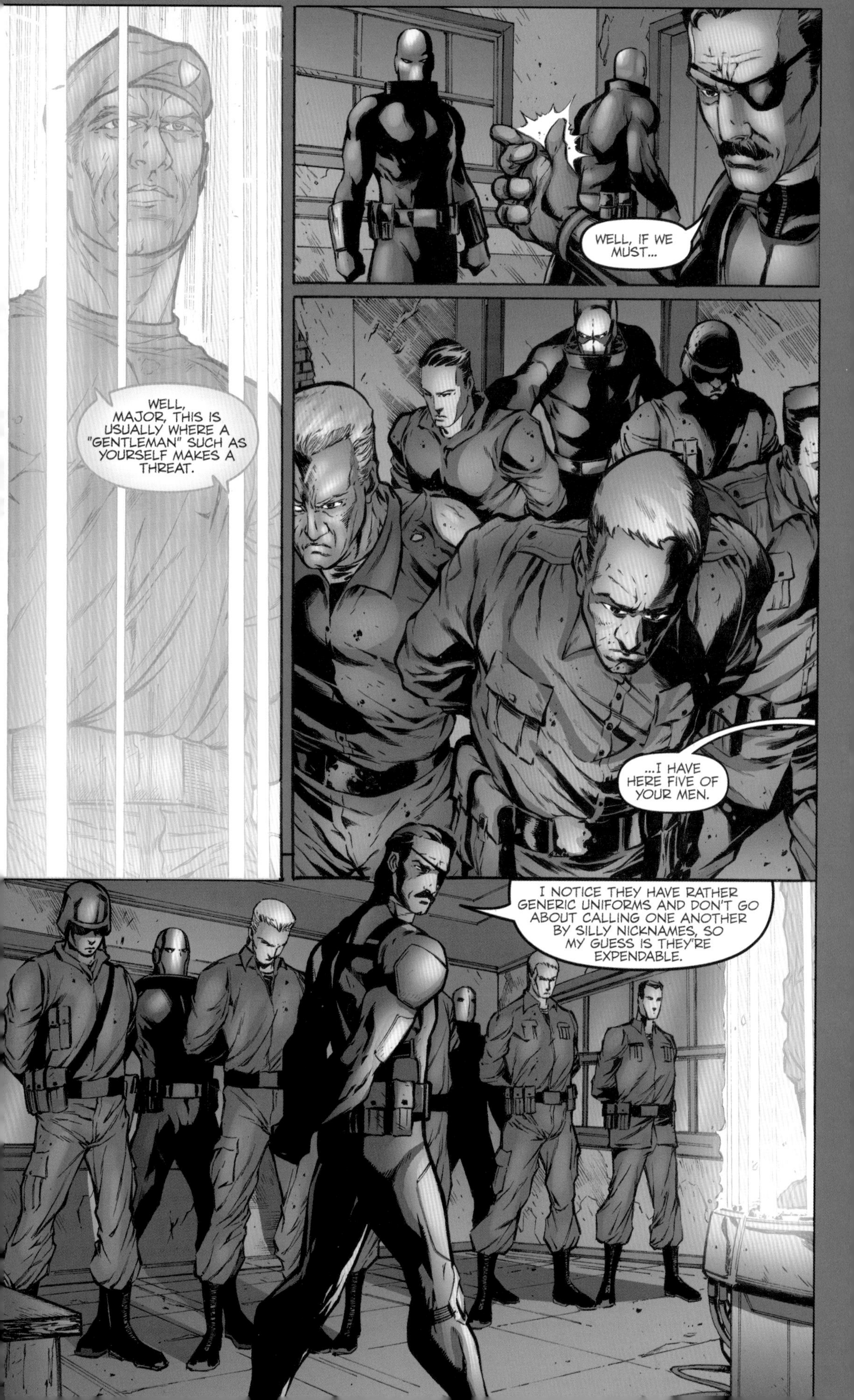

WELL, MAJOR, THIS IS USUALLY WHERE A "GENTLEMAN" SUCH AS YOURSELF MAKES A THREAT.
WELL, IF WE MUST...
...I HAVE HERE FIVE OF YOUR MEN.
I NOTICE THEY HAVE RATHER GENERIC UNIFORMS AND DON'T GO ABOUT CALLING ONE ANOTHER BY SILLY NICKNAMES, SO MY GUESS IS THEY'RE EXPENDABLE.

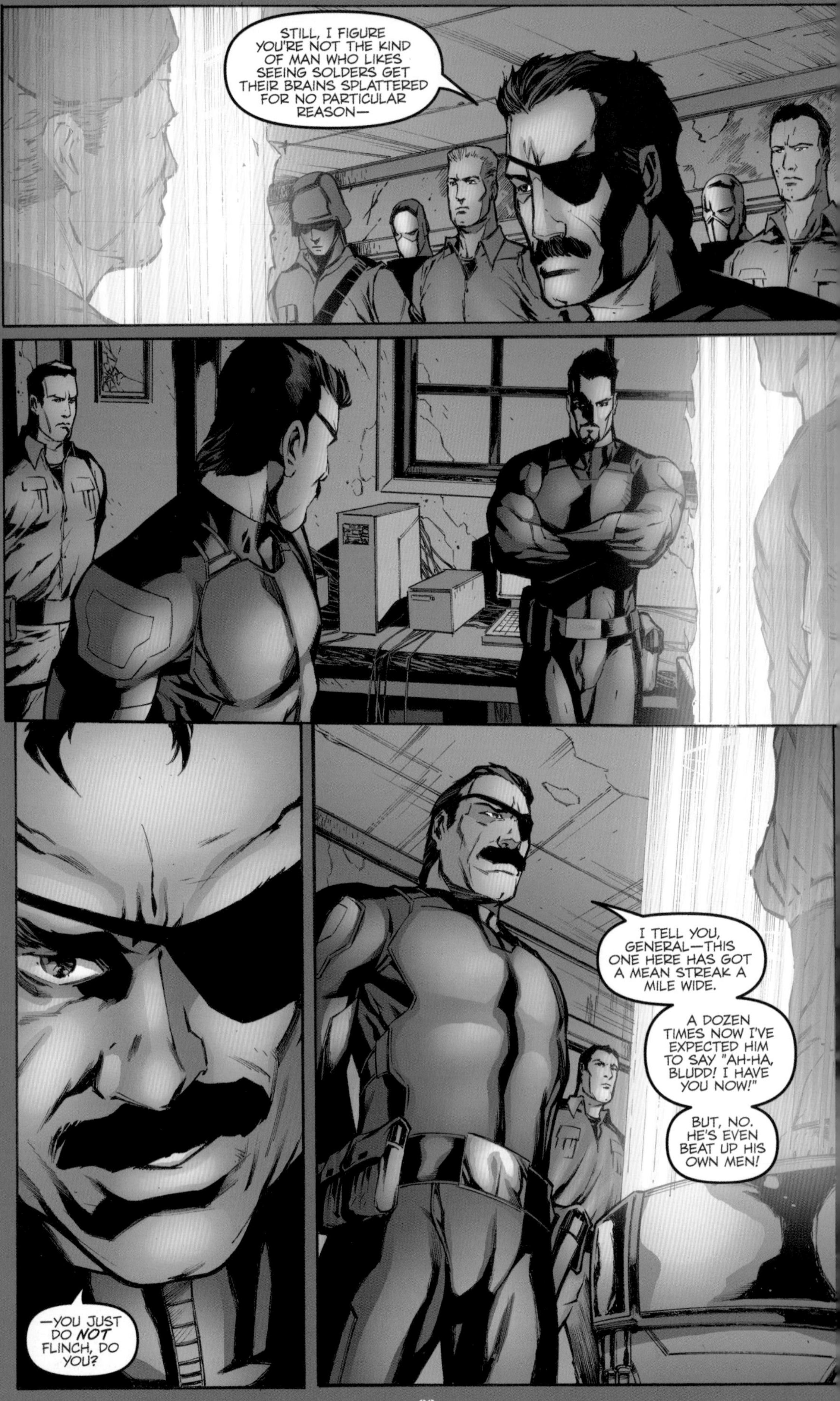

STILL, I FIGURE YOU'RE NOT THE KIND OF MAN WHO LIKES SEEING SOLDERS GET THEIR BRAINS SPLATTERED FOR NO PARTICULAR REASON—
—YOU JUST DO ***NOT*** FLINCH, DO YOU?
I TELL YOU, GENERAL—THIS ONE HERE HAS GOT A MEAN STREAK A MILE WIDE.
A DOZEN TIMES NOW I'VE EXPECTED HIM TO SAY "AH-HA, BLUDD! I HAVE YOU NOW!"
BUT, NO. HE'S EVEN BEAT UP HIS OWN MEN!

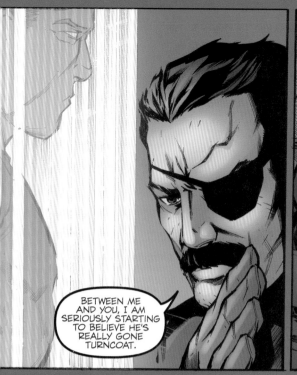

I DO NOT KNOW THAT MAN, MAJOR.

BUT I KNOW THE OTHERS YOU HAVE THERE.

BETWEEN ME AND YOU, I AM SERIOUSLY STARTING TO BELIEVE HE'S REALLY GONE TURNCOAT.

THEY ARE GOOD MEN, EVERY ONE.

SERGEANT PINES.

CAPTAIN JONES.

MAJOR ANDERSON.

COLONEL LO—

WAIT... COLONEL?

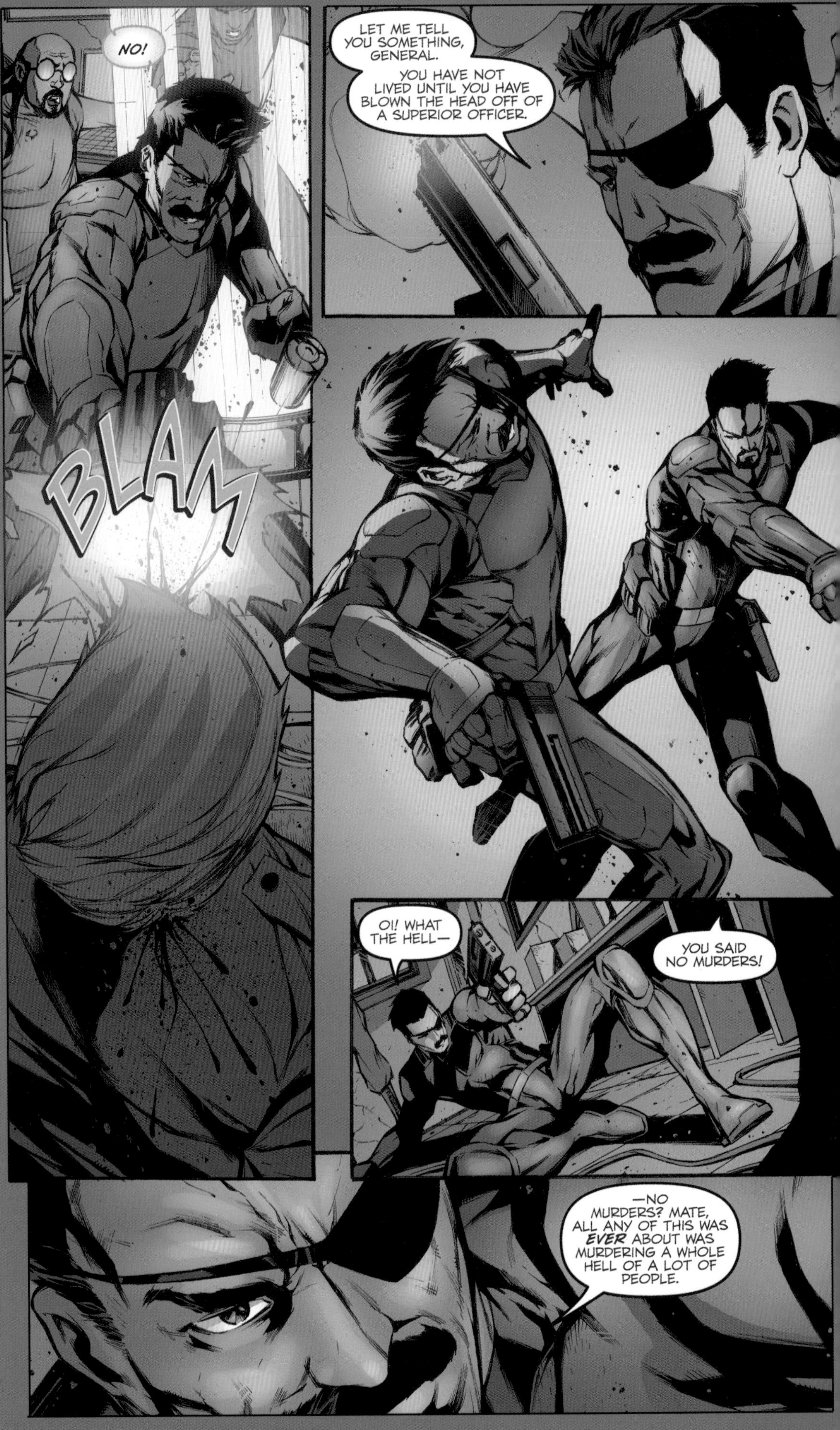
NO!
LET ME TELL YOU SOMETHING, GENERAL.
YOU HAVE NOT LIVED UNTIL YOU HAVE BLOWN THE HEAD OFF OF A SUPERIOR OFFICER.
BLAM
OI! WHAT THE HELL—
YOU SAID NO MURDERS!
—NO MURDERS? MATE, ALL ANY OF THIS WAS *EVER* ABOUT WAS MURDERING A WHOLE HELL OF A LOT OF PEOPLE.

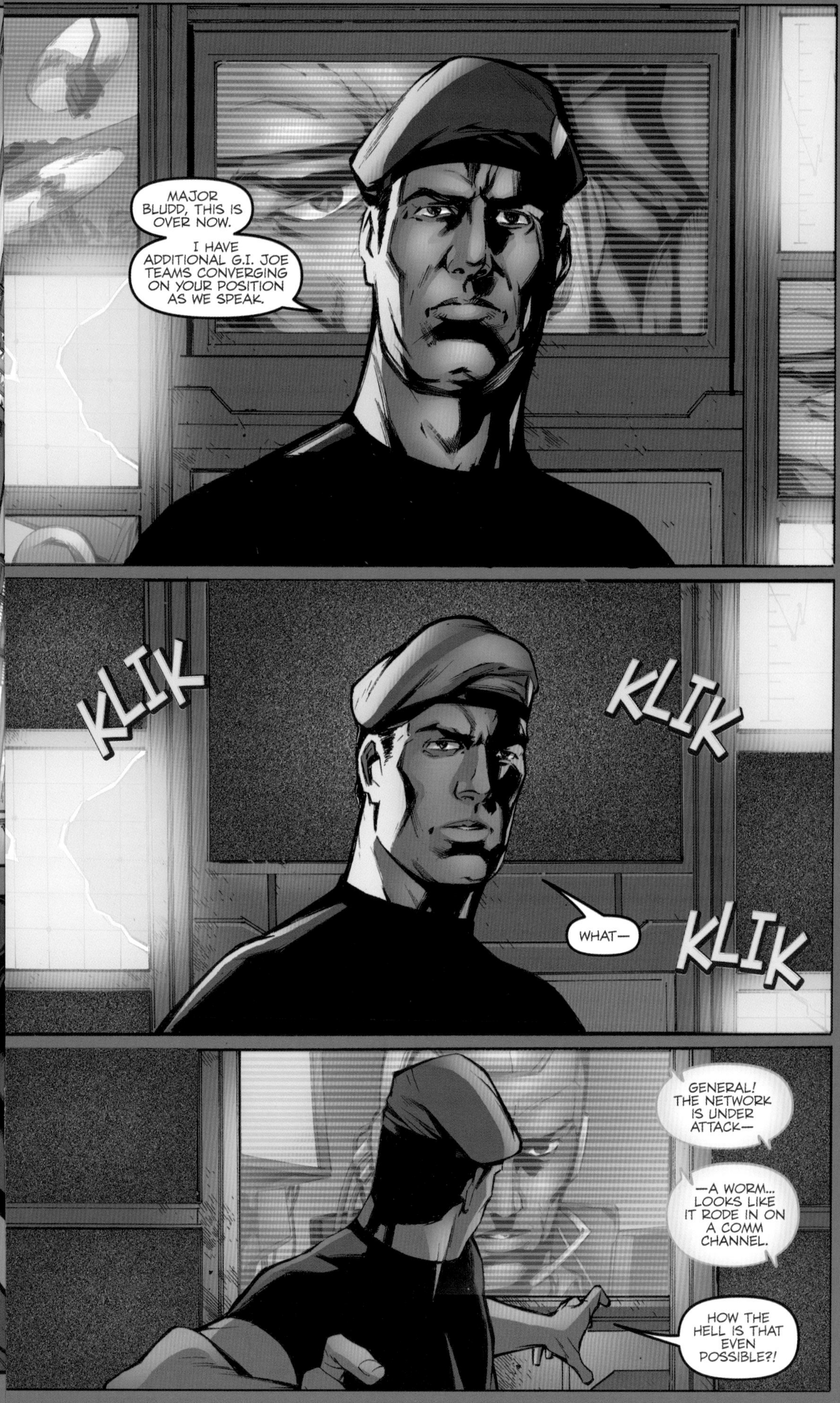
MAJOR BLUDD, THIS IS OVER NOW.
I HAVE ADDITIONAL G.I. JOE TEAMS CONVERGING ON YOUR POSITION AS WE SPEAK.
KLIK
KLIK
WHAT—
KLIK
GENERAL! THE NETWORK IS UNDER ATTACK—
—A WORM... LOOKS LIKE IT RODE IN ON A COMM CHANNEL.
HOW THE HELL IS THAT EVEN POSSIBLE?!

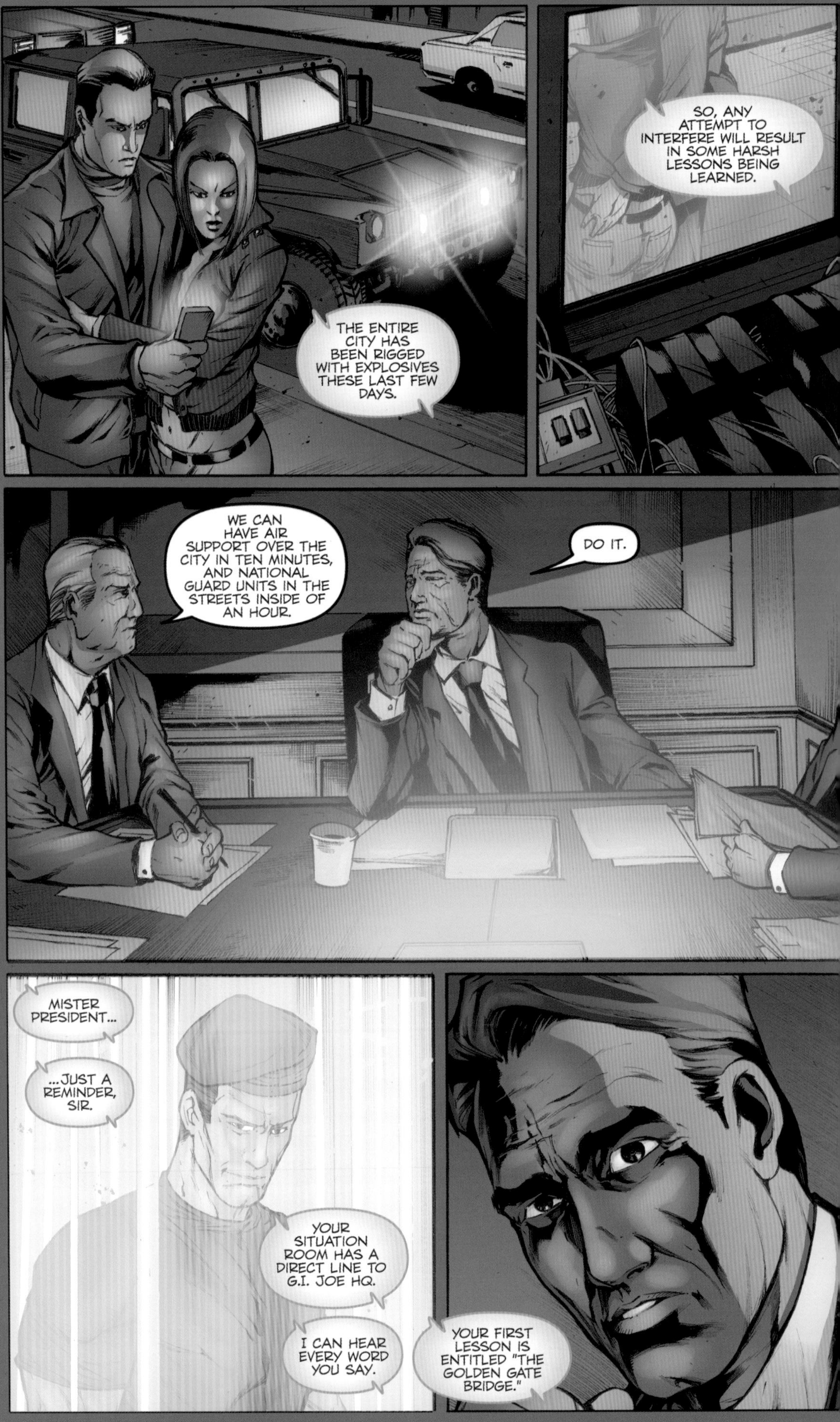
SO, ANY ATTEMPT TO INTERFERE WILL RESULT IN SOME HARSH LESSONS BEING LEARNED.
THE ENTIRE CITY HAS BEEN RIGGED WITH EXPLOSIVES THESE LAST FEW DAYS.
WE CAN HAVE AIR SUPPORT OVER THE CITY IN TEN MINUTES, AND NATIONAL GUARD UNITS IN THE STREETS INSIDE OF AN HOUR.
DO IT.
MISTER PRESIDENT...
...JUST A REMINDER, SIR.
YOUR SITUATION ROOM HAS A DIRECT LINE TO G.I. JOE HQ.
I CAN HEAR EVERY WORD YOU SAY.
YOUR FIRST LESSON IS ENTITLED "THE GOLDEN GATE BRIDGE."

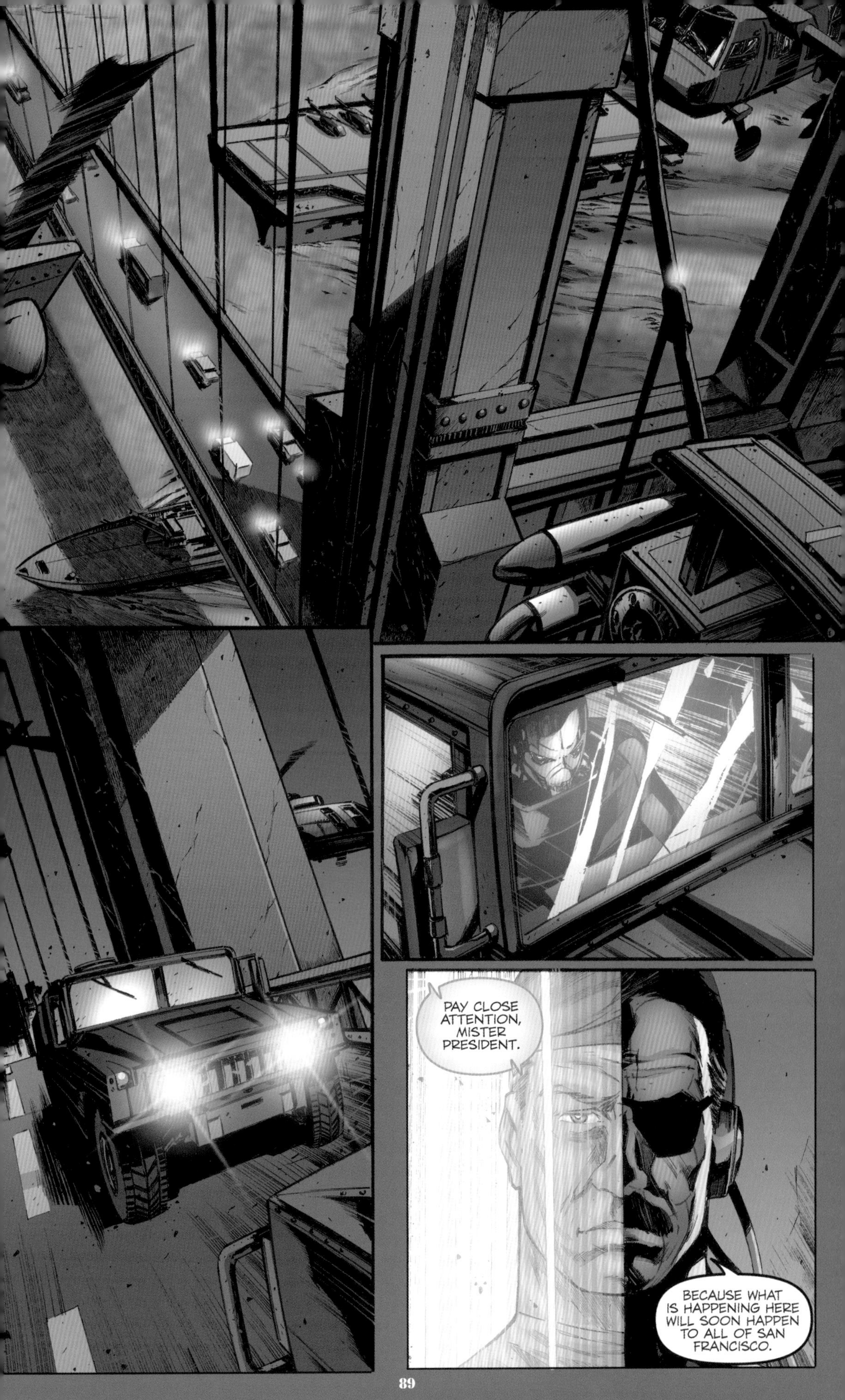
PAY CLOSE ATTENTION, MISTER PRESIDENT.
BECAUSE WHAT IS HAPPENING HERE WILL SOON HAPPEN TO ALL OF SAN FRANCISCO.

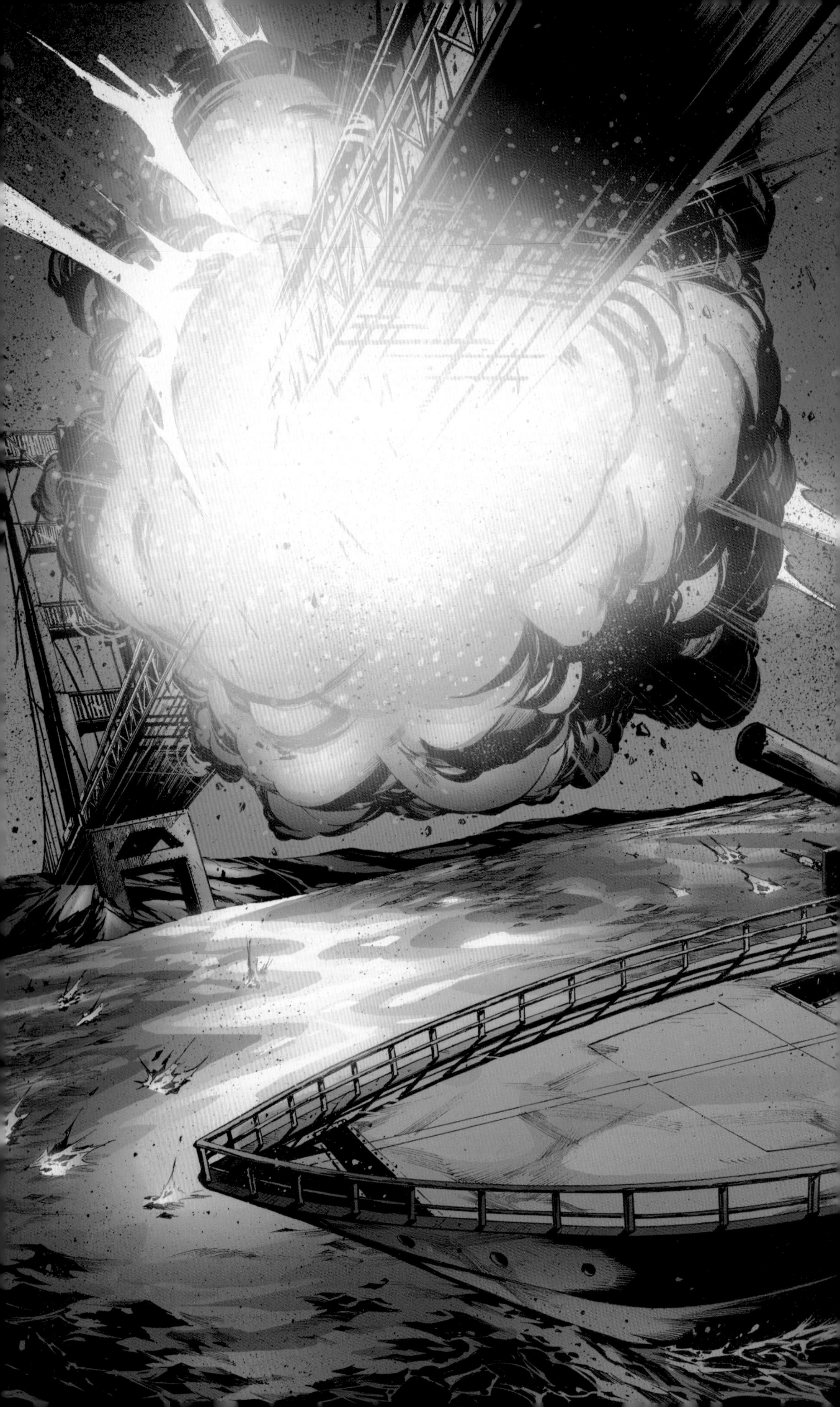

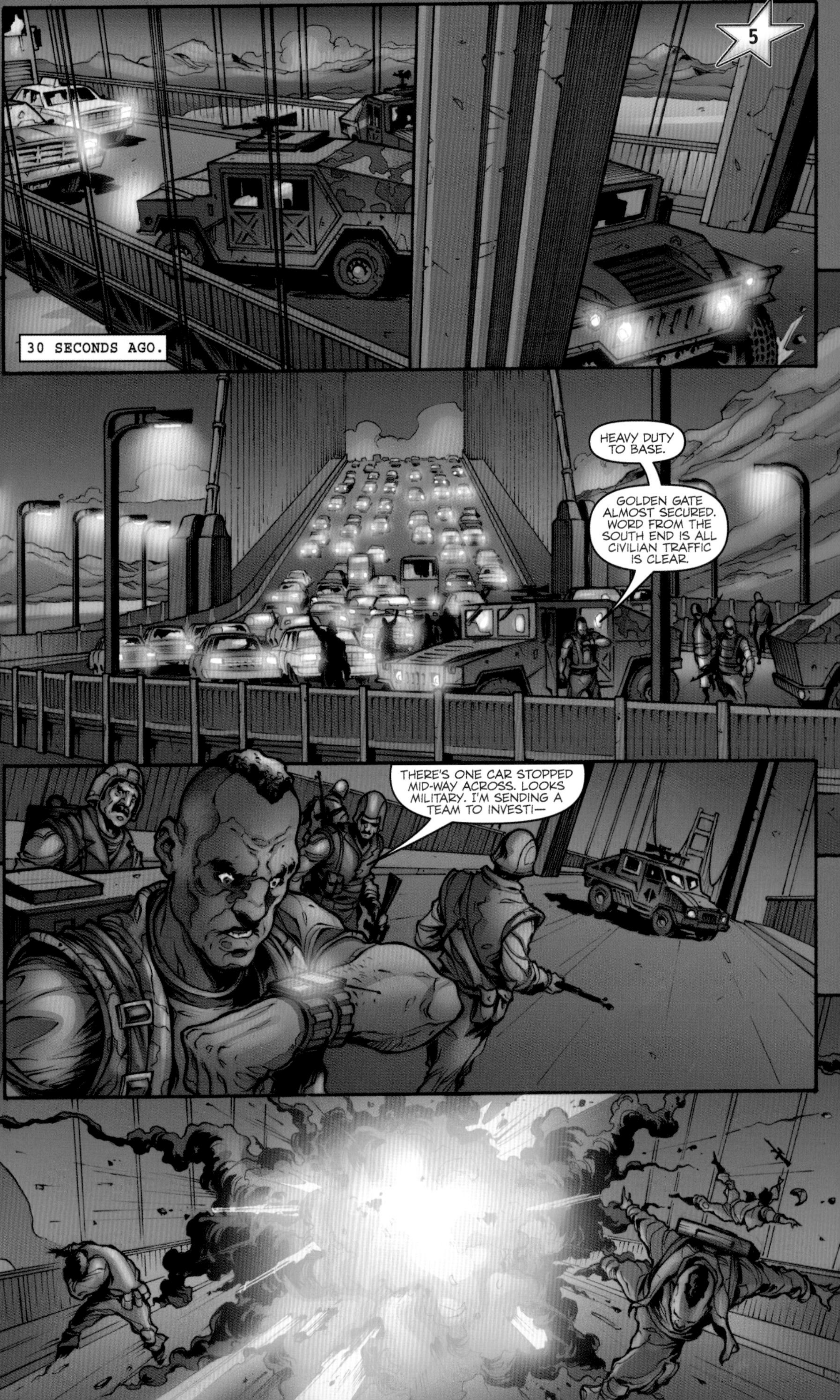
5
30 SECONDS AGO.
HEAVY DUTY TO BASE.
GOLDEN GATE ALMOST SECURED. WORD FROM THE SOUTH END IS ALL CIVILIAN TRAFFIC IS CLEAR.
THERE'S ONE CAR STOPPED MID-WAY ACROSS. LOOKS MILITARY. I'M SENDING A TEAM TO INVESTI—

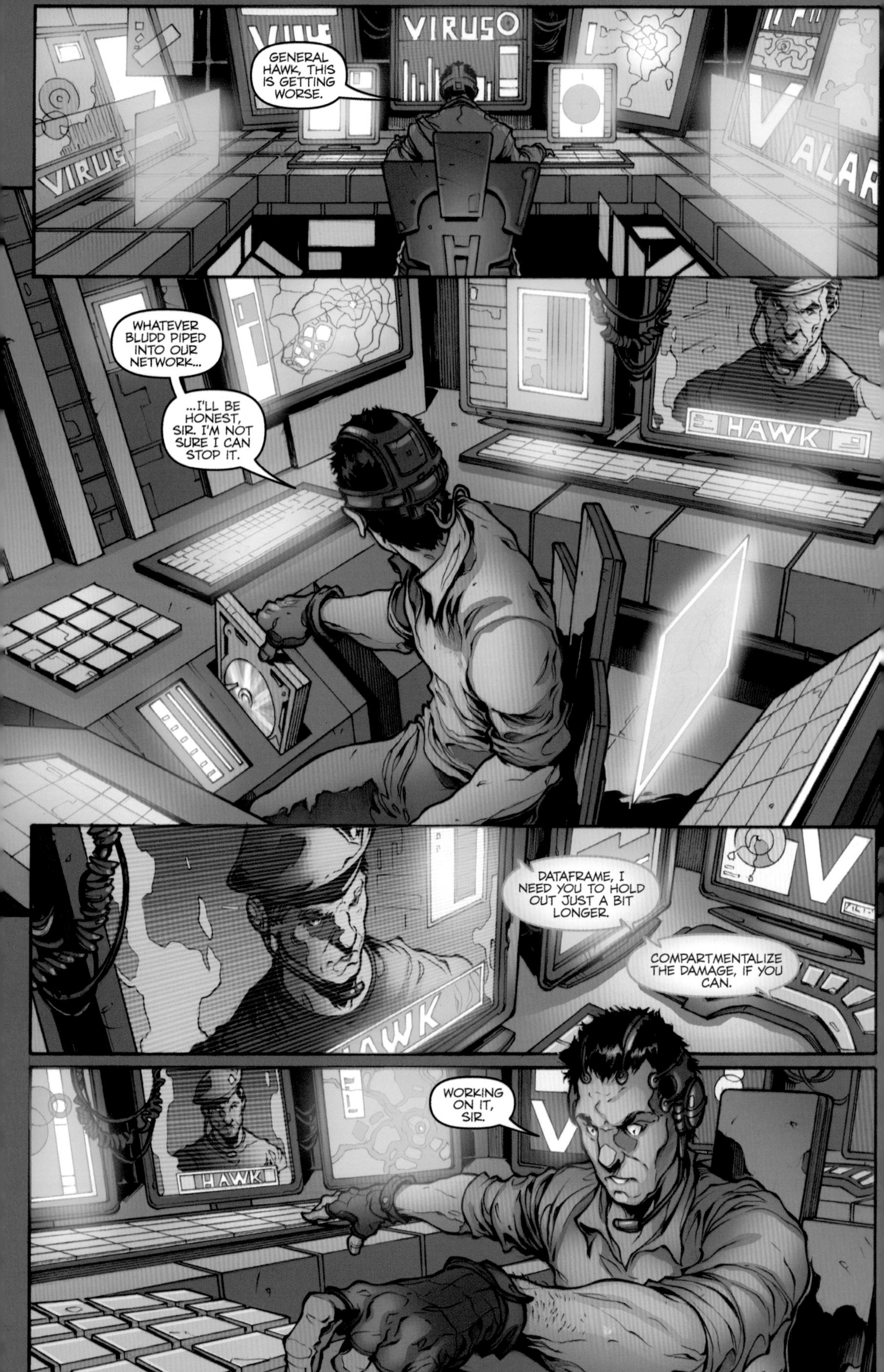
VIRUSO
GENERAL HAWK, THIS IS GETTING WORSE.
WHATEVER BLUDD PIPED INTO OUR NETWORK...
...I'LL BE HONEST, SIR. I'M NOT SURE I CAN STOP IT.
HAWK
DATAFRAME, I NEED YOU TO HOLD OUT JUST A BIT LONGER.
COMPARTMENTALIZE THE DAMAGE, IF YOU CAN.
WORKING ON IT, SIR.
HAWK

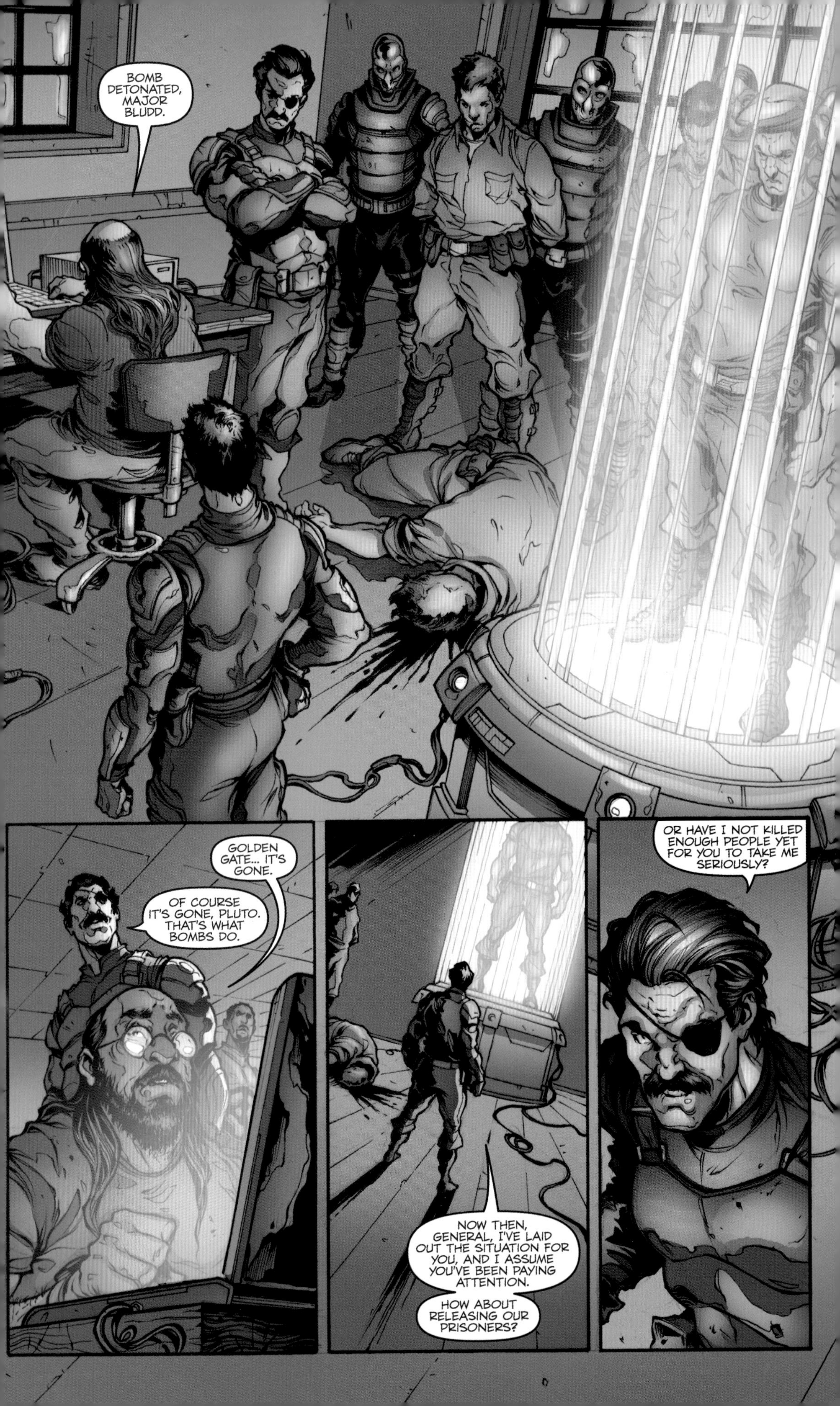
BOMB DETONATED, MAJOR BLUDD.
GOLDEN GATE... IT'S GONE.
OF COURSE IT'S GONE, PLUTO. THAT'S WHAT BOMBS DO.
NOW THEN, GENERAL, I'VE LAID OUT THE SITUATION FOR YOU, AND I ASSUME YOU'VE BEEN PAYING ATTENTION.
HOW ABOUT RELEASING OUR PRISONERS?
OR HAVE I NOT KILLED ENOUGH PEOPLE YET FOR YOU TO TAKE ME SERIOUSLY?

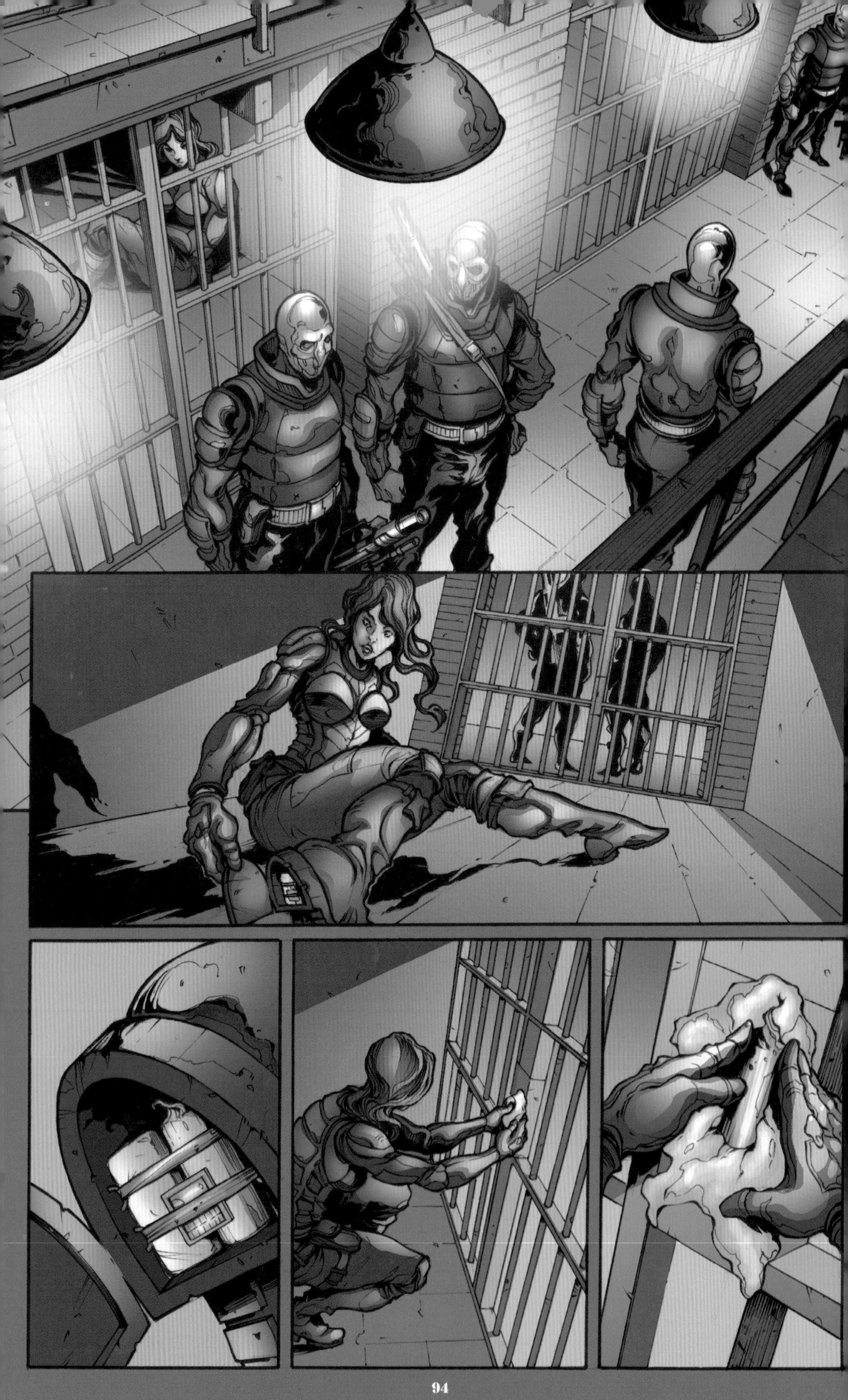

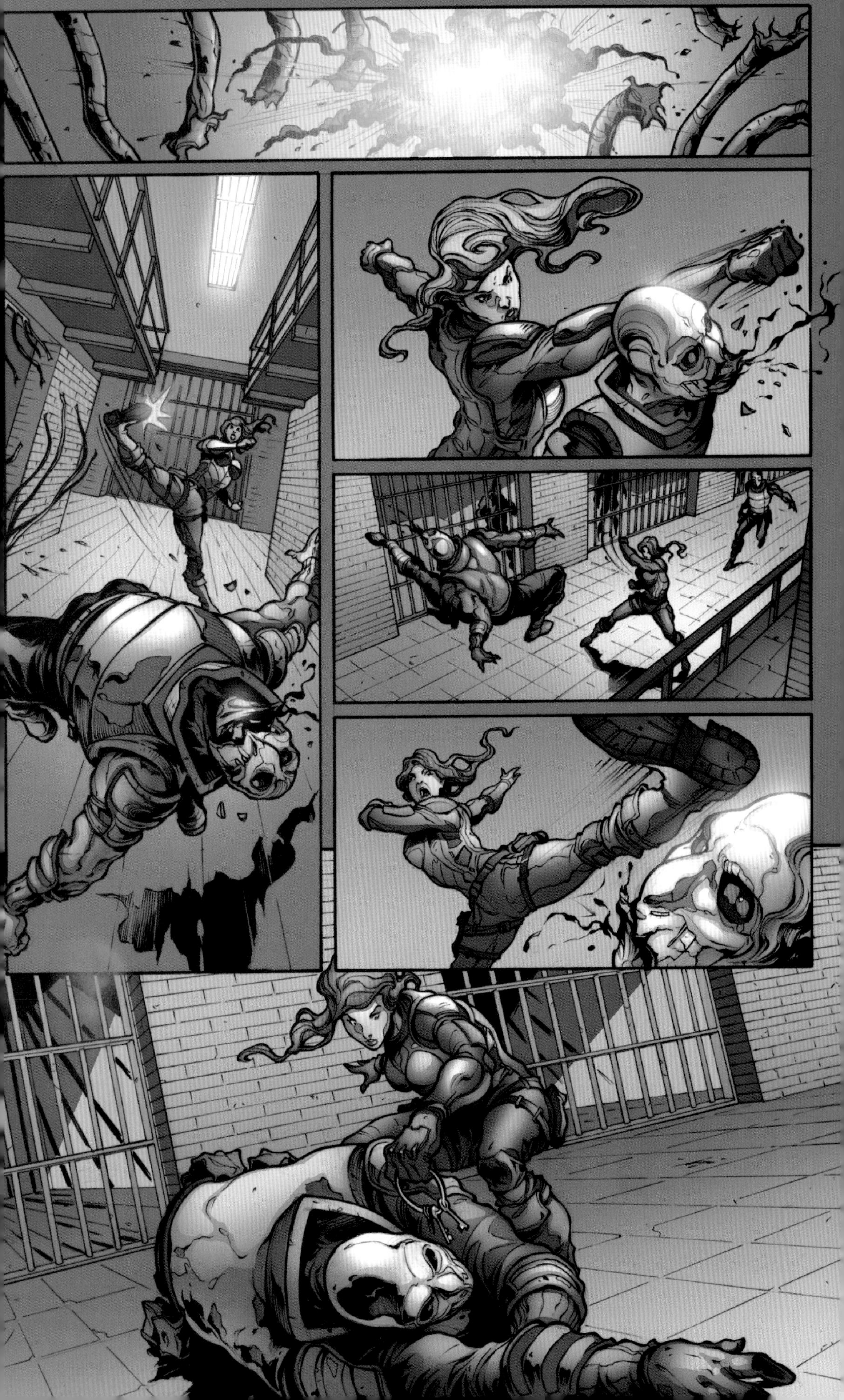

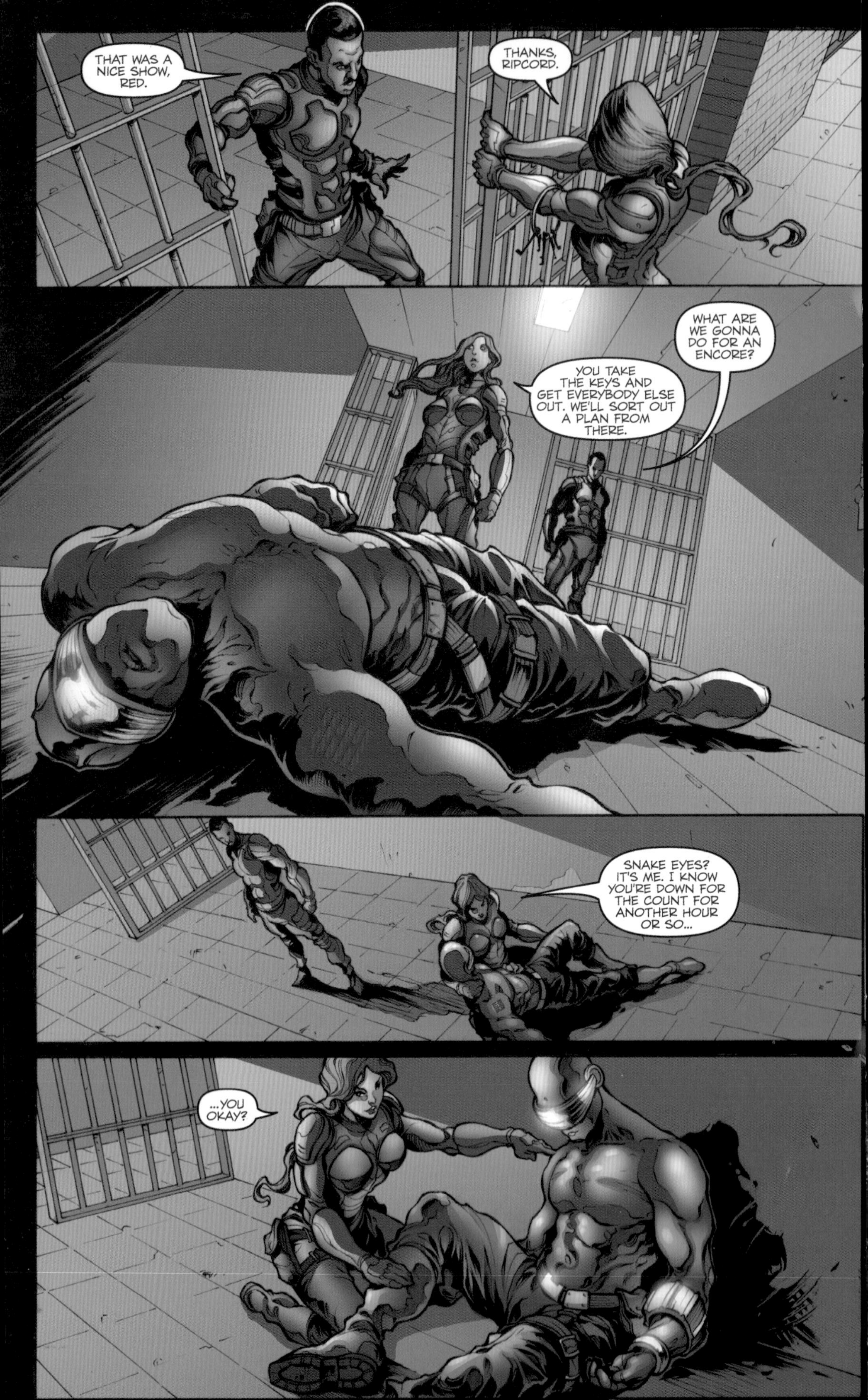
THAT WAS A NICE SHOW, RED.
THANKS, RIPCORD.
WHAT ARE WE GONNA DO FOR AN ENCORE?
YOU TAKE THE KEYS AND GET EVERYBODY ELSE OUT. WE'LL SORT OUT A PLAN FROM THERE.
SNAKE EYES? IT'S ME. I KNOW YOU'RE DOWN FOR THE COUNT FOR ANOTHER HOUR OR SO...
...YOU OKAY?

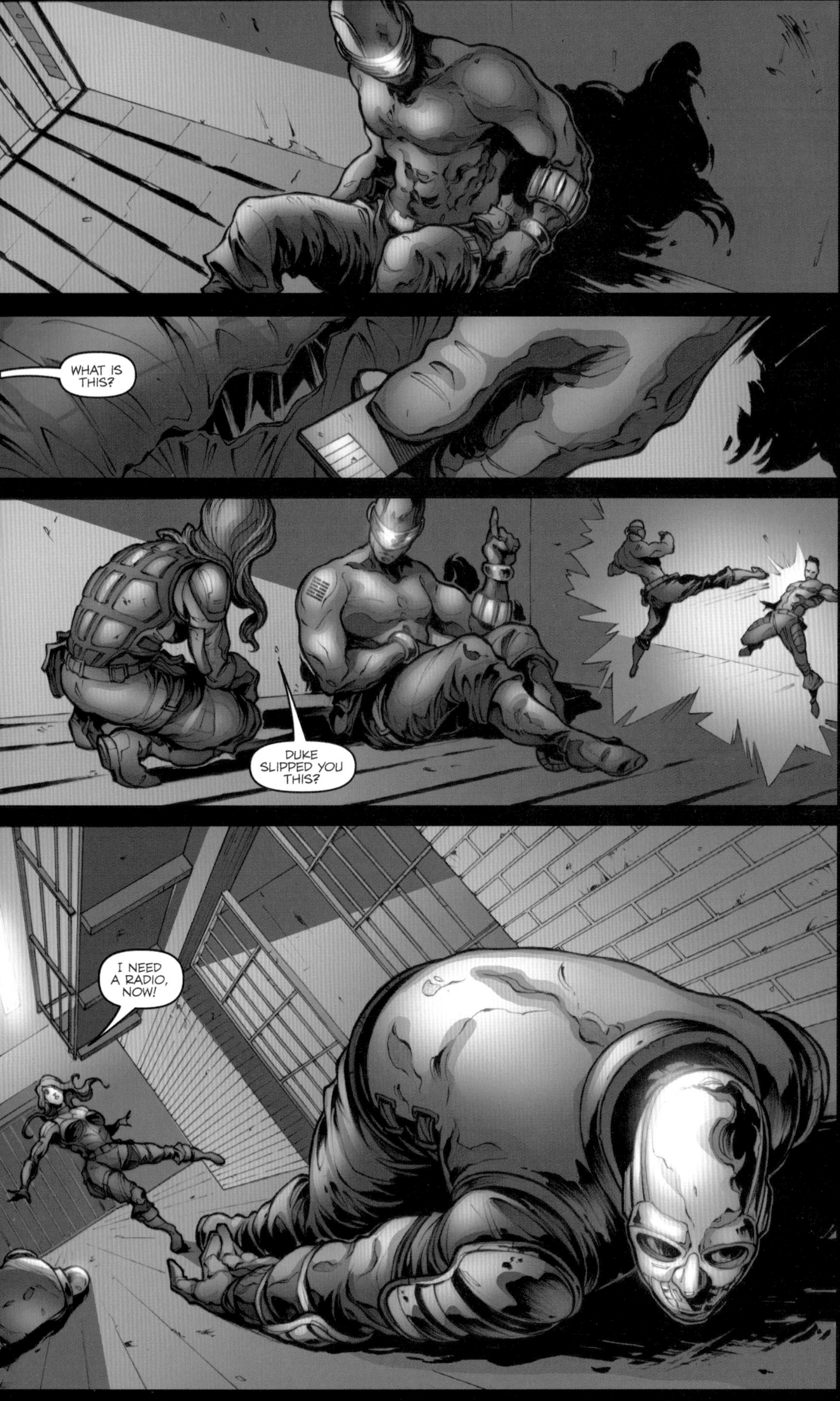
WHAT IS THIS?
DUKE SLIPPED YOU THIS?
I NEED A RADIO, NOW!

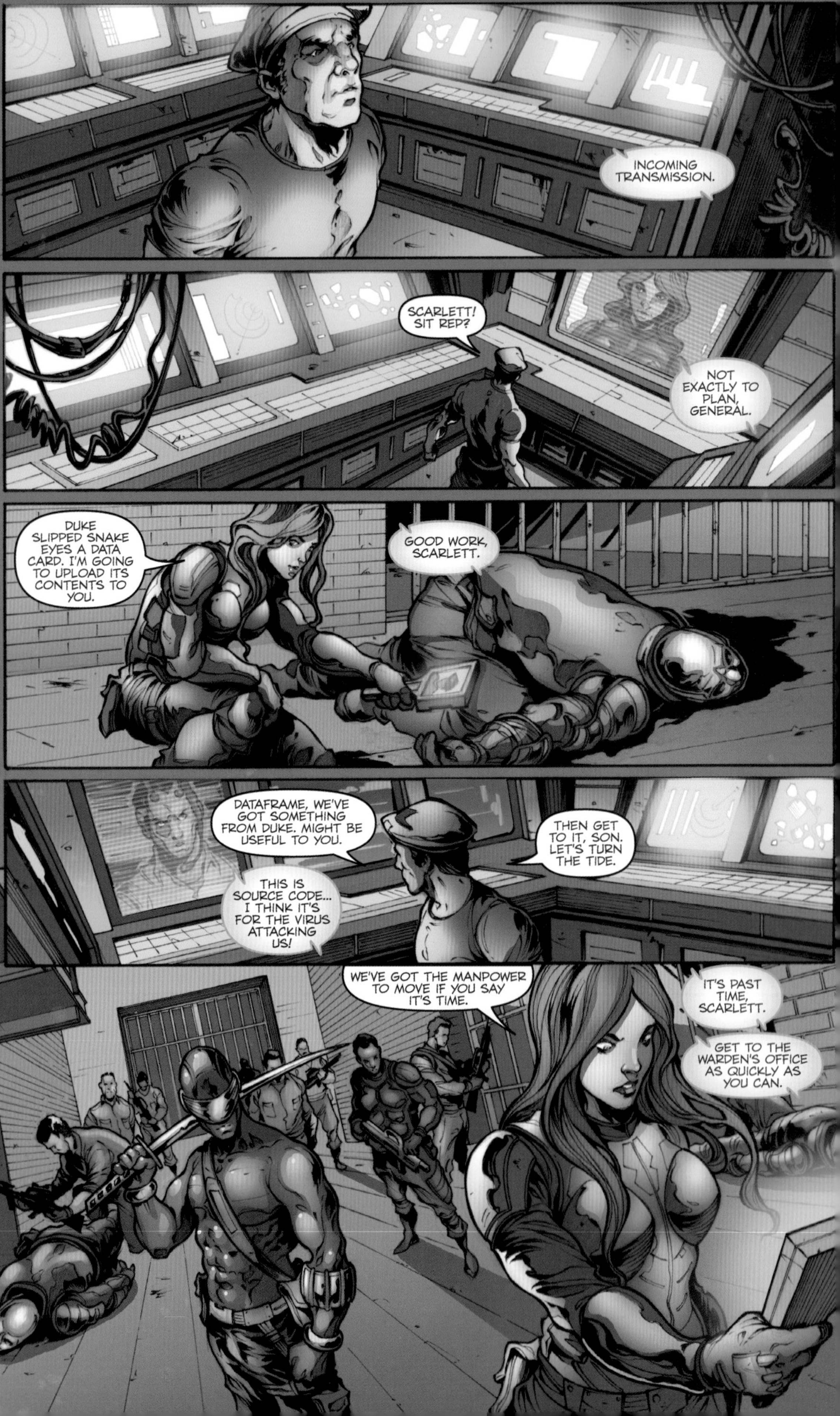
INCOMING TRANSMISSION.
SCARLETT! SIT REP?
NOT EXACTLY TO PLAN, GENERAL.
DUKE SLIPPED SNAKE EYES A DATA CARD. I'M GOING TO UPLOAD ITS CONTENTS TO YOU.
GOOD WORK, SCARLETT.
DATAFRAME, WE'VE GOT SOMETHING FROM DUKE. MIGHT BE USEFUL TO YOU.
THIS IS SOURCE CODE... I THINK IT'S FOR THE VIRUS ATTACKING US!
THEN GET TO IT, SON. LET'S TURN THE TIDE.
WE'VE GOT THE MANPOWER TO MOVE IF YOU SAY IT'S TIME.
IT'S PAST TIME, SCARLETT.
GET TO THE WARDEN'S OFFICE AS QUICKLY AS YOU CAN.

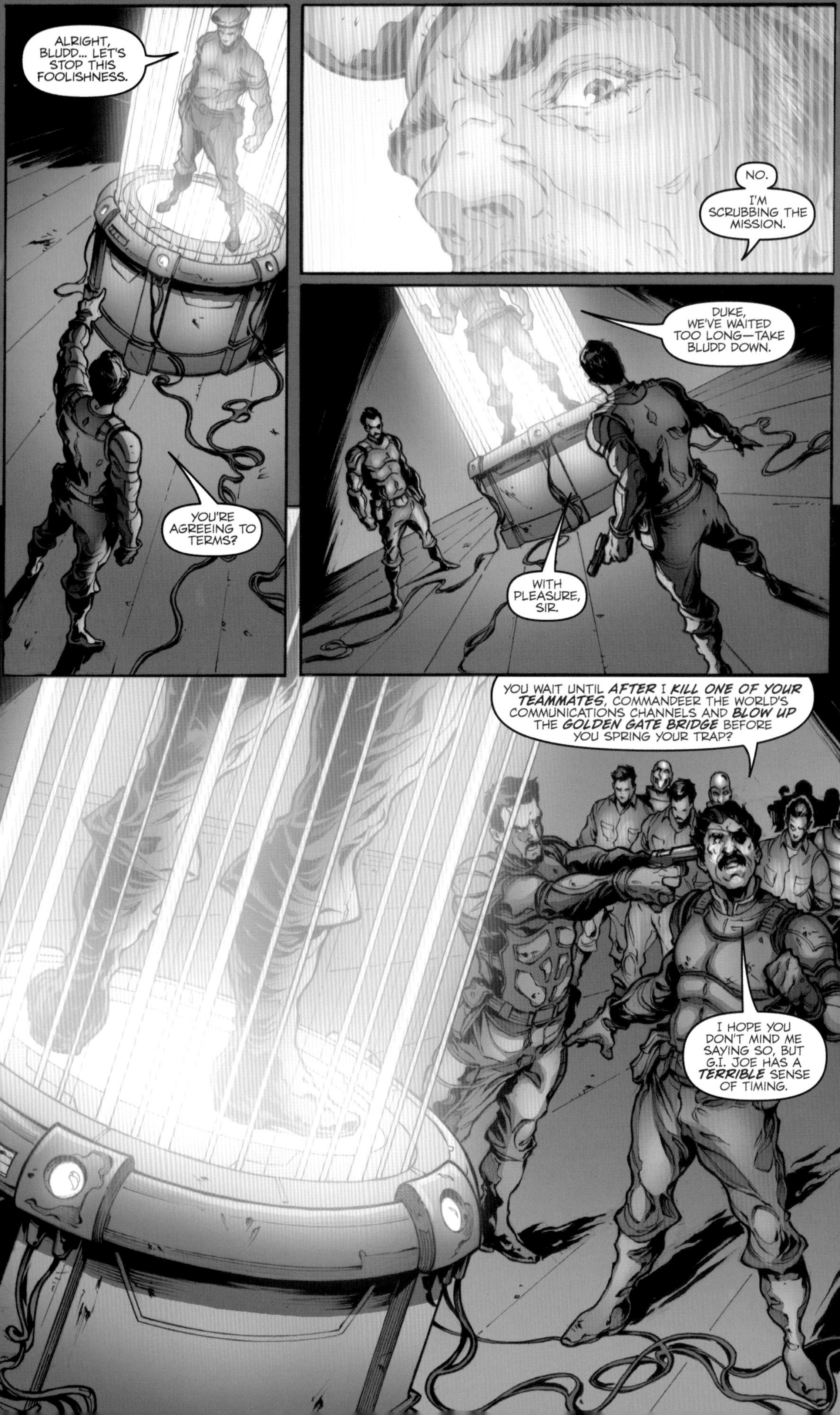
ALRIGHT, BLUDD... LET'S STOP THIS FOOLISHNESS.
YOU'RE AGREEING TO TERMS?
NO.
I'M SCRUBBING THE MISSION.
DUKE, WE'VE WAITED TOO LONG—TAKE BLUDD DOWN.
WITH PLEASURE, SIR.
YOU WAIT UNTIL AFTER I KILL ONE OF YOUR TEAMMATES, COMMANDEER THE WORLD'S COMMUNICATIONS CHANNELS AND BLOW UP THE GOLDEN GATE BRIDGE BEFORE YOU SPRING YOUR TRAP?
I HOPE YOU DON'T MIND ME SAYING SO, BUT G.I. JOE HAS A TERRIBLE SENSE OF TIMING.

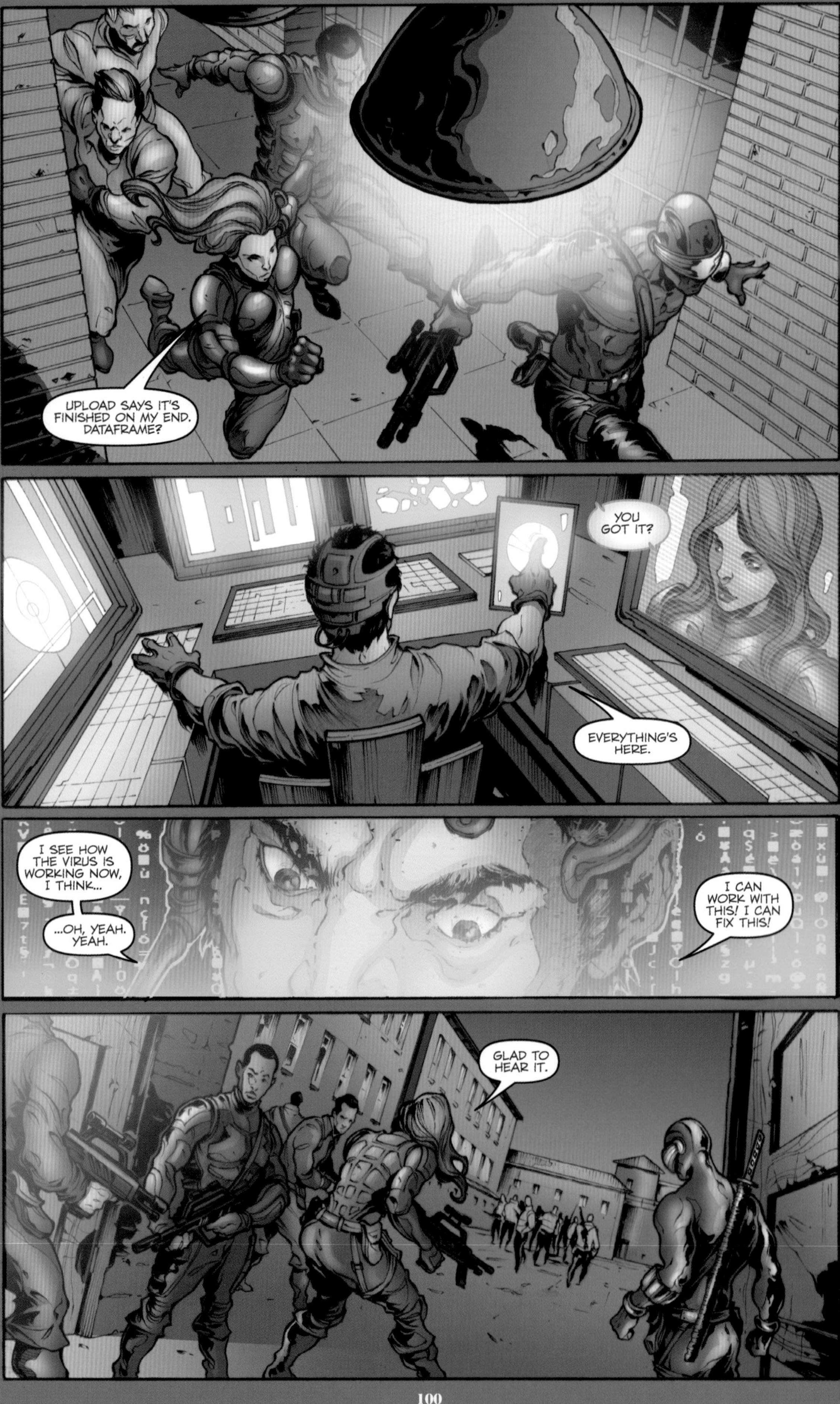
UPLOAD SAYS IT'S FINISHED ON MY END. DATAFRAME?
YOU GOT IT?
EVERYTHING'S HERE.
I SEE HOW THE VIRUS IS WORKING NOW, I THINK...
...OH, YEAH. YEAH.
I CAN WORK WITH THIS! I CAN FIX THIS!
GLAD TO HEAR IT.

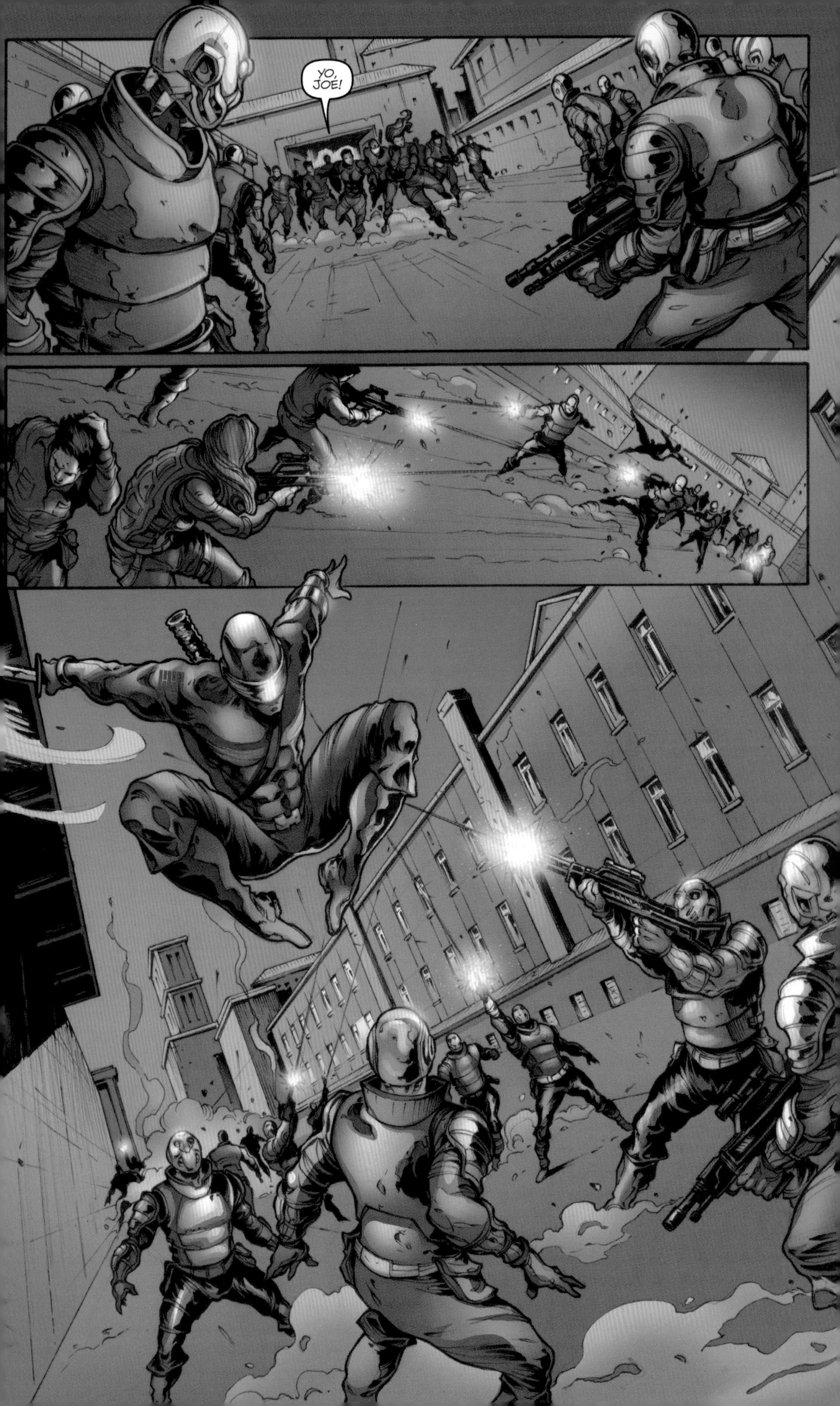
YO, JOE!

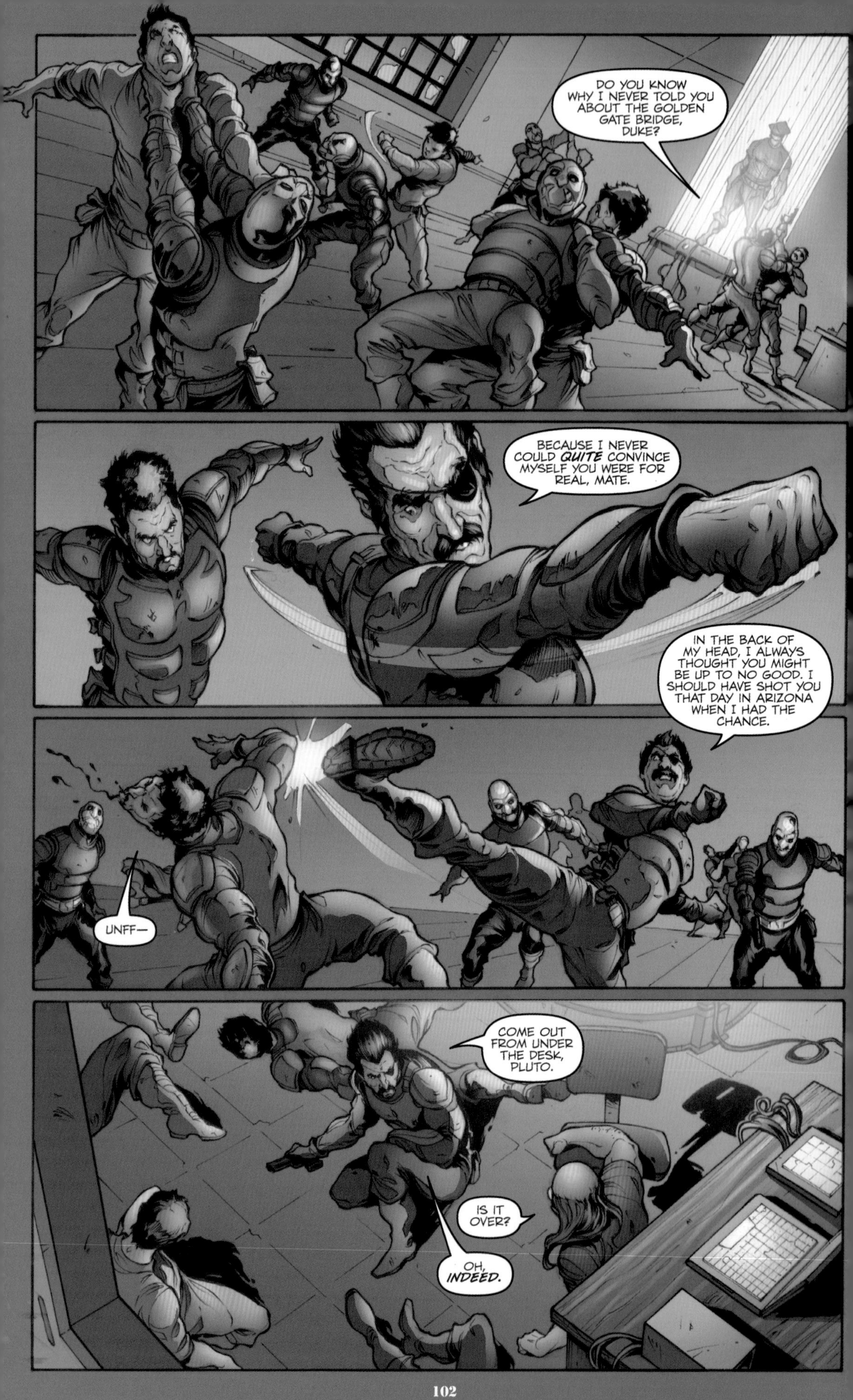
DO YOU KNOW WHY I NEVER TOLD YOU ABOUT THE GOLDEN GATE BRIDGE, DUKE?
BECAUSE I NEVER COULD *QUITE* CONVINCE MYSELF YOU WERE FOR REAL, MATE.
IN THE BACK OF MY HEAD, I ALWAYS THOUGHT YOU MIGHT BE UP TO NO GOOD. I SHOULD HAVE SHOT YOU THAT DAY IN ARIZONA WHEN I HAD THE CHANCE.
UNFF—
COME OUT FROM UNDER THE DESK, PLUTO.
IS IT OVER?
OH, ***INDEED.***

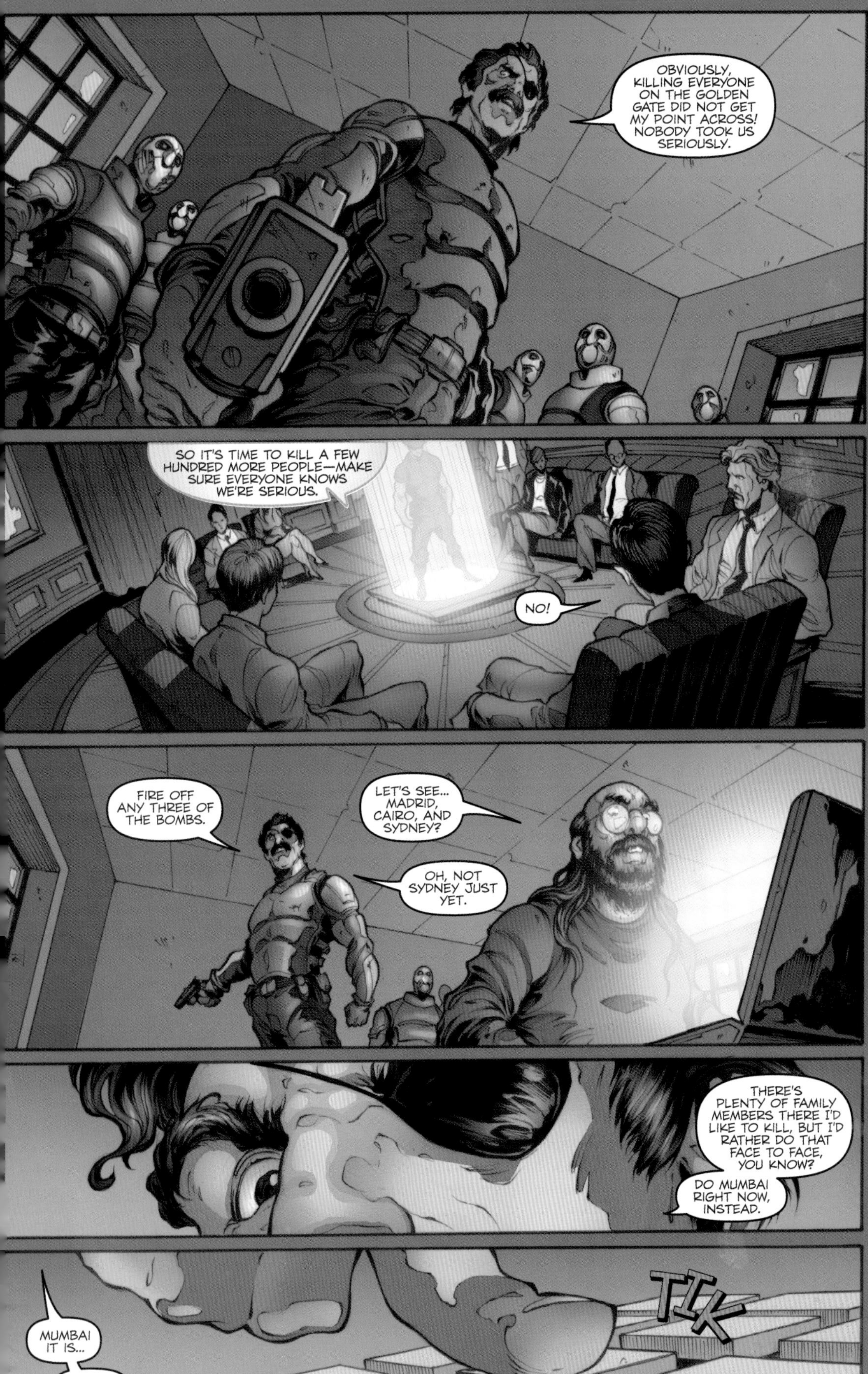

OBVIOUSLY, KILLING EVERYONE ON THE GOLDEN GATE DID NOT GET MY POINT ACROSS! NOBODY TOOK US SERIOUSLY.
SO IT'S TIME TO KILL A FEW HUNDRED MORE PEOPLE—MAKE SURE EVERYONE KNOWS WE'RE SERIOUS.
NO!
FIRE OFF ANY THREE OF THE BOMBS.
LET'S SEE... MADRID, CAIRO, AND SYDNEY?
OH, NOT SYDNEY JUST YET.
THERE'S PLENTY OF FAMILY MEMBERS THERE I'D LIKE TO KILL, BUT I'D RATHER DO THAT FACE TO FACE, YOU KNOW?
DO MUMBAI RIGHT NOW, INSTEAD.
TIK
MUMBAI IT IS...
...BOOM!

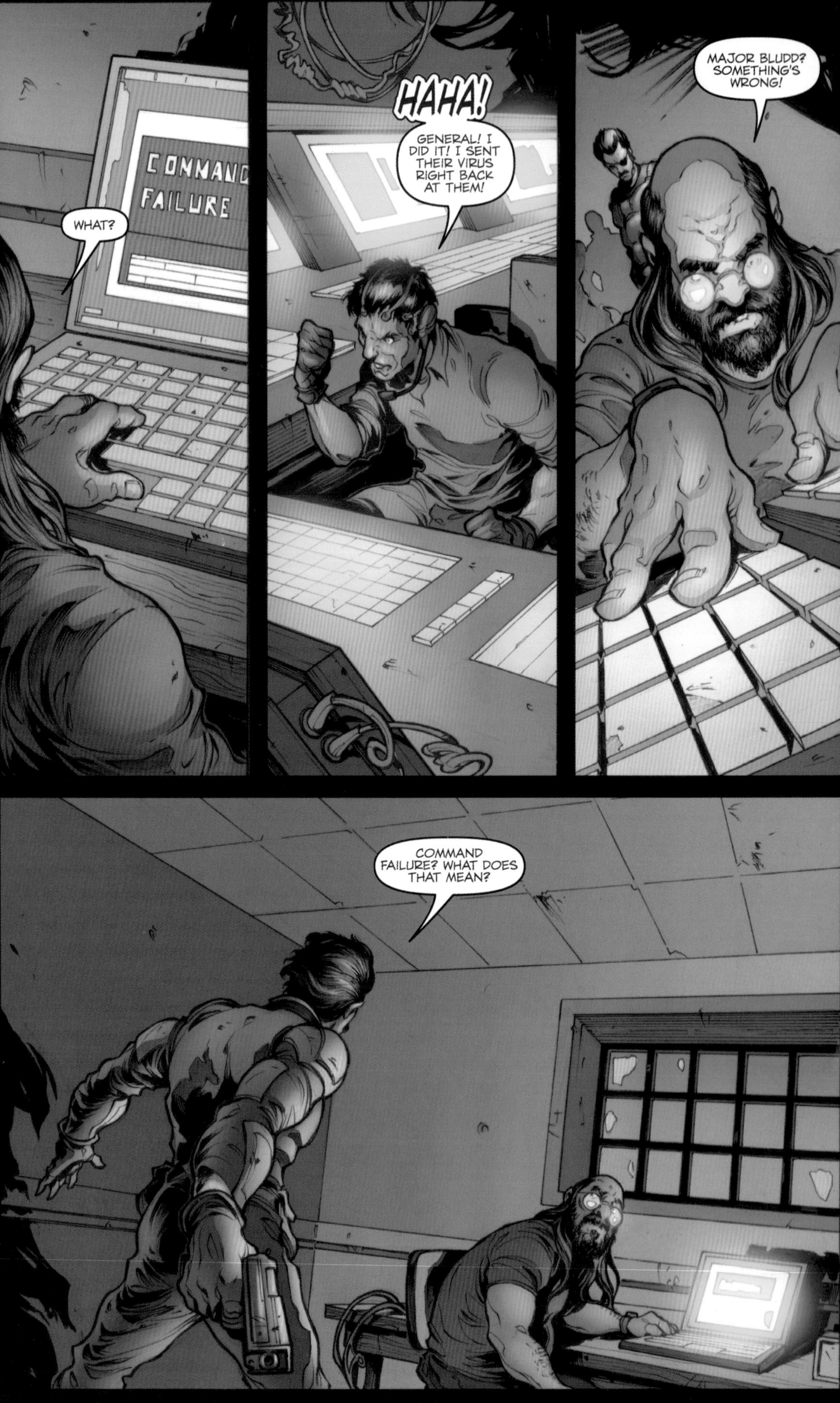
COMMAND FAILURE
WHAT?
HAHA!
GENERAL! I DID IT! I SENT THEIR VIRUS RIGHT BACK AT THEM!
MAJOR BLUDD? SOMETHING'S WRONG!
COMMAND FAILURE? WHAT DOES THAT MEAN?

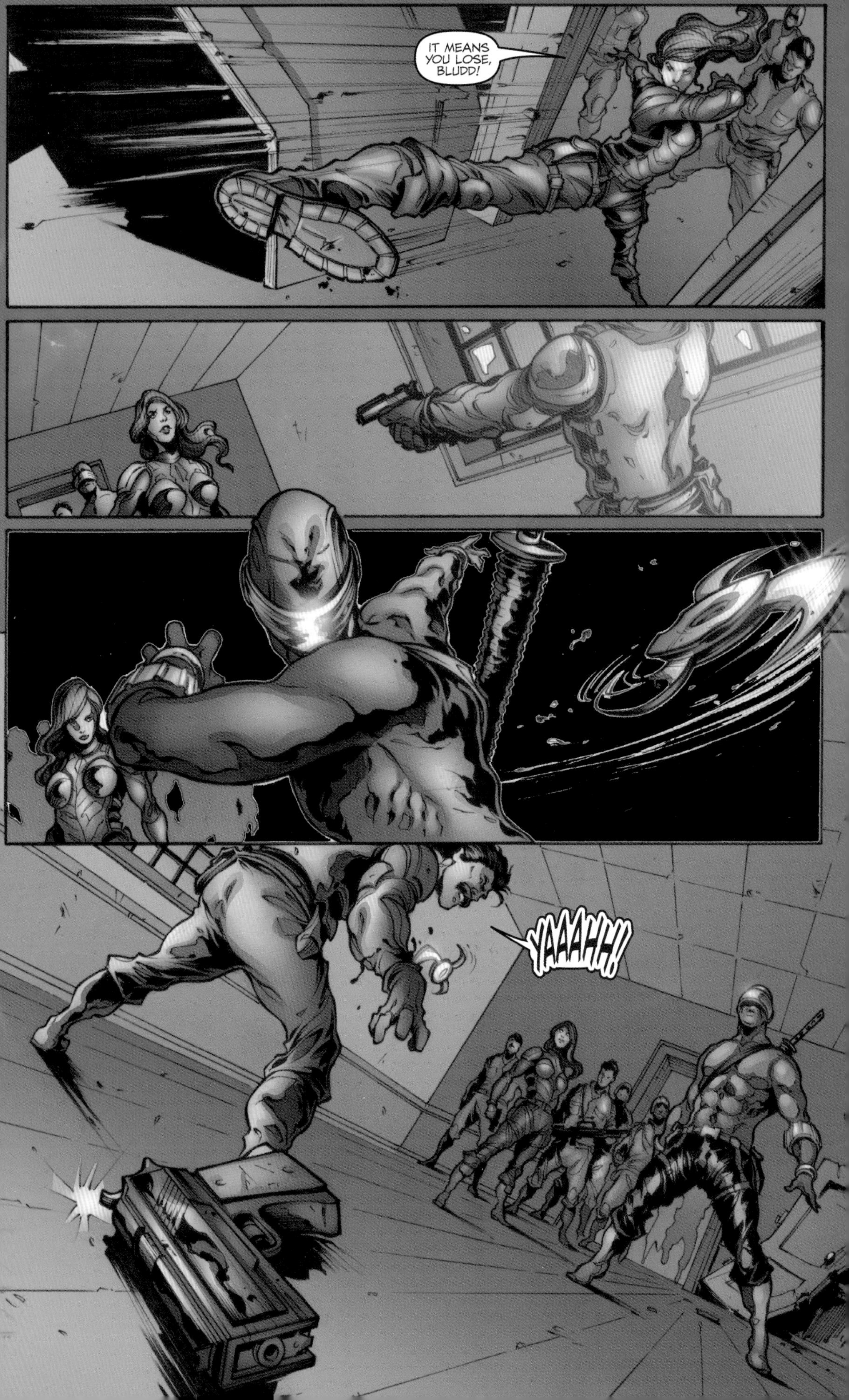
IT MEANS YOU LOSE, BLUDD!
YAAAHH!

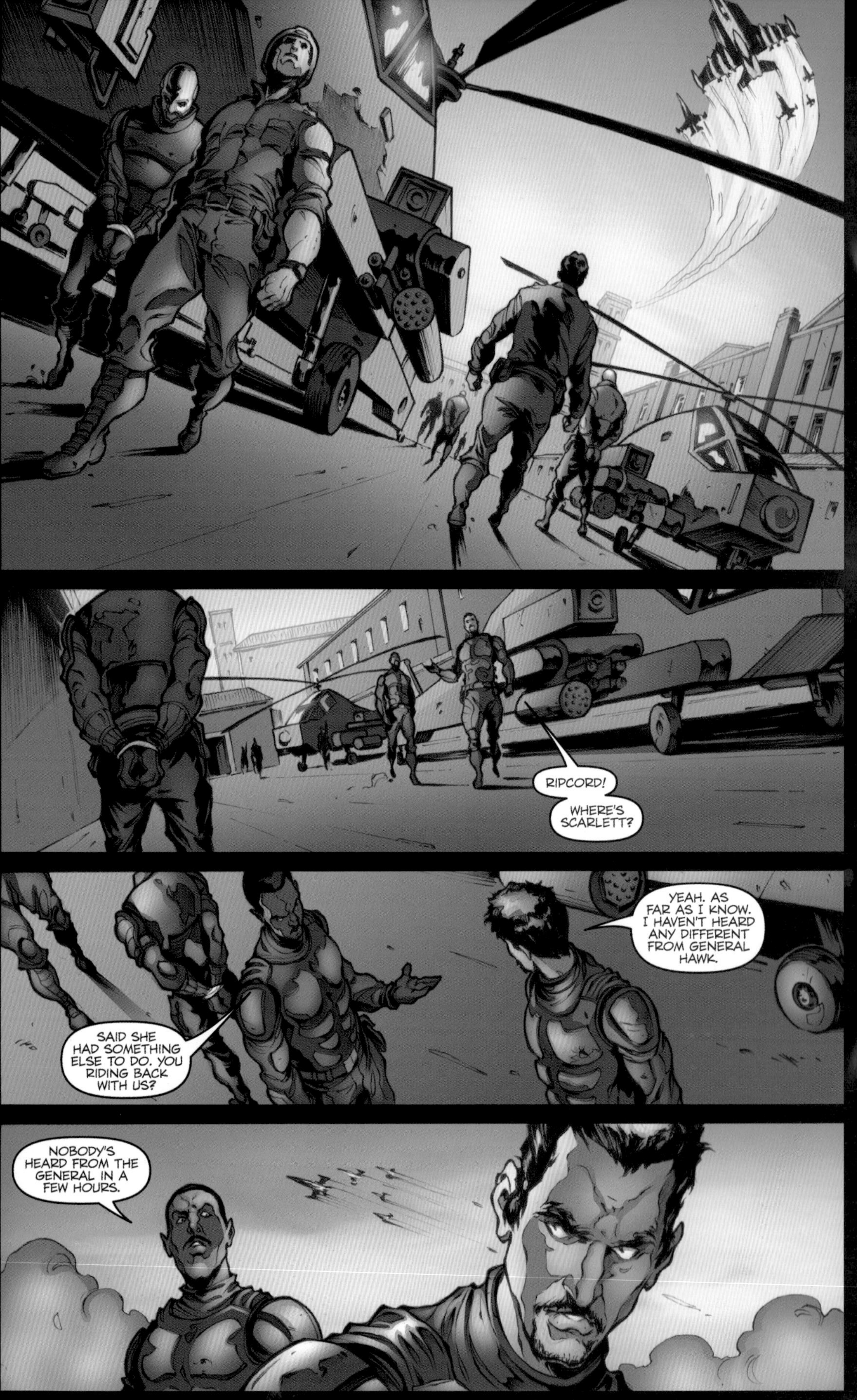
RIPCORD!
WHERE'S SCARLETT?
SAID SHE HAD SOMETHING ELSE TO DO. YOU RIDING BACK WITH US?
YEAH. AS FAR AS I KNOW. I HAVEN'T HEARD ANY DIFFERENT FROM GENERAL HAWK.
NOBODY'S HEARD FROM THE GENERAL IN A FEW HOURS.

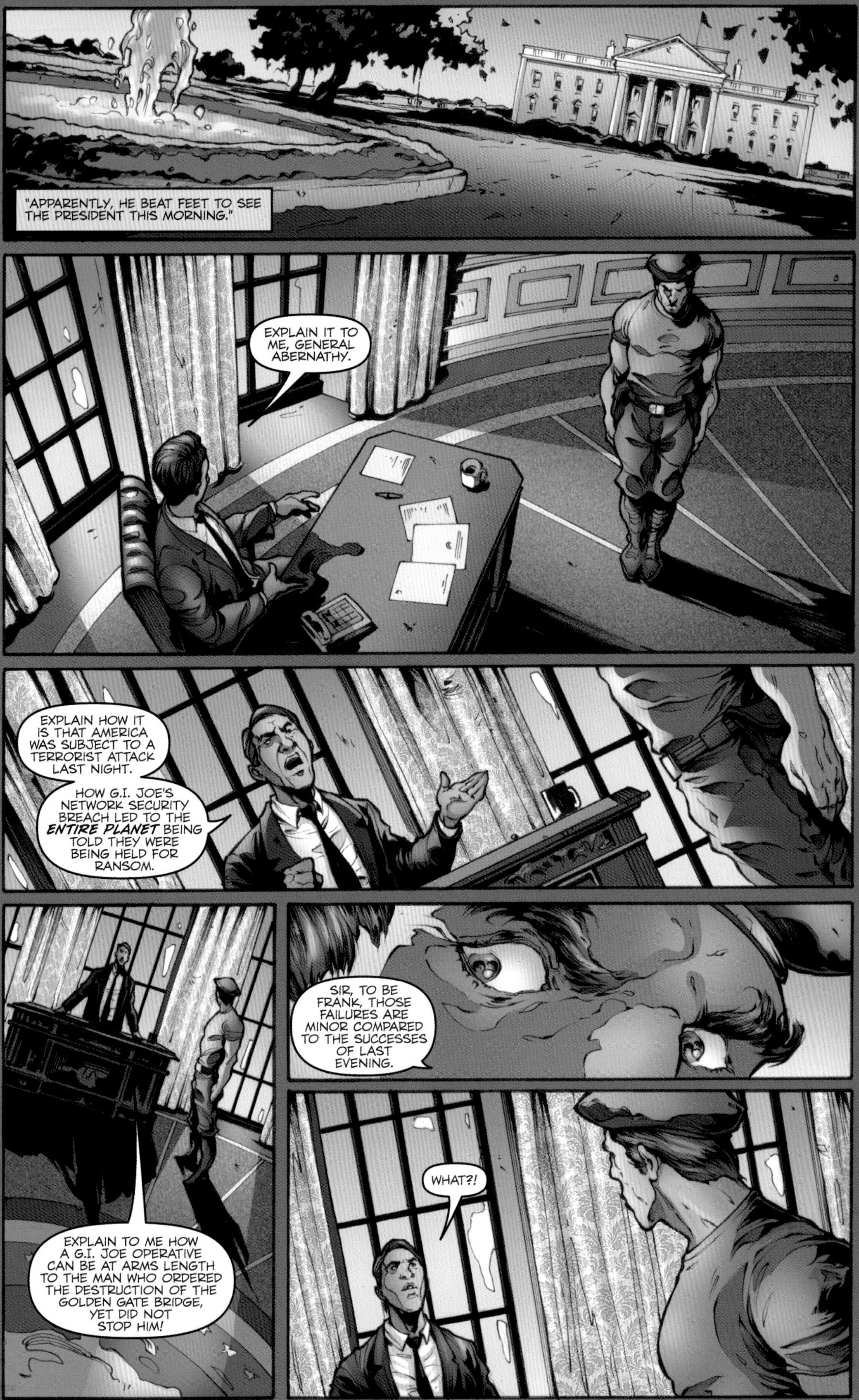
"APPARENTLY, HE BEAT FEET TO SEE THE PRESIDENT THIS MORNING."
EXPLAIN IT TO ME, GENERAL ABERNATHY.
EXPLAIN HOW IT IS THAT AMERICA WAS SUBJECT TO A TERRORIST ATTACK LAST NIGHT.
HOW G.I. JOE'S NETWORK SECURITY BREACH LED TO THE ENTIRE PLANET BEING TOLD THEY WERE BEING HELD FOR RANSOM.
EXPLAIN TO ME HOW A G.I. JOE OPERATIVE CAN BE AT ARMS LENGTH TO THE MAN WHO ORDERED THE DESTRUCTION OF THE GOLDEN GATE BRIDGE, YET DID NOT STOP HIM!
SIR, TO BE FRANK, THOSE FAILURES ARE MINOR COMPARED TO THE SUCCESSES OF LAST EVENING.
WHAT?!

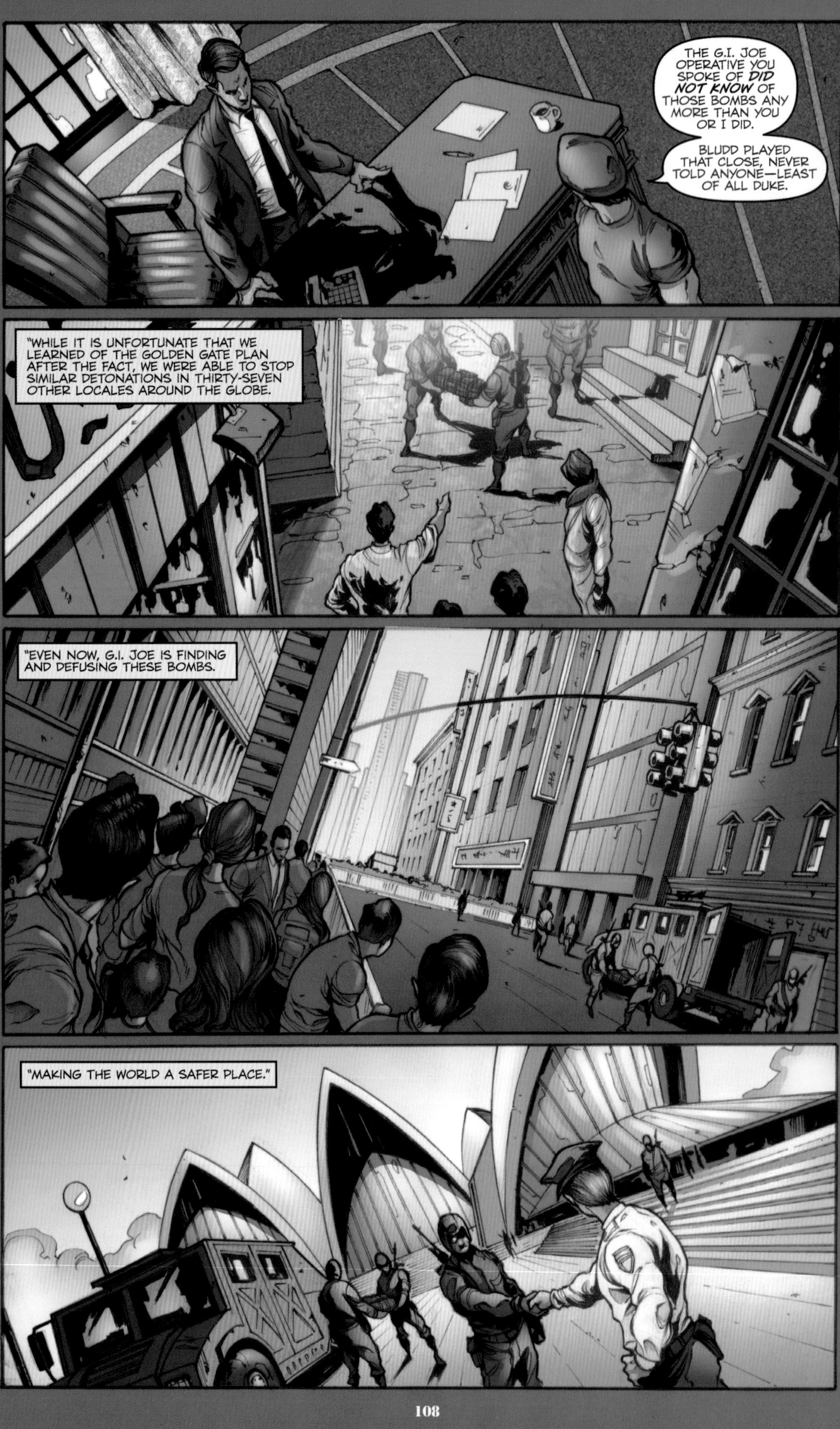
THE G.I. JOE OPERATIVE YOU SPOKE OF *DID NOT KNOW* OF THOSE BOMBS ANY MORE THAN YOU OR I DID.
BLUDD PLAYED THAT CLOSE, NEVER TOLD ANYONE—LEAST OF ALL DUKE.
"WHILE IT IS UNFORTUNATE THAT WE LEARNED OF THE GOLDEN GATE PLAN AFTER THE FACT, WE WERE ABLE TO STOP SIMILAR DETONATIONS IN THIRTY-SEVEN OTHER LOCALES AROUND THE GLOBE.
"EVEN NOW, G.I. JOE IS FINDING AND DEFUSING THESE BOMBS.
"MAKING THE WORLD A SAFER PLACE."

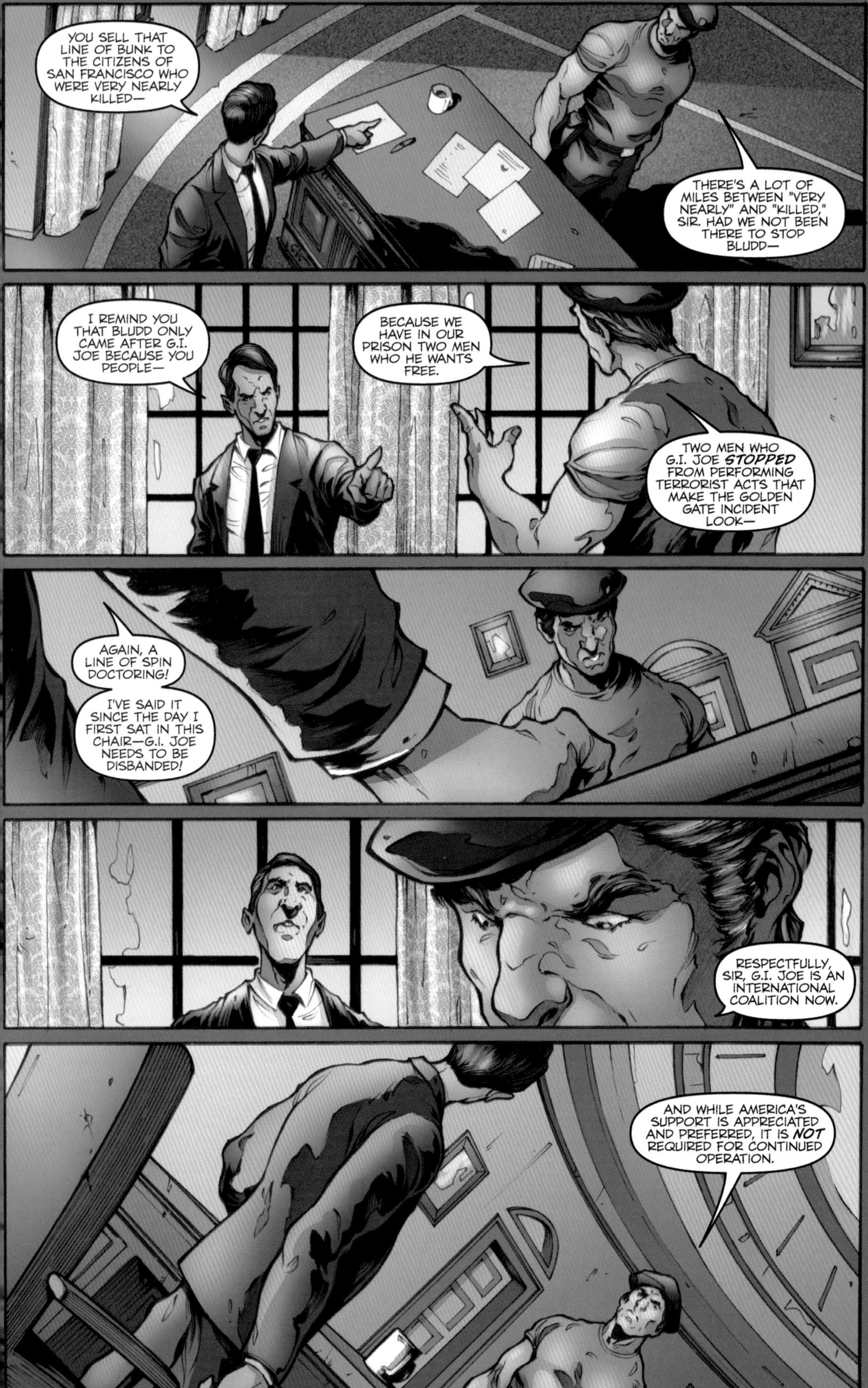
YOU SELL THAT LINE OF BUNK TO THE CITIZENS OF SAN FRANCISCO WHO WERE VERY NEARLY KILLED—
THERE'S A LOT OF MILES BETWEEN "VERY NEARLY" AND "KILLED," SIR. HAD WE NOT BEEN THERE TO STOP BLUDD—
I REMIND YOU THAT BLUDD ONLY CAME AFTER G.I. JOE BECAUSE YOU PEOPLE—
BECAUSE WE HAVE IN OUR PRISON TWO MEN WHO HE WANTS FREE.
TWO MEN WHO G.I. JOE *STOPPED* FROM PERFORMING TERRORIST ACTS THAT MAKE THE GOLDEN GATE INCIDENT LOOK—
AGAIN, A LINE OF SPIN DOCTORING!
I'VE SAID IT SINCE THE DAY I FIRST SAT IN THIS CHAIR—G.I. JOE NEEDS TO BE DISBANDED!
RESPECTFULLY, SIR, G.I. JOE IS AN INTERNATIONAL COALITION NOW.
AND WHILE AMERICA'S SUPPORT IS APPRECIATED AND PREFERRED, IT IS *NOT* REQUIRED FOR CONTINUED OPERATION.

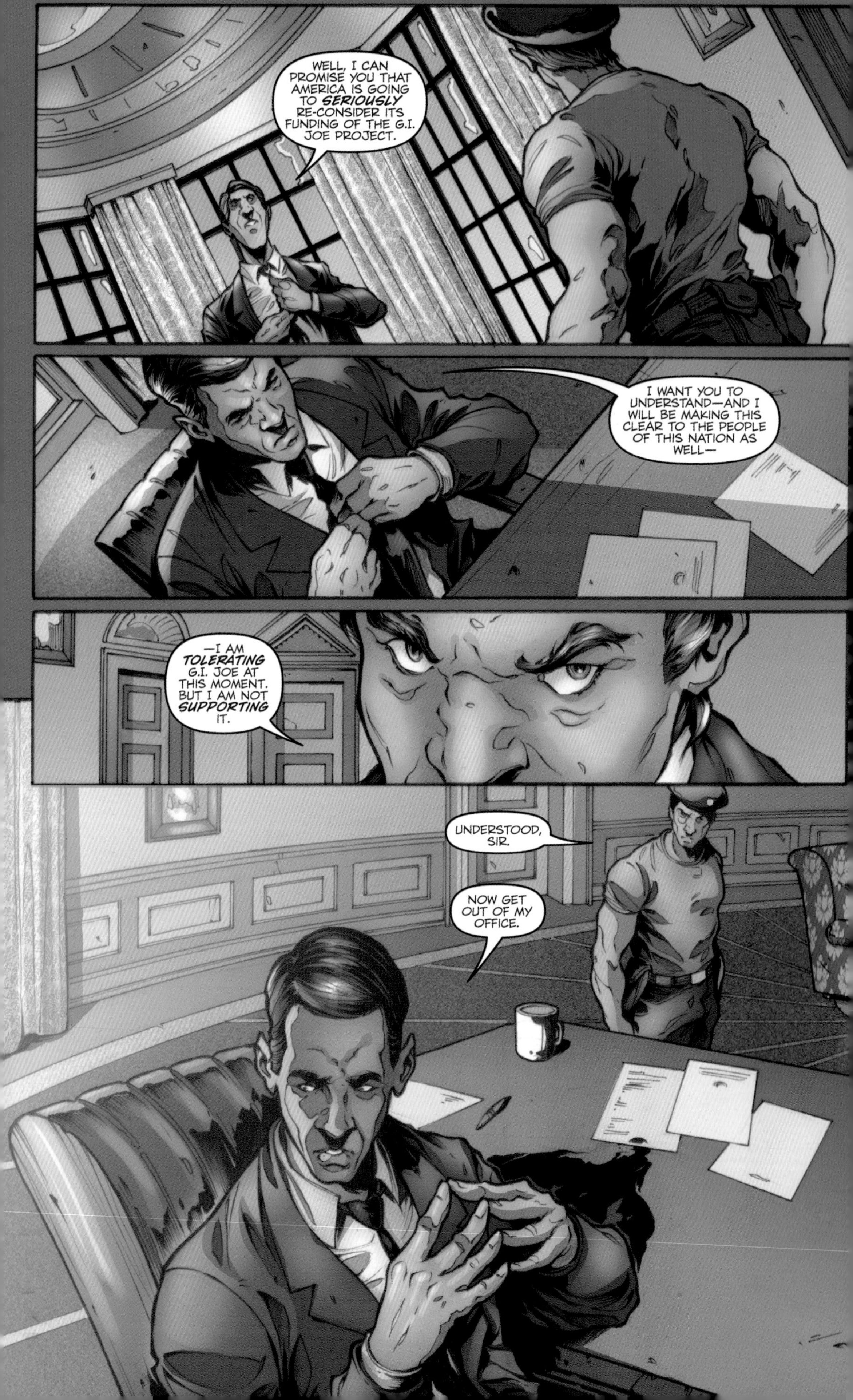
WELL, I CAN PROMISE YOU THAT AMERICA IS GOING TO SERIOUSLY RE-CONSIDER ITS FUNDING OF THE G.I. JOE PROJECT.
I WANT YOU TO UNDERSTAND—AND I WILL BE MAKING THIS CLEAR TO THE PEOPLE OF THIS NATION AS WELL—
—I AM TOLERATING G.I. JOE AT THIS MOMENT. BUT I AM NOT SUPPORTING IT.
UNDERSTOOD, SIR.
NOW GET OUT OF MY OFFICE.

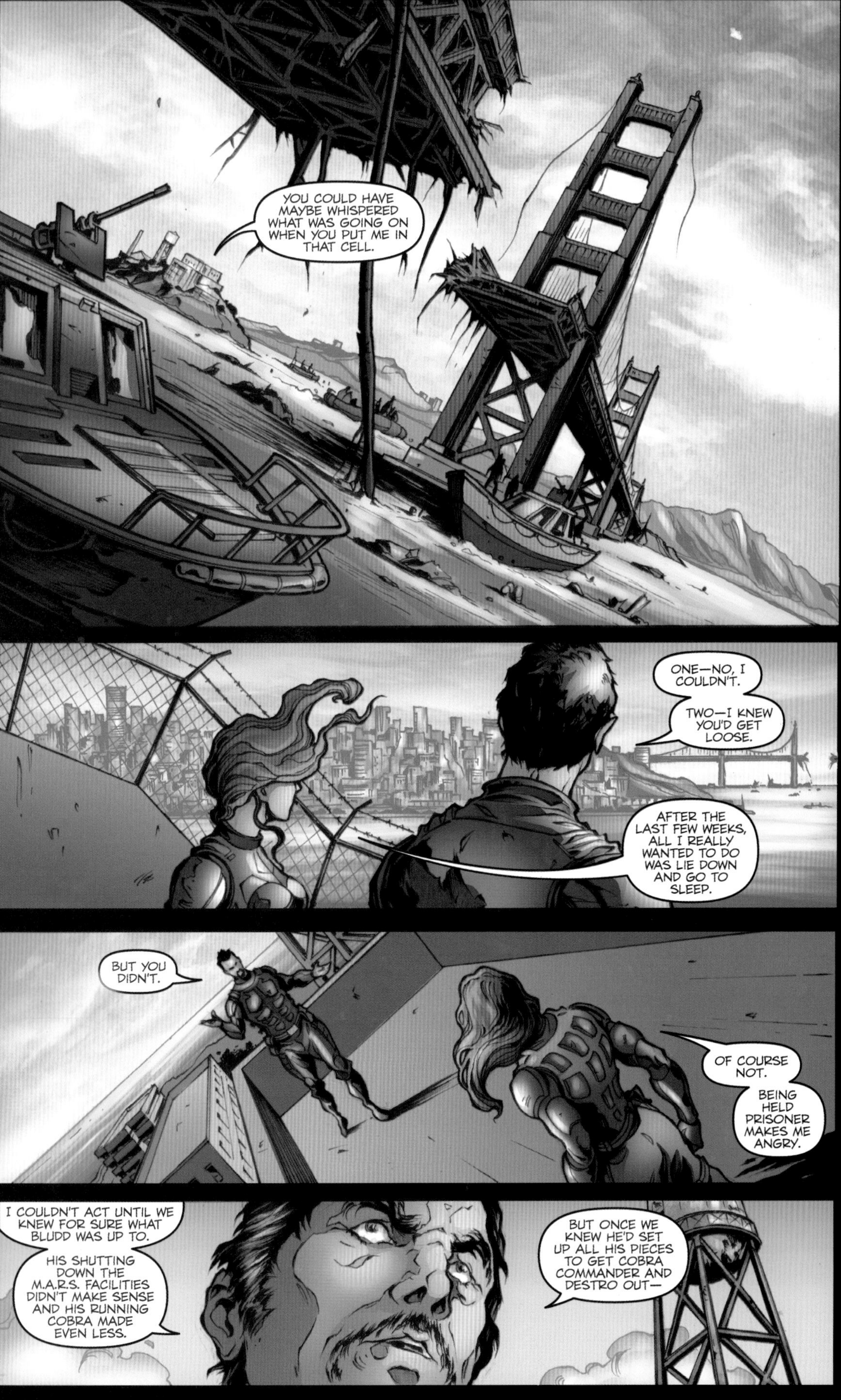
YOU COULD HAVE MAYBE WHISPERED WHAT WAS GOING ON WHEN YOU PUT ME IN THAT CELL.
ONE—NO, I COULDN'T.
TWO—I KNEW YOU'D GET LOOSE.
AFTER THE LAST FEW WEEKS, ALL I REALLY WANTED TO DO WAS LIE DOWN AND GO TO SLEEP.
BUT YOU DIDN'T.
OF COURSE NOT.
BEING HELD PRISONER MAKES ME ANGRY.
I COULDN'T ACT UNTIL WE KNEW FOR SURE WHAT BLUDD WAS UP TO.
HIS SHUTTING DOWN THE M.A.R.S. FACILITIES DIDN'T MAKE SENSE AND HIS RUNNING COBRA MADE EVEN LESS.
BUT ONCE WE KNEW HE'D SET UP ALL HIS PIECES TO GET COBRA COMMANDER AND DESTRO OUT—

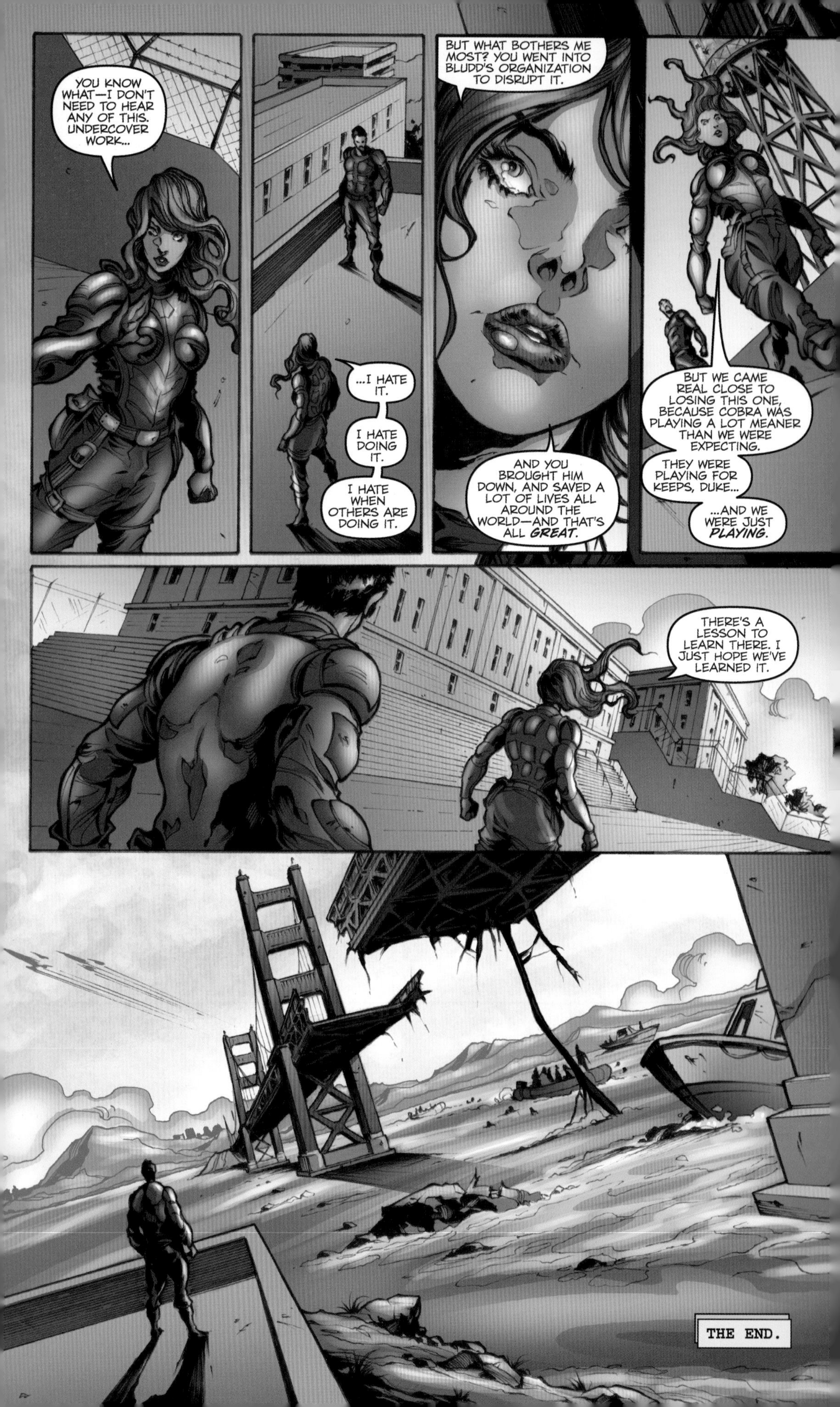
YOU KNOW WHAT—I DON'T NEED TO HEAR ANY OF THIS. UNDERCOVER WORK...
...I HATE IT.
I HATE DOING IT.
I HATE WHEN OTHERS ARE DOING IT.
BUT WHAT BOTHERS ME MOST? YOU WENT INTO BLUDD'S ORGANIZATION TO DISRUPT IT.
AND YOU BROUGHT HIM DOWN, AND SAVED A LOT OF LIVES ALL AROUND THE WORLD—AND THAT'S ALL *GREAT*.
BUT WE CAME REAL CLOSE TO LOSING THIS ONE, BECAUSE COBRA WAS PLAYING A LOT MEANER THAN WE WERE EXPECTING.
THEY WERE PLAYING FOR KEEPS, DUKE...
...AND WE WERE JUST *PLAYING*.
THERE'S A LESSON TO LEARN THERE. I JUST HOPE WE'VE LEARNED IT.
THE END.

ART BY **AGUSTIN PADILLA**
COLORS BY **J. BROWN**

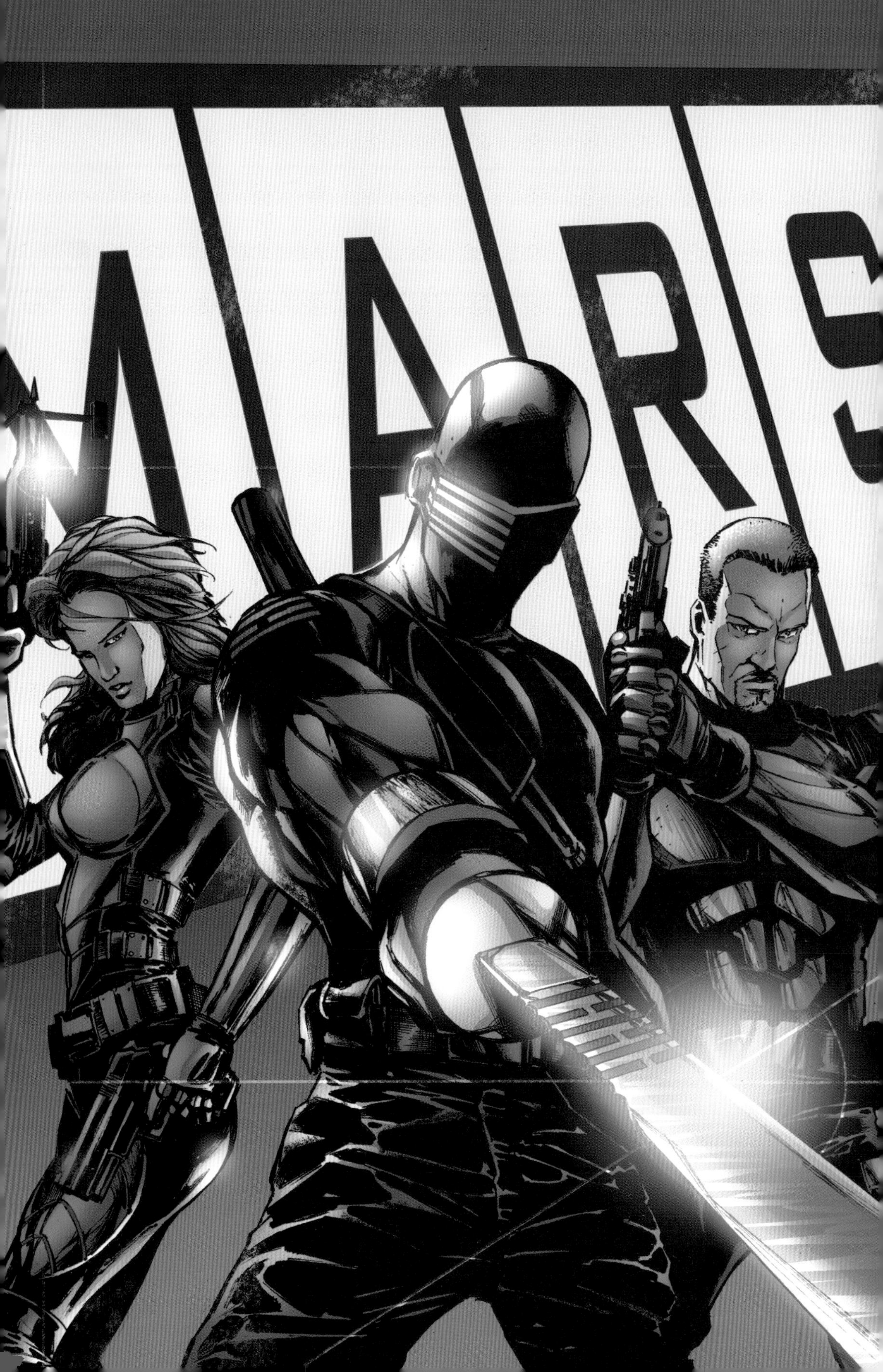

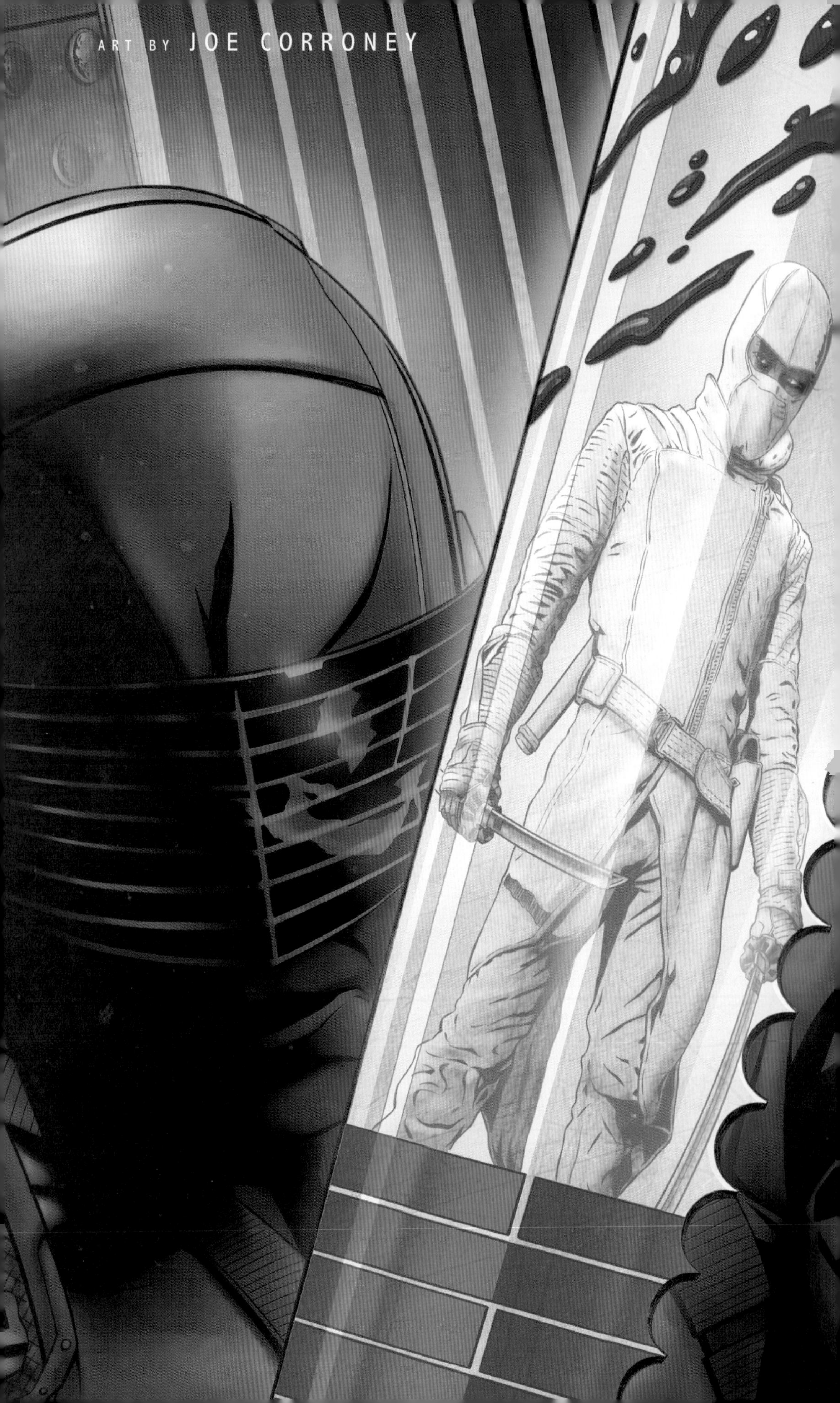
ART BY JOE CORRONEY

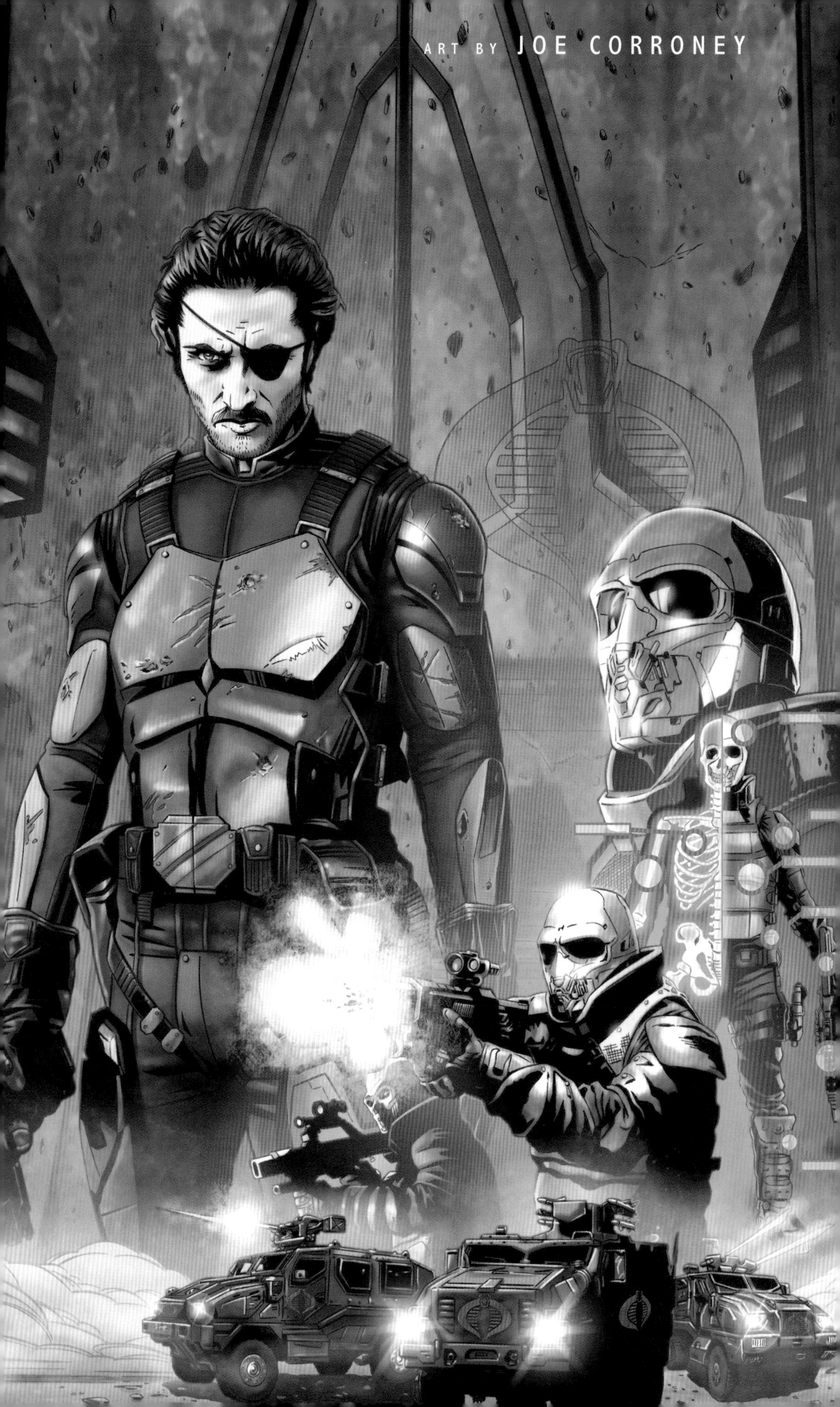
ART BY JOE CORRONEY

ART BY JOE CORRONEY

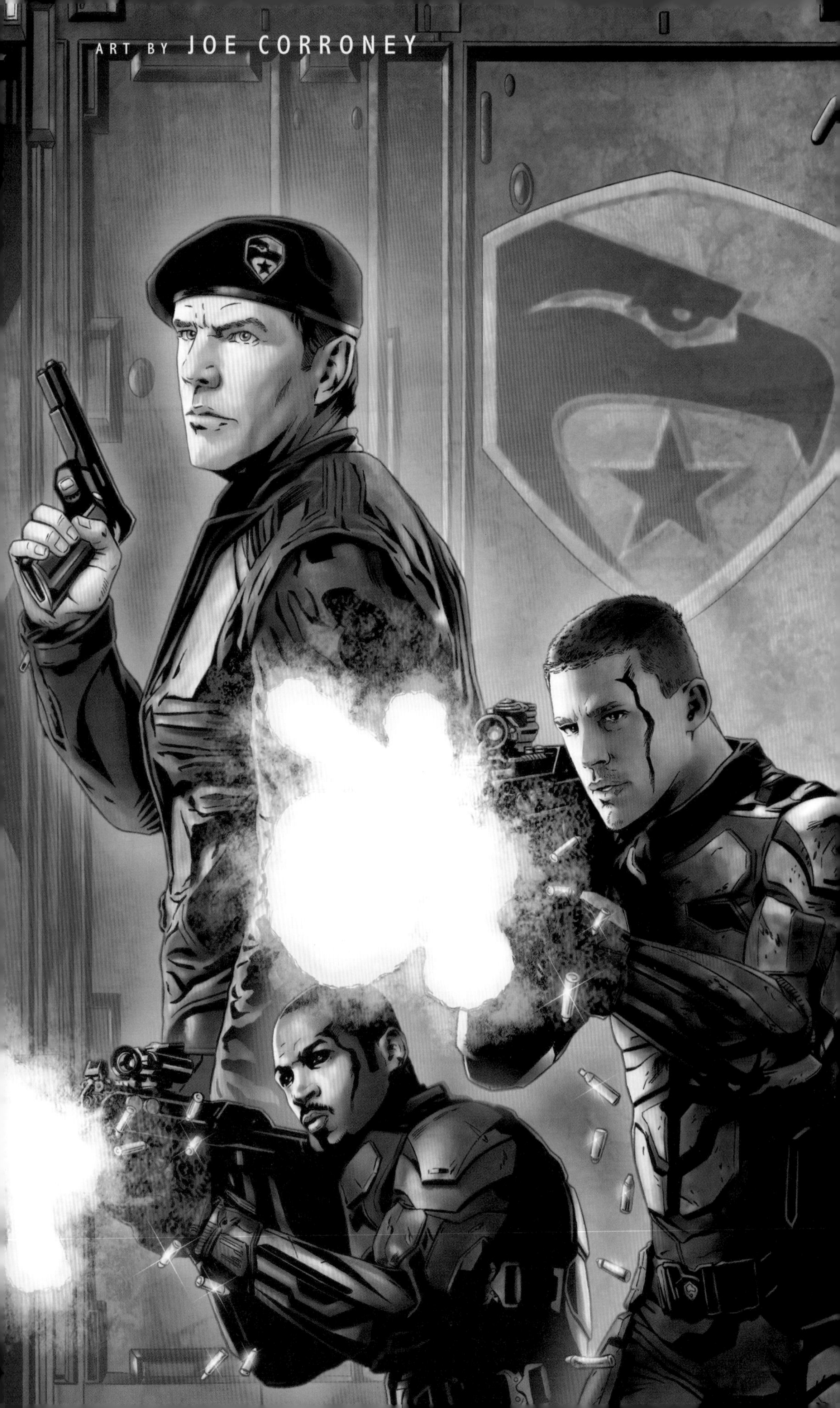

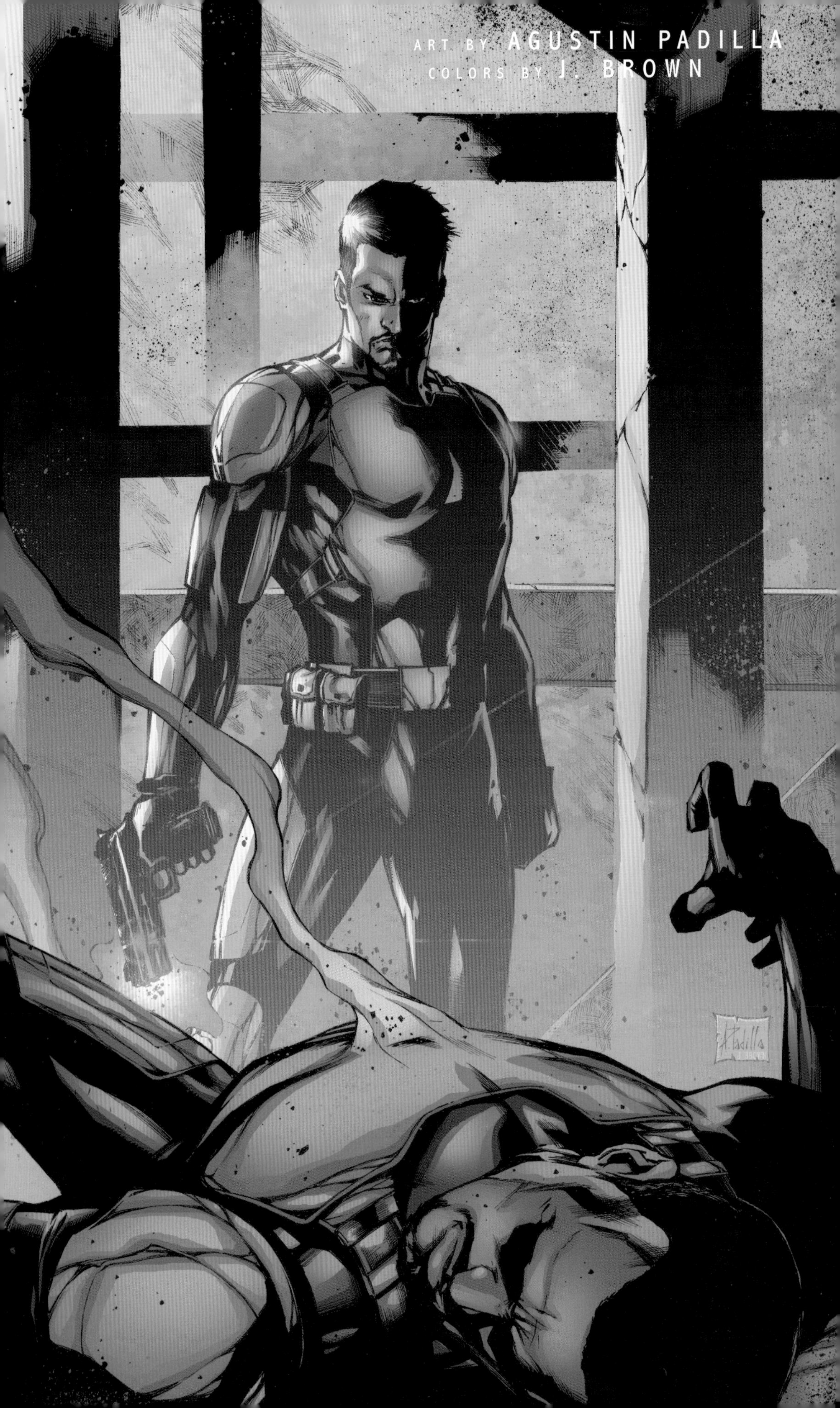
ART BY AGUSTIN PADILLA
COLORS BY J. BROWN
A. Padilla

ART BY JOE CORRONEY

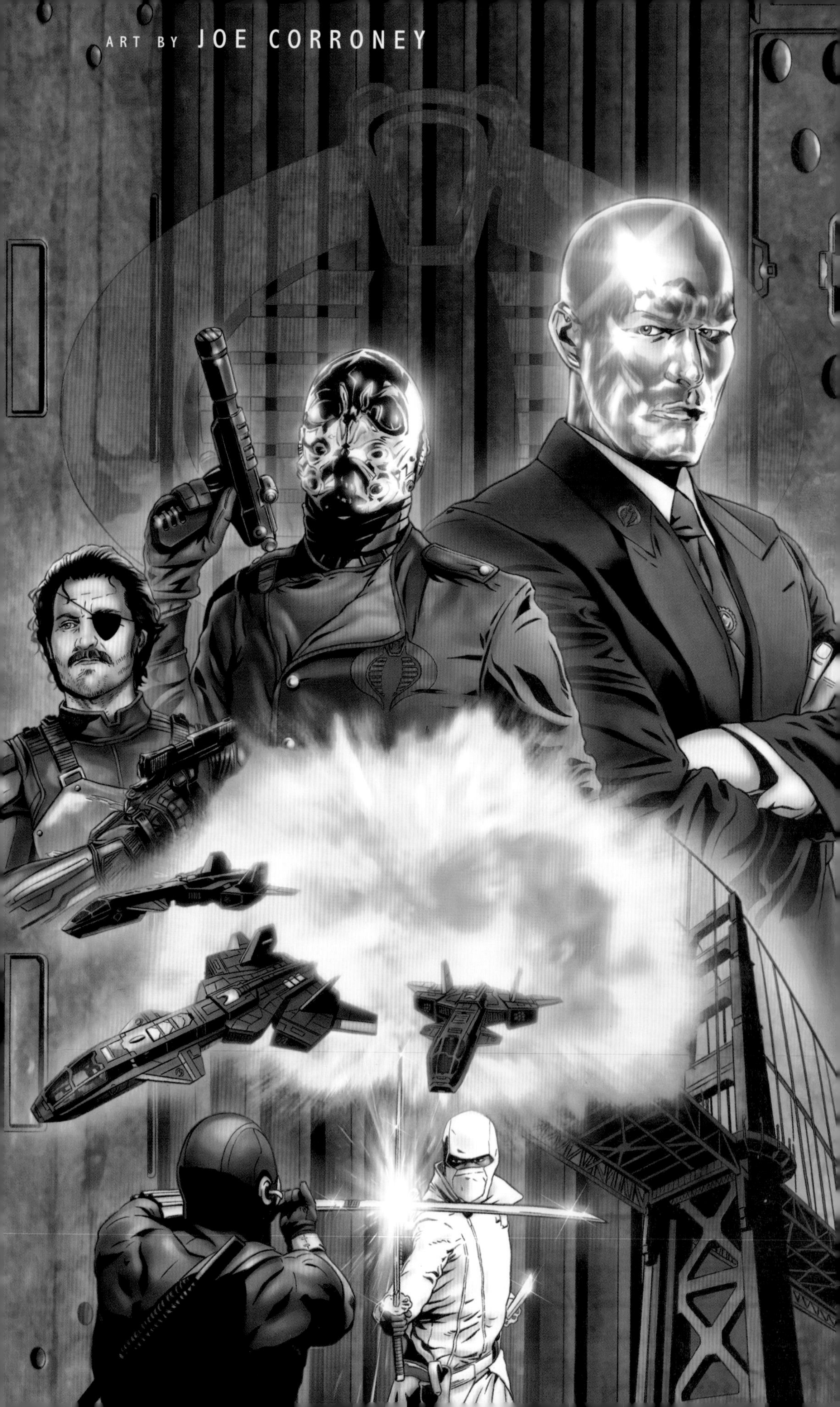

ART BY JOE CORRONEY

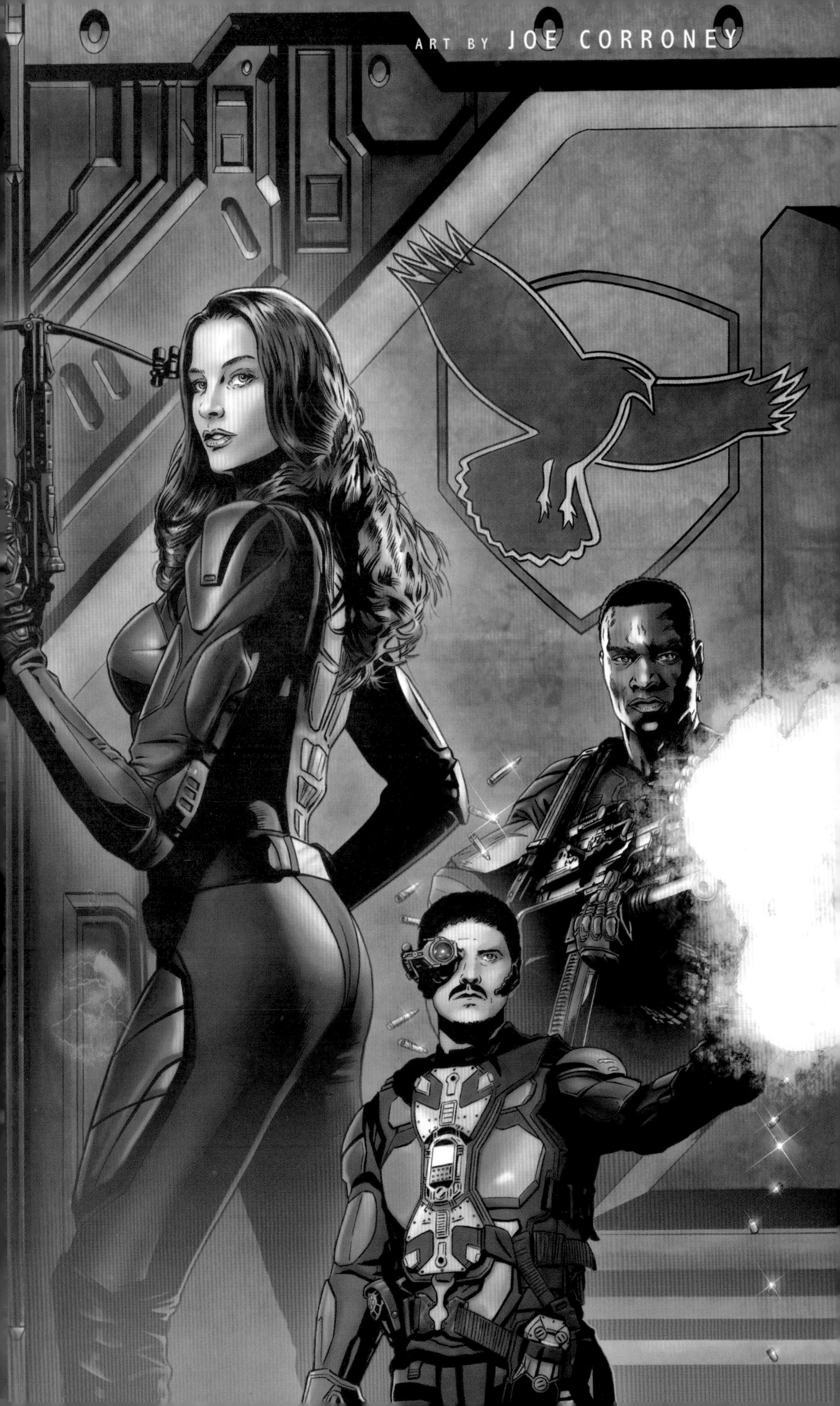

G.I. JOE

OPERATION HISS

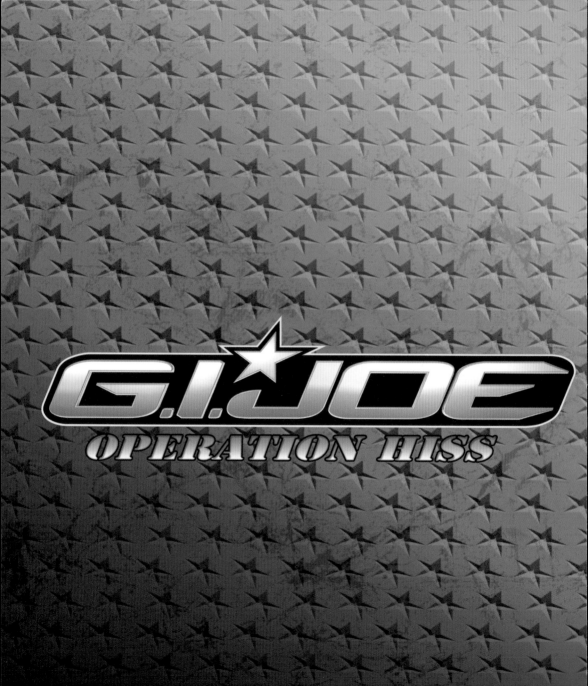